MW00603600

The PhD Parenthood Trap

The **PhD Parenthood Trap**

Caught between Work and Family in Academia

KERRY F. CRAWFORD
AND LEAH C. WINDSOR

GEORGETOWN UNIVERSITY PRESS / WASHINGTON, DC

© 2021 Georgetown University Press. All rights reserved. No part of this book may be reproduced or utilized in any form or by any means, electronic or mechanical, including photocopying and recording, or by any information storage and retrieval system, without permission in writing from the publisher.

The publisher is not responsible for third-party websites or their content. URL links were active at time of publication.

Library of Congress Cataloging-in-Publication Data

Names: Crawford, Kerry F., author. | Windsor, Leah C., author.
Title: The PhD parenthood trap : caught between work and family in academia / Kerry F. Crawford and Leah C. Windsor.
Description: Washington, DC : Georgetown University Press, 2021. | Includes bibliographical references and index.
Identifiers: LCCN 2020048525 | ISBN 9781647120665 (hardcover) | ISBN 9781647120672 (ebook)
Subjects: LCSH: Women college teachers—United States—Social conditions. | Women in higher education—United States—Social conditions. | Women graduate students—United States—Social conditions. | Working mothers—United States. | Work and family—United States. | Work-life balance—United States.
Classification: LCC LB2332.3 .C73 2021 | DDC 378.1/2082—dc23
LC record available at https://lccn.loc.gov/2020048525

∞ This paper meets the requirements of ANSI/NISO Z39.48-1992 (Permanence of Paper).

22 21   9 8 7 6 5 4 3 2 First printing

Printed in the United States of America

Cover design by Erin Kirk
Interior design by BookComp, Inc.

For our children:

Cathryn
Lucca
Lucy
Emilia
Isabella

Without them, this book would have been impossible.
Because of them, it took a very long time to write.

Contents

Figures

Acknowledgments

More than three hundred academic parents completed the anonymous survey that forms the heart of this book. While we cannot name them, we owe them a tremendous debt of gratitude. The vignette contributors have given the book its pulse and passion. We extend our sincere thanks to Susan Hannah Allen, Kelly Baker, David Andersen-Rodgers, Courtney Burns, Christina Fattore, Jael Goldsmith Weil, Kathleen Hancock, Kelly Kadera, Carolyn Kaldon, Lily Moloney, Madeleine Moloney, Maxwell Moloney, Sara McLaughlin Mitchell, Amanda Murdie, Erin Olsen-Telles, Whitney Pirtle, Nancy Rower, Susan Sell, Sahar Shafqat, Sarah Shair-Rosenfield, Krista Wiegand, Reed Wood, and several anonymous writers.

A legion of friends and colleagues made this book possible by commenting on various parts of the survey and manuscript. In particular, we would like to thank Jacqueline DeMerritt, Amelia Hoover Green, Sara McLaughlin Mitchell, and Cameron Thies. We are also grateful to the mentorship networks that have sustained us through our early careers and inspired this project.

We wish to thank Don Jacobs and the staff at Georgetown University Press, as well as the book's anonymous reviewers.

As always, our deepest gratitude goes to our children, partners, and families.

Introduction

"Don't ever let them tell you when to have your babies." In the fall of 2011, we attended the Journeys in World Politics workshop for junior women scholars. While there, we received this life-shaping advice from a senior scholar who spoke with the kind of optimistic exasperation that is born of years spent battling the academic status quo.[1] This moment arose during an informal discussion on life as women in academia, a conversation in which the mentors participating in the workshop answered questions our group would never dare to ask in other venues. It was clear to all of us that the norms within our new profession required us to make tenure at a prestigious university our top priority. Other things might have to take a back seat. For both of us, those "other things"—partners and then spouses, a child and then children—did not take a back seat. In fact, we flagrantly and unabashedly defied the conventional wisdom and chose to have families *and* to pursue academic careers. And we are still here.

In the years that followed, we had—with each other and others—multiple conversations on the theme of families and "work-life balance" with graduate students and fellow junior faculty in different settings. A doctoral student reported to one of us that her advisor admonished the students for spending any fewer than eighty hours per week on coursework; life, the advisor warned, can wait until after the PhD. A student at another university asked one of us, with visible disbelief, if we had *intended* to give birth in graduate school or if the child was an accident, noting that *no woman* in her department has ever had a child, not even among the faculty, and asking whether the risk was worth it. Each time we discussed these exchanges, we replied to one another that we needed to write a book so early-career scholars could commiserate, feel empowered to make major life choices without guilt, simply know that they are not alone, and—most importantly—start conversations among established faculty and administrators that will make the academic profession more inclusive through formal and informal support for scholar parents.

On Academic Chutes and Ladders

Academia has a big problem. Too many women exit the profession before they earn tenure or reach senior academic ranks, not because they are not capable scholars and teachers, but because the system creates barriers to their retention, advancement, and success, a phenomenon often dubbed the "leaky pipeline." We have seen this happen to friends and colleagues. And we have observed that the toll taken by lower-order processes—messy, daily realities, decisions, and constraints—related to gender bias and parenting drive many women to leave their graduate programs and tenure-track positions before they have had a chance to land permanent positions and earn promotions. The weight of the expectation to work like they do not have children and parent like they do not have a career is crushing. An absence of women at the highest ranks, in turn, leaves junior scholars without role models and mentors with similar life experiences. The academic boys' club rules still set the cultural standard in many ways.

A wealth of literature focuses on academic mothers and the difficulties they face (Connelly and Ghodsee 2011; Evans and Grant 2008; Mason, Wolfinger, and Goulden 2013). It is important to emphasize that this story is not *just* about women and mothers. Bias, inequality, and the leaky pipeline—or, as we prefer to call it, the game of Academic Chutes and Ladders—also affect men and nonbinary parents. All academic parents who subvert or transgress traditional gender roles suffer penalties. To the extent that the system in which we all learn and work perpetuates specific ideas about who bears the burden of unseen and unpaid care work and who will be more or less productive as a result of parental status, everyone suffers, especially those who do not fit the mold. A father who is the primary caregiver or plays an active role in his infant's early days will fail to meet the expectation that his research productivity and responsiveness to students will not decrease after his child's birth. Non-birth parents may lack access to parental leave policies designed chiefly to accommodate people who give birth. Much of our discussion of the literature on the leaky pipeline in academia and bias with respect to family formation focuses on women and mothers, but we broaden the discussion to include parents of all genders.

In these pages we issue a call for colleges and universities to move beyond the ground floor of existing policies toward a cultural shift in academia that makes the profession inclusive of all scholars, including those who choose to have children before, during, and after they start an academic career. Existing parental leave policies—which vary widely across and even within campuses—provide only a basic level of decency for people who give birth, whose partners give birth, and who welcome their children through adoption. To the extent that formal parental leave policies exist, they tend to be limited to a certain amount of time with reduced teaching, research, or service responsibilities. Where parental leave policies exist, they are not always universally applied, transparent, or clearly communicated. The demands of raising families are not limited to the weeks or months immediately following a child's birth or adoption, and the failure to recognize and accommodate parents'—especially mothers'—needs for flexibility has created a system in which talented scholars fall through the proverbial cracks before they have a chance to advance through the professional ranks. It is also important to recognize that the flaws in the system are not unique to academia. Support for new parents is woefully insufficient in the United States, where family leave policies fall far below parental leave and family support policies in other wealthy, industrialized democracies. This problem is bigger than academia, but colleges and universities can and should serve as platforms for innovation and norm change. We can do better, and this requires culture change across campuses and society (James 2017).

Our call to do better is a call for systemic change. We have to understand how the lower-order processes we foreground in this book contribute to the well-documented higher-order outcomes endemic to the leaky pipeline. Much ink has been spilled on the question of whether women can "have it all" (but not whether men can do the same), when and how they should "lean in," and what "life hacks" they can utilize to balance the competing demands of work and family. We argue that academia needs more than life hacks and leaning in—especially when one is asked to lean in without the support that will prevent her from falling on her face. Our colleagues also need to "lean out" so the burden of change is not borne solely by women. In addition to personal drive and persistence, the work of making the academy a more inclusive place to work, study, and thrive must be carried out by all of us: senior scholars, faculty who supervise and mentor students, department and unit heads, campus administrators, and the leaders of professional associations.

In short, we must work together to decrease the burden on the individual and place it on the profession as a whole. We advocate for best practices that increase support for academics and their families, and that do so in a way that is equitable and transparent. At the heart of each of these best practices is the notion that when individuals do not know what their rights are, they are already at a disadvantage. By improving awareness of existing policies, and creating or improving policies and support systems themselves, campuses can attract and retain more diverse faculty and enable scholars to "have it all," regardless of their gender and parental status. It is important to us that this book speaks to individuals across levels of and roles in academia. In addition to offering best practices for administrators and mentors, we offer advice for academic parents who are in the trenches raising children and for prospective parents who are unsure of the compatibility of parenthood and academic careers.

No matter where you sit in the academic profession, we are writing for you.

Our Focus and a Few Caveats

Through this book we highlight gaps in support for academic parents—especially mothers—and provide evidence of best practices for academics of all ranks. Our goal is nothing short of institutional reform that will make the game of Academic Chutes and Ladders fairer for all players. The project began with a survey that we publicized and disseminated through political science and international relations groups and associations, as well as social media groups for academic parents across disciplines. The responses we gathered were shocking in some cases and inspiring in others. In analyzing the survey responses, we learned about universities and departments with supportive formal and informal policies in place, and advisors and department chairs whose behavior toward new parents (students and faculty alike) borders on abuse. We gleaned respondents' tips and tricks for making it through the day-to-day chaos of working in academia while raising young children, negotiating with administrators for parental leave, and providing support through mentorship. We found that respondents felt a sense of relief in recounting their experiences and that the survey served as a catharsis for some and a way for others to pay it forward and help future generations of scholar parents. In chapter 1, we discuss the survey sample and key findings. We integrate survey responses on specific topics throughout the thematic chapters.

Implicit bias and precarity take many forms in academia and society as a whole. While our focus here is on the experiences of academic parents, and especially academic mothers, we recognize that the challenges facing individuals and families will vary widely on the basis of gender, race, family structure, job security, socioeconomic status, first-generation college student status, and other salient factors. As we discuss in chapters 2, 5, and 9, the increasing reliance on non-tenure-track faculty in the academy creates a system in which many scholars are struggling to balance a crushing workload with little job security and the demands that come along with family formation and parenting. Precarity stemming from job security, racial discrimination, financial insecurity, and other constraints exacerbates the gender gap in academia. Race and ethnicity are highly salient factors that intersect with gender and parenthood to compound bias in the academy and in society more broadly. We finalized this book in the spring and summer of 2020, during which the movement to reckon with racial injustice and discrimination in the United States gained more traction on a national level through sustained protests and calls for change. The literature on academic parenthood to date centers whiteness, and white mothers in particular, too often overlooking the effects of race and ethnicity on parents' or women's career trajectories. As colleges and universities across the United States rename buildings and remove statues that glorify racist individuals and institutions, we must also realize that the academy as a whole has significant work to do to support equal opportunities for success for Black, indigenous, and people of color in the profession now and in the future. At the core of our book's central argument is the notion that the patriarchal structure of the academy disadvantages anyone who does not fit the mold of the ideal-typical man scholar. Patriarchy is also at the core of white supremacy. Dismantling the academy's patriarchal structure, then, benefits academic parents of all genders, races, and ethnicities.

We hope the book will be of particular benefit to early-career scholars, including graduate students and those who received their PhD or other terminal degree within the last several years, as they navigate graduate school, the academic job market, the tenure track, or short-term or non-tenure-track positions. Just as importantly, we intend for department chairs, deans, and other administrators to learn from the experiences and best practices uncovered by the survey and discussed in the book. Our aim is that graduate students, faculty, and campus decision-makers will have substantive conversations about accommodating and normalizing parenthood in the academy that lead to better, clearer, and more consistently applied policies.

Where We Focus

This book is not just for mother scholars. We recognize that there are an increasing number of non-birth parents in academia—parents whose partners gave birth to their child or whose families grew through adoption, surrogacy, or foster parenting—who assume heavy childcare workloads and whose lives and careers are affected by the process of family formation. Accordingly, we seek to go beyond the usual focus in the literature on the "mom penalty" rooted in pregnancy and childbirth and the effects of parenting and household responsibilities on women's careers, while recognizing that women still carry a disproportionate burden in these areas and face significant obstacles rooted in gender-based discrimination. We address the contingent of non-birth partners most directly in chapter 5, "Doctor, Parent," but integrate consideration of parents of all genders as frequently as possible in the other chapters. Throughout the book, we use the terms "women" and "woman" in lieu of "female," and "men" and "man" instead of "male" where possible. Gender—the personal sense of self and related social expectations of and roles derived from masculinity and femininity—is much broader than the traditional male/female dichotomy.

Nevertheless, we must acknowledge the difficulties imposed by existing literature on the subject of academic parenthood, which nearly universally centers white cisgender women in heterosexual relationships. While we have attempted to use gender-inclusive and non-heteronormative language throughout the book, our efforts are somewhat constrained by the language, categories, and assumptions used in previous research. Where the terms "female" or "male" appear in the scholarship or survey responses we cite, those terms remain in place to stay true to the original authors' text. Further, the majority of our survey respondents and vignette contributors self-identified as women. (See chapter 1 for a more complete discussion of recruitment and demographics.) The book's insights, then, are heavily based on women's lived experiences. Still, we hope that this book and other studies that seek to move beyond the gender binary will encourage individuals and institutions to adopt a more inclusive view of academic parents.

This book is for academic families of all types and in all stages and for all who want to work toward a more inclusive academia. We focus most directly on the early years of parenting, as our survey responses point to these years as the ones during which academic parents are in the proverbial trenches, attempting to find and maintain a precarious balance between work and family. As we discuss throughout the book, "work-life balance" is more appropriately dubbed the "work-life myth." In considering these early years, we refer to "family formation." We use this term to describe the process through which an individual or a couple expands their family through childbirth, adoption, marriage to a partner who has a child or children, fostering, or any other means by which a child joins a family, whether the first time, second time, or seventh time. We recognize, however, that "family" begins before children, whether that sense of family starts when someone chooses a partner or makes the decision to become a parent (with or without a partner). An anonymous vignette contributor in chapter 5 observes the importance of choosing a supportive partner, and we agree that this is the point at which family begins. Our use of "family formation" as a term to refer to the process through which a child joins a family is an effort to simplify the reference to the diverse range of experiences.

Beyond the Book's Scope

We hope to broaden the conversation on academic parenthood and how campuses can best support students and faculty to promote diversity and inclusion and create a more balanced and humane academic culture. We aim to highlight the obstacles women academics face as a result of deeply entrenched gender biases while also pushing past the usual focus on women who give birth. We recognize that much of the gender-based discrimination related to professional parents arises in large part because our society associates the burden of parenthood solely with motherhood.

Still, the scope of our book on family formation in academia has its limits. In focusing on specific phases of family formation and parenting along the trajectory of an academic career, we have not incorporated specific parent identities. Despite our efforts to cast a wide net in recruitment for our survey and vignette contributors, three groups of academics left out of the spotlight in this book deserve specific mentions here.

We do not have a section of the book dedicated solely and specifically to caregivers. We recognize that caregiving in its many forms carries many of the same challenges as family formation and giving birth to or adopting a child. An individual who becomes the caregiver of a child or children, whether unexpectedly and suddenly or with training and notice, will encounter many or all of the obstacles, lower-order processes, and messy daily realities we discuss. Similarly, many academics are sandwiched between caring for children and caring for aging parents who present similar challenges and demands. Our hope is that caregivers and legal guardians of all kinds will benefit from the positive changes and increased support for families we strive to inspire. Families are families regardless of how they originate.

Similarly, we do not have a chapter or section devoted solely to single parents, but two vignettes in chapter 2 discuss single academic parenthood directly. As these vignettes demonstrate, single parents, especially single mothers, encounter all of the obstacles and challenges that we discuss in this book but they do so while handling the entire household workload. Creating a more hospitable academia that embraces parents will benefit single parents, especially if campuses create adequate parental leave policies, a culture of mentorship and support, and a child-friendly environment (or at the very least a calendar that aligns with that of the local school system).

Third, we have not included a chapter on academics without children. Our colleagues who do not have children—whether by choice or circumstance—are our colleagues; any changes designed to make academia more hospitable to parents should not unduly burden academics who are not parents. Further, a scholar who does not have children may have other caregiving duties—parents, siblings, a partner, pets, or other family members whose well-being depends on their support. Everyone carries some burden. In this book, our focus is on the burdens, challenges, and opportunities that come along with parenting. In chapter 3, however, we engage the gender gap in citations and the unequal service burden, both of which are rooted in gender-based discrimination and create obstacles for women in academia regardless of their status as parents. Much of the literature we discuss on the leaky pipeline is written with a focus on women, not exclusively mothers. Addressing the problems facing academic parents will ideally mitigate some of the gender bias that limits the opportunities women and nonbinary scholars encounter.

We approach the subject of raising children as a type of public good. Colleges and universities, in particular, depend on a robust stream of future generations for their continued viability as institutions and businesses. It is the height of irony, then, if these institutions that depend on the recruitment of thousands of bright young people every year should snub the faculty, staff, and students who choose to grow their own families.

A final group that is largely absent from our survey and vignettes, but one that we have worked to acknowledge in several chapters, is the legion of scholars who have left academia at any stage of the process. While we do have a number of survey respondents and one vignette contributor who have opted to leave the academic profession, it is worth noting that many of the experiences of these scholars remain unknown. We refer to this absence as a form of survivorship bias throughout the book: our work necessarily speaks to those who have stayed in the pipeline or the game because of the experiences and accounts that have informed this research. The book looks largely at how those who *have* stayed in academic were able to do so, with an eye toward helping future generations of scholars overcome and eliminate the obstacles that past generations faced.

Gender and Scholarship in the Time of COVID-19

We completed work on this book during the start of the COVID-19 pandemic, in early 2020. As we were finalizing chapter drafts, our universities were beginning the transition to online teaching and our kids' schools and daycares shut down. This dramatic shift in "work-life balance" and the attendant effects on the gender gap in academia brought all of the work for this book full circle. The effects of the COVID-19 pandemic will not be seasonal—they will be decadal. The mentorship networks, fostered through in-person face-to-face interaction, that women scholars rely on for footholds on the academic ladder have faltered due to canceled conferences, competing childcare demands of academic parents, and shifts in priorities as scholars have been forced to reallocate time to move courses online while also caring for children at home. Some scholars without children have become primary caregivers because of the pandemic, providing new or increased care to aging or ailing family members. Some scholar parents have also provided new or increased care to older loved ones *in addition* to twenty-four-seven care for their children during the pandemic. While academics broadly may have more job flexibility and security—although this is not universally the case—the pandemic will have pernicious and non-random effects on scholarship.

Now, five months into the pandemic, it is clear that the effects on academics'—most especially academic parents'—productivity will be felt for many years. Early in the pandemic, submissions to academic journals by women scholars were already demonstrably lower than previous years' trends (Kitchener 2020). New research by fellow political scientists suggests that the biggest determinant in productivity is not gender but parental status. In other words, parents are likely to fare worse than nonparents as a result of the pandemic. As the pandemic deepened, submissions by women declined by as much as 19 percent from previous years (Minello 2020; Viglione 2020; Wiegand et al. 2020).

We demonstrate in this book that bias in family formation in academia is gendered, and the proverbial deck is stacked against academic parents. The COVID-19 pandemic has not created these problems, but it has amplified and multiplied them. It is especially difficult for women, who often perform much of the cognitive and emotional labor both in their departments and institutions and at home. The pandemic has exacerbated the gender gap in academia, which will likely manifest in gendered tenure and promotion rates for years to come. Some universities have provided across-the-board tenure clock extensions, but this may only serve to widen the gap for academic parents and scholars with caregiver roles that impinge on research time.

The effects of the pandemic on many facets of academia are yet unknown, including changing norms of work-life harmony, mental health, financial challenges, and childcare. Mentorship—the lifeline for women academics—will have to adjust to new demands, such as the backlog of jobless, qualified PhDs competing for fewer jobs since universities have closed financial gaps by eliminating new positions or closing unfilled ones. Now, more than ever, we must recognize the obstacles and opportunities that come along with academic parenting.

Plan of the Book

This book's proceeding nine chapters cover a range of topics central to academic parenthood. We ground our explorations of these topics in both the literature and scholar parents' lived experiences. In each chapter we discuss findings from the corresponding section of our survey of academic parents, highlighting prominent themes and experiences as well as direct excerpts from responses. Each chapter features at least two vignettes from anonymous and named contributors; these extended narratives provide rich accounts of the good, bad, messy, and uplifting moments academic parenthood brings. The vignettes are set apart in the text to make it clear that the experiences, insights, and recommendations shared are the contributors'. These firsthand narratives provide rich context to the discussion of the lower-order processes and messy daily realities of parenthood in academia.

We thread a discussion of the literature on the game of Academic Chutes and Ladders, formerly discussed as the "leaky pipeline," and the many forms of gender bias in academia throughout the book. While all of these issues featured in the literature—from discriminatory hiring practices to the gender citation gap—affect all or most stages of academic life, we place them in the context of the phases in which they have the strongest influence on the lower-order processes or daily decisions and realities of academic parenting. To connect the literature and our research to policies and practices in academia, we conclude each chapter with a discussion of best practices that individuals, department or unit heads, and administrators can adopt to make academia more inclusive of parents and families. We have derived these recommendations from responses to our survey, insights from mentorship networks and panels focused on helping women and early-career scholars succeed, the experiences shared in the vignettes, and our own experiences as academic parents. We turn now to a brief overview of the book's chapters.

Chapter 1, "Surviving or Thriving in the Academy? Insights from a Survey on Family Formation and Parenthood," introduces the survey of academic parents that forms the backbone of this book. In this chapter we discuss the results of the survey, which we opened in fall 2017 to assess experiences with family formation and parenthood in the academy. Approximately three hundred participants answered questions about a range of topics, including their ability to negotiate and take parental leave for the birth or adoption of a child, their perception of the family-friendliness of their university and home department, and professional rank held at the time of their first child's birth or adoption. Chapter 1 introduces lower- and higher-order processes as they relate to academic parenthood and lays the foundation for the discussions in the subsequent chapters, which focus on specific opportunities and obstacles arising from academic parenthood.

Chapter 2, "Thesis Baby: Getting Student Parents the Support They Need," explores the unique set of opportunities and challenges facing parents in graduate school. The overarching theme is that it is perfectly acceptable for graduate students to have personal lives—and children!—in addition to their academic commitments. The chapter explores possible accommodations and support systems for graduate student parents and discusses the potential for bias against women and parents in new faculty hiring decisions. We write here not only for graduate students seeking assurance and commiseration but also for faculty and administrators who work with graduate students and wish to consider best practices to guarantee the support student parents need to complete their degrees and find academic employment. Chapter 2 features four vignettes that speak to starkly contrasting experiences.

Chapter 3, "How to Scale the Ladders while Sidestepping the Chutes: On Parenting without the Security of Tenure," examines the effects of family formation and parenting on early-career faculty. We examine the obstacles to progress toward tenure and promotion and the constraints imposed on parents by non-tenure-track positions. The probationary period generally lasts six years, during which time scholars are expected to balance service to the department and discipline, teaching, and research to meet both internal and external goals. In light of these competing demands, we underscore the need for systemic changes to support scholar parents, including universal, transparent, and clearly communicated formal parental leave policies and informal efforts to create flexibility within departments and campuses. We connect these parent-specific concerns with the broader literature on gender bias and the disproportionate service burden and gender gap in citations to shed light on the mechanisms at work in the game of Academic Chutes and Ladders. Chapter 3 features two vignettes from senior scholars who have successfully navigated the tenure track while parenting.

Chapter 4, "The Elusive Work-Life Balance: Daily Challenges in Academic Parenting," discusses efforts to manage academic work, family life, and personal health. In this chapter we directly engage the popular advice that women should "lean in," arguing that a more effective approach involves systemic change that better supports women and parents' efforts to have both a family and a career. This chapter contains two vignettes from junior faculty members.

In chapter 5, "Doctor, Parent: Recognizing the Range of Experiences," we focus on university and peer support for parents who do not give birth, including partners, biological fathers, and adoptive parents. The chapter also looks at the factors influencing a partner, coparent, or adoptive parent's willingness or ability to take parental leave or continue working upon the birth or adoption of a child, as discussed by our survey respondents. This chapter explores the experiences of partners and adoptive parents of all genders, expanding the conversation beyond its usual focus on mothers who have given birth. We center our vignette contributors' experiences in this chapter even more than in the others; our goal is to devote this chapter's pages to the vignette authors' varied experiences with parenting and the path to parenthood. To this end, the chapter features four vignettes by five scholars—three solo-authored vignettes and one vignette written by a dual-academic couple.

Chapter 6, "Sick and Tired: The Physical Toll of Parenthood," discusses the effects of physical health challenges on the academic career. Linking pregnancy difficulties and work modification, maternity leave, family physical and emotional health after the birth of a child, and postpartum issues for new parents to the academic career, the chapter explores university support for new parents and families as well as productivity (or lack thereof) during the first twenty-four months after childbirth or adoption. The effects of early pregnancy hormones, as well as the change in hormones from infertility treatments, affect women before the pregnancy is disclosed, presenting a unique set of professional challenges. Similarly, fatigue and morning sickness may decrease women's academic productivity prior to giving birth. Given the coincidence of the years in which many people choose to start families and the academic job search and time on the tenure track, physical limitations can have profound effects on the academic career. Chapter 6 explores some of these concerns through two vignettes.

Chapter 7, "Love, Loss, and Longing: Fertility Struggles, Adoption, Miscarriage, and Infant and Child Loss," explores the difficult subjects of infertility and pregnancy and infant loss. We discuss infertility and the sometimes long road to parenthood, early- and later-term pregnancy loss, infant sickness and loss, and the availability of institutional support—whether formal or informal—for these difficult family situations. These scenarios isolate all parents as they are generally taboo to discuss; many miscarriages are unreported to family, friends, and colleagues because women often wait until after the vulnerable first trimester to share news of the pregnancy. Family leave policies begin near or at the time of delivery, but the onset of physiological and psychological changes happens months before that. In American society broadly there is little support for pregnancy and infant loss; the academic environment mirrors this deficit. Furthermore, the onset of an academic career often coincides with ideal family formation time, setting up a competition between work and family as women enter the academic faculty track. Two anonymous vignette contributors share their stories of strength, loss, and love.

Chapter 8, "Express Yourself: Breastfeeding and Lactation in the Ivory Tower," focuses on nursing or lactating parents and the challenges or support they encounter on campus and at academic conferences. Breastfeeding is time-consuming and represents an opportunity cost for scholars who must attend to feeding their babies. While not all parents choose or are able to breastfeed, those who do contend with medically supported reasons for regular milk expression, including the threat of dwindling milk supply and health complications such as mastitis. Milk expression, whether by pumping milk or by breastfeeding, averages thirty minutes per session, with an average of two to four sessions during the day. Time spent expressing milk is time spent not working, networking, researching, and engaging with peers and colleagues. Parents who rely on formula to feed their babies report obstacles related to social stigma, pressure, and guilt, all of which also complicate the early days of parenthood; accordingly, we explore the needs and perspectives of parents who choose to or have no choice but to formula feed their babies.

In this concluding chapter, chapter 9, "Looking Back, Moving Forward: Conversation Starters for a More Inclusive Academic Environment," we center vignettes from senior scholars who reflect on why they stayed in the pipeline and what the profession meant to them as they started raising families and what it means to them now. We also incorporate survey respondents' answers to a question about the best advice they received or the advice they did not receive but wish they had. The advice touches on broad themes, including self-care, partnership roles, multitasking, the profession, parenting, and the messy realities of academic parenthood. This chapter is intended to provide inspiration for readers, pointing to the experiences of those who found ways to balance academic work and family life successfully. Finally, and most importantly, we close with a list of best practices universities, colleges, and the departments within them should discuss as potential avenues for attracting and retaining faculty members. We intend for this chapter to serve as a call to action, a starting point for practical conversations surrounding implicit bias against parents and families within the academy.

Note

1. Journeys in World Politics connects junior and senior women specializing in international relations research through an annual workshop at the University of Iowa. Organizers Kelly Kadera and Sara Mitchell are dedicated to advancing the status of women in the discipline and both have written vignettes for this book. Information on Journeys in World Politics is available at http://www.saramitchell.org/journeys.html.

1 Surviving or Thriving in the Academy?

Insights from a Survey on Family Formation and Parenthood

"I didn't have maternity leave. I had a meeting a week after giving birth. I taught a week and a half after giving birth. It was incredibly difficult," wrote one survey respondent. Academia has a leaky pipeline problem, and talented scholars are exiting the profession before they have had a chance to advance through the faculty ranks. The leaky pipeline is a metaphor that demonstrates how women achieve tenure and promotion at lower rates than men. The academic pipeline begins in undergraduate, then graduate school, through the job market to non-tenure-track and tenure-track positions, and on through tenure and promotion from assistant to associate to full professor. Challenges accumulate along the pipeline, and many factors cause scholars to exit the profession in the early stages of their careers—usually women scholars and often due to family obligations. This leads to a dearth of role models and mentors in senior ranks: if fewer women persist in the academic pipeline, fewer senior women scholars will be in positions to serve as mentors for junior colleagues. Family-unfriendly policies unduly burden women, whose careers are often taking off during optimal childbearing years. With fewer women (or parents in general) holding leadership positions on campus, academic parents who wish to pursue both family and career have fewer potential champions in their corner to advocate for better policies. The status quo of systemic biases persists against women and families in the early academic career stages, with broader implications for mentorship, diversity, and inclusivity. To expose the underlying systemic biases and less visible issues that place parents—especially women—at a disadvantage in academia, we share insights from survey respondents alongside vignettes from other academic parents, some anonymously. We also offer early-career scholars in the process of starting families useful tools to evaluate the policies in their departments and institutions and advocate for improvements. Early-career scholars, especially women and families, deserve more equitable accommodations and fairer policies which, over time, can chip away at the existing biases that penalize scholars who pursue the dual goals of family and career.

We explore and provide evidence for the lower-order processes or daily experiences and decisions that manifest in higher-order phenomena or trends seen in particular disciplines or the profession as a whole that we can more easily observe. Lower-order processes are less visible, such as health consequences of fertility and infertility, childbirth, and the early, sleep-deprived years of childrearing. Many of the lower-order processes contribute to the higher-order outcomes, and to address the inequalities at the top we must acknowledge the problems at the foundation. Higher-order phenomena include outcomes such as women achieving tenure and promotion to full professorship at lower rates than their peers who are men, disparate service assignments, and unequal salaries. The higher-order phenomena are determined by critical life events that compete with scholars' professional obligations and benchmarks that are required to remain in—and progress through—the academy. All parents are affected by family formation, but women tend to suffer professionally more than men (whose careers by comparison often benefit from the process).

The academic profession as a whole will become more inclusive when campuses normalize and embrace parenthood. Normalizing parenthood means making individual, departmental, and institutional changes to existing official policies and informal practices that unfairly penalize women. Embracing parenthood means doing all of this willingly in pursuit of a more equitable and humane profession. To this end, we seek to make the invisible but messy daily realities of family formation and parenting visible and acceptable.

We are both political scientists and mothers. We have experienced the challenges of navigating the early-career years while in the process of starting families and raising young children. We have also been fortunate to participate in mentoring circles where senior women scholars have told their stories and shared their lessons learned and strategies for success. Arguably the most important aspect of normalizing parenthood in the academy is access to mentorship, but if women—or parents of any gender—exit the pipeline too quickly, there are too few mentors to inspire, guide, and support early-career scholar parents. Mentorship represents meaningful social connection, an inoculation against the profound isolation that academic parents often face.

A View from the Top: Higher-Order Processes

Higher-order processes describe the divergent paths for men and women in academia. Gender bias in teaching evaluations, gender gaps in citations in articles and syllabi, gender gaps in tenure and rank attainment: higher-order attributes are easily observable phenomena that provide evidence of the leaky pipeline (Breuning and Sanders 2007; Clark Blickenstaff 2005; Hesli, Lee, and Mitchell 2012; London School of Economics and Political Science 2014; Mitchell and Hesli 2013). Other factors include unequal service assignments, a propensity among women toward qualitative work that tends to take longer from inception to publication, and disparity in publication citations among other metrics used to evaluate academic progress. Coauthored scholarship is one way junior scholars get more publications out the door; the benefits for men and women are again unequal, however (Broderick and Casadevall 2017; Casadevall et al. 2019). Moreover, women receive less credit than men do for collaborative work (Sarsons 2017). Letters of recommendation also expose gender bias: writers tend to emphasize quantifiable positive achievements for men but reference women's personality and social characteristics. These gendered processes create obstacles for women's advancement in academia regardless of parental status, but the effects of parenthood and gender on academic success are inextricably linked.

So to answer the questions—*why* women achieve tenure and promotion at lower rates than men do and *why* they drop out of academia altogether more often—we need to explore the more subtle ways family formation during an early academic career disadvantages women. Higher-order processes are amply quantified, in large part because they are observable and thus measurable. Lower-order processes are often invisible, and yet they serve as the tributaries that strain the careers of academic parents. Higher-order processes are the benchmarks and measurable achievements in an academic's life. Lower-order processes are the less observable and often gender-specific life events and circumstances that steer the divergent courses of men's and women's careers. Think about the path to professorship as a board game, where you roll the dice and move forward toward tenure and promotion, or draw "life happens" cards and move backward as you navigate the early years of your professional career while starting a family. Take two steps forward if you have high-quality mentorship. Take a step back for every miscarriage. Draw a card: *your new job is ten hours away from family and support systems, and your child is sick for the third time this month. Take a step back because you miss an important conference to care for your kid.* Take a step forward if you have favorable family formation policies in your department and institution. Take five steps forward if you're from a top-ten institution. Draw a card: *Your long-awaited and desired adoption fell through, again. Take a step back.* Roll the dice, land on *Your chair or dean refuses to negotiate family leave with you.* Take two steps back. Draw a card: *Your partner has a tenure-track job, and you take an instructorship position. Skip twelve turns.*

Lower-Order Processes
- Infertility, miscarriage, and infant and child loss (Gregory 2015; Silver-Greenberg and Kitroeff 2018; von Stein 2013; Winegar 2016)
- Medically complicated pregnancies (Hoekzema et al. 2017)
- Postpartum depression and anxiety (Brenhouse 2013; Griffiths 2019)
- Mental load and emotional labor (Kim, Fitzsimons, and Kay 2018; Wong 2018)
- Use of parental leave (Antecol, Bedard, and Stearns 2016; Wolfers 2017)
- Illnesses of early childhood (Wolfinger 2013)
- Childcare difficulties (Anderson 2016; Epifanio and Troeger 2013)
- Geographic isolation (Kulis and Sicotte 2002)
- Dual-career academics ("two-body problem") (Wolf-Wendel, Twombly, and Rice 2004)
- Breastfeeding and lactation (Davidson and Langan 2006)
- Inequitably applied family leave policies (Kittilson 2008; Masuoka 2017; Powell 2019)

Higher-Order Processes
- Student evaluations (Merritt 2008; K. M. W. Mitchell and Martin 2018)
- Letters of recommendation (Madera, Hebl, and Martin 2009; Trix and Psenka 2003)
- Access to formal and informal mentorship (Leeds et al. 2014)
- Publication count (Voeten 2013)
- The gender gap in citations (Ainley, Danewid, and Yao 2017; Maliniak, Powers, and Walter 2013; S. M. Mitchell, Lange, and Brus 2013)
- Discipline prestige (R. Oprisko 2012; R. L. Oprisko 2012)
- Unequal service assignments (Epifanio and Troeger 2013)
- Tenure, promotion, and rank disparity (Armenti 2004; Chenoweth et al. 2016; Chronister et al. 1997)
- Gendered salary gaps (Claypool et al. 2017; Ginther and Hayes 2003)

- Discriminatory hiring practices (Yakowicz n.d.)
- Penalties for flouting gender norms (S. M. Mitchell and Hesli 2013)

Although the "leaky pipeline" is the standard reference for explaining disparate and gendered trends in academia, the board game metaphor more accurately describes how lower- and higher-order factors shape women's academic careers. The leaky pipeline metaphor assumes that everyone progresses along on a linear path through the academic ranks, which we know intuitively and empirically is not the case. The path to tenure and promotion—especially for women and those starting families simultaneously—is fundamentally nonlinear. It's a game not unlike Chutes and Ladders, where quality mentorship and equitable and favorable family formation policies can improve your chances of "winning," and lack of adequate support can send you backward. Through their stories, our survey respondents and vignette contributors have helped us understand in greater detail what fosters career advancement and what stifles it in academia.

Demographics of Survey Respondents

In November 2017 we launched an online survey to assess experiences with family formation and parenthood in academia. The full text of the survey is in the appendix. Approximately three hundred respondents answered questions about a range of topics, including their ability to negotiate and take parental leave for the birth or adoption of a child, their perception of the family-friendliness of their university and home department, and the professional rank they held at the time of their first child's birth or adoption. Their responses confirmed what the research suggests: that the "primary parent" faces professional and personal penalties that contribute to leaks in the academic pipeline. The demographics of our survey respondents alone provide important insights into the experiences of academic parents, so we turn now to a brief discussion of who answered the call for participants.

Our survey on family formation and parenting in academia and the call for vignette authors were open to academics, including graduate students, in any discipline and geographic location. We disseminated the call for survey participants and vignettes through social networking groups focused on parenting in the academy, formal and informal LISTSERVs composed of academics (broadly speaking) or academic parents (more narrowly focused), presentation of the research and advertisement of the survey at the International Studies Association annual meeting in April 2018, and direct recruitment of colleagues and their personal networks. In recruiting for both the survey and the vignettes, we sought to cast a wide net. In promoting the project in parenthood-focused groups we hoped to gain a diverse respondent pool by recruiting from inclusive spaces with members in all stages of the academic career (from graduate student through full professor), in multiple countries, and who identify with a range of genders, races, and ethnicities.

Our survey respondents are based in a variety of academic institutions and occupy both contingent and more secure appointments. The largest percentage (34 percent) work in research universities, with the next largest group (27 percent) based in public institutions. About 17 percent work on liberal arts campuses, while 7 percent are in private institutions. Roughly 10 percent of respondents work in comprehensive universities, while 3 percent are in minority-serving institutions, and 2 percent are in community colleges. Assistant professors comprise the largest share of survey respondents (36 percent), with associate professors forming the second-largest group (28 percent). Full professors account for 13 percent of our respondents. Contingent faculty and researchers make up roughly 18 percent of the sample: 4 percent are adjunct faculty, 6 percent are instructors, 3 percent are postdoctoral fellows, 2 percent are visiting assistant professors, and 3 percent are research assistant professors. Five percent of respondents are unemployed (or were at the time of the survey). Graduate students are counted among the adjunct faculty, instructors, and unemployed.

About 2 in 5 respondents to our survey (44 percent) are in political science, almost 1 in 5 are in other social sciences (17 percent), and more than a quarter (29 percent) are in other fields including medicine and STEM-related disciplines. The heavy concentration of respondents in political science and the social sciences is due to the nature of the LISTSERVs, conference, and professional connections where we publicized the survey. The issues facing parents in academia are not particular to political science; these problems cross disciplinary and institutional boundaries. The lower-order and higher-order problems—and the solutions we identify—apply beyond the field of political science. Many of the problems, however, appear to be unique to academics in the United States. Respondents from non-US institutions noted that problems of equitable application of policies—and the ready availability and publicity of these policies—are non-issues outside the United States. The striking contrasts provided by non-US respondents have helped reveal the nature and depth of problems facing women and families in academia in the United States. These responses point to broad societal differences between support for parents and families in the United States and in other countries. Lack of support for parents and families in the United States relative to other wealthy industrialized democracies is not just an issue within academia.

The demographics of our survey respondents reflect the characteristics of the population we expect would be most concerned with issues surrounding bias, gender, and parenting within academic institutions. More than half of the respondents (55 percent) are in their thirties, and one-third of the respondents are in their forties. The majority of respondents (85 percent) identify as women, and most respondents (89 percent) are white. The racial and ethnic makeup of the survey population underscores the broader under-representation of people of color within the faculty ranks. We asked respondents to write in the race or ethnicity with which they identify and provided a text box (rather than a list of options) to avoid excluding or overlooking any race or ethnicity. Our respondents overwhelmingly self-identified as white (73.5 percent), which limits the extent to which we can speak to issues of race and racial bias in the academy. Roughly 10 percent self-identified as members of minority groups: 0.6 percent self-identified as Black, 1.8 percent self-identified as Latinx; 1.5 percent self-identified as Asian; 1.8 percent self-identified as Jewish; 0.3 percent self-identified as Middle Eastern; 2.4 percent self-identified as multiracial. Of the respondents who answered the question, 1.2 percent self-identified as "other" or stated that they did not identify with any race or ethnicity. Importantly, a large portion of respondents (16.8 percent) declined to answer the question.

Research on demographic questions in surveys points to a higher rate of nonresponse to such questions among participants who identify as racial or ethnic minorities. Stacey Patton's research highlights the mixed perception of race-focused demographic questions on forms and job applications; some individuals feel that race should not matter when weighing a candidate's credentials and decline to disclose their race, while others "check the box" hesitantly, as a matter of habit, or proudly. In their research, Maichou Lor and colleagues (2017) find that adding context to demographic survey questions yields a modest improvement in the response to demographic questions among racial and ethnic minority groups. While the anonymous nature of our survey precludes us from inferring the identities of the 20 percent of respondents who declined to answer the race and ethnicity question, existing research suggests that the portion of respondents who identify as people of color is likely higher than the data suggest.

Most respondents are from North America (83 percent). This regional concentration is due again to the networks through which we disseminated the survey. Examining the location of respondents in the United States more closely, almost half of respondents are in the Midwest (22 percent) or the

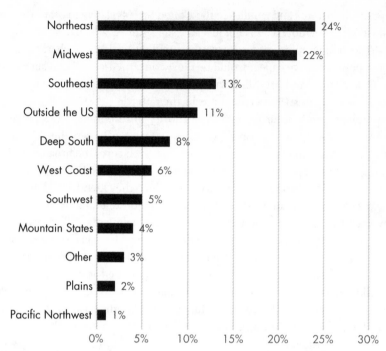

Figure 1.1. If your primary residence is the United States, which region best describes where you live? (n = 277)

Northeast (24 percent). Just over one-tenth (13 percent) are in the South, and just under 1 in 5 (16 percent) are in the West (mountain states, 4 percent; Pacific Northwest, 1 percent; Southwest, 5 percent; West Coast, 6 percent). Figure 1.1 illustrates the geographic region of respondents within the United States. Roughly 11 percent of respondents identified their region as outside of the United States. We recognize the wide variation in national parental leave policies, and specifically the lack of a federal parental leave policy in the United States, but we have kept academics from outside of the United States in the sample precisely because their insights into effective parental leave policies inform recommendations for best practices. On the other hand, we also know that gendered expectations for parents are consistent across regions and cultures, and gender-based discrimination is not a phenomenon limited to the academic profession within the United States.

In terms of family size, most respondents' households have either one (46 percent) or two (38 percent) children, while just over 10 percent have three or more children. More than two-thirds of respondents had their first child in their thirties (68 percent), and about a quarter of people had their first child in their twenties (24 percent). Of respondents with more than one child, the majority (55 percent) had their second child in their thirties. The overwhelming majority of respondents (95 percent) are married or in a relationship. More than 4 in 5 respondents have a doctorate, and almost 1 in 10 have a master's degree. Respondents across ranks in both tenure-track and non-tenure-track positions had approximately the same average number of children.

Only *10 percent* of respondents earned tenure before having their first child, suggesting that the vast majority of our survey respondents were not in positions with a high degree of job security when they started their families. This finding stands in stark contrast to much of the informal (and impractical) advice given to early-career women scholars: wait until after tenure to have children. We have seen the impacts of this advice firsthand. For example, during a workshop for early-career scholars a graduate student approached one of us in wide-eyed disbelief and exclaimed, "You said you had your child while finishing your dissertation. Did you mean to? Were you using birth control? There are no mothers in my department! Female students and professors just don't have children." This graduate student had observed the dearth of academic mothers in her immediate network and internalized the advice that scholars should hold off until their careers are safely established before having children. We hypothesize that this advice is prevalent because the journey to tenure and promotion with children on board is so fraught with challenges.

Finally, we wish to reiterate that the survey overrepresents academics—students, researchers, and faculty—who are currently in the profession. As we noted in the introduction, the survey sample does not adequately represent the experiences of individuals who have left academia, given the channels we used to recruit participants. One of the limitations of this survivorship bias is that we cannot parse the factors that led those who left academia to do so. Instead, our survey sample largely represents best-case scenarios. Our survey data tell the stories of the "lucky ones" who stayed in the profession despite significant challenges. While the survey's reach is limited to those within or still connected to the academy, the responses point to factors that force some academics out of the profession. If our survey respondents survived the difficult experiences they recounted, it stands to reason that circumstances were even worse for those who left. While we cannot fully explore the factors that drove many academics out of the profession, we *can* underscore the urgent need for reforms.

Family-Unfriendly Policies Are at Odds with the Academy's Goal of Fostering Diversity

Due to the way society envisions parenthood and family responsibilities—with the disproportionate share of the work done by women—it is impractical to decouple the dynamics surrounding parenthood from those related to gender. Women are expected to work as though they do not have family commitments and parent as though they do not work outside the home. We cannot, then, discuss normalizing parenthood without engaging the effort to normalize *women* in the academy and to diversify college and university campuses in all senses.

In the past, revealing family concerns has often been viewed as unprofessional. The underlying assumption is that masculinity equals professionalism, where job candidates are expected to reveal only the qualifications related to their prospective employment. Candidates are expected to portray themselves as unencumbered by family distractions. Women are counseled to remove wedding bands for job interviews and not disclose their family status. To guard against potential discrimination, identity-based questions such as religion, sexual orientation, and family status are illegal during job interviews. However, this policy and general approach is at odds with recent job market trends of institutions and departments "encouraging women and minorities to apply."

Academia says it wants more diversity, but there is a gap between acknowledging the goals of diversification and the means to achieving it long term. Women in particular are more likely to stay at institutions that embrace and support the process of family formation. Many colleges and universities are working to improve diversity among students, faculty, staff, and administrators, adjusting admissions and hiring practices to mitigate the effects of bias in pursuit of the benefits inclusivity conveys for all members of a campus community (Griffin n.d.; Lor et al. 2017; Patton 2014). As university administrators seek to improve retention of individuals from traditionally underrepresented groups, they must acknowledge and address issues pertaining to implicit bias and obstacles to professional success. Simply bringing in women and minorities without changing broader campus culture does too little. Research by Mary Ann Mason and Marc Goulden (2002) found that only 58 percent of early-career mothers earned tenure, while 78 percent of early-career fathers did. To retain and promote women, especially minority women, academic disciplines and campuses must engage in serious reconsideration of institutional, college-level, and departmental policies related to family formation.

The website hosting company GoDaddy pursued a strategy targeting cultural and policy subtleties to make its workplace more equitable for women (Duhigg 2017) by focusing on implicit bias around employee evaluation and salary negotiations (Greenwald and Krieger 2006). Similarly, we address issues of implicit bias in depth in the following section. Diversity, underrepresentation, and bias cut many ways. We focus here on obstacles to the success and retention of faculty who are (or hope to become) parents, especially women in the early stages of their careers. These individuals may also encounter bias related to their racial, religious, ethnic, national, regional, or socioeconomic identities, and as these biases arise so too do additional obstacles to professional advancement and overall well-being. The scope of this book, however, is limited to an academic's gender identity and identity as a parent (or prospective parent). In this section we explore the existing research on common gender-related professional obstacles and setbacks and discuss the ideas presented therein in the context of our survey on parenting in the academy.

In the academic game of Chutes and Ladders, women enter graduate school cohorts in numbers roughly equal to men but drop off from the higher ranks of the academic profession; this results in a gender imbalance among tenured faculty (Hesli, Lee, and Mitchell 2012; London School of Economics and Political Science 2014). Hesli, Lee, and Mitchell (2012, 486) find that while women are less likely to achieve the rank of associate professor and the accompanying benefit of tenure, those who do "survive the tenure process are as likely as men (given relevant controls) to move up the academic ladder to full professor." Yet, as Ward and Wolf-Wendel (2012, 7) observe in their study of women on the tenure track, the ideal academic career trajectory from graduate school through the tenure track to promotion with tenure "can present a woman who enters the academic ranks childless, but wanting children, a feeling that she confronts what can seem like irreconcilable differences between parenthood and a career as a tenure-line faculty member." The key is getting to and through the tenure process unscathed. As Mason, Wolfinger, and Goulden (2013, 48) note, roughly half of assistant professors (regardless of parental status) will not achieve tenure, and tenure is more attainable at colleges and universities that place less emphasis on research and publications. Hesli, Lee, and Mitchell (2012, 486) find that neither partnership or marital status nor the number of children clearly affects promotion, but they also note that the extant research on the subject suggests that the evidence is mixed. For instance, men enjoy benefits from "marriage to a spouse without a professional degree," including greater likelihood of earning tenure (Morrison, Rudd, and Nerad n.d., 545).

Hesli, Lee, and Mitchell (2012, 487) also urge caution in interpreting the effects of marriage and parenthood on promotion and tenure, noting that "women with heavy family responsibilities may have already left academia," a trend we call survivorship bias.[1] They find that a greater number of publications help men's careers, but the number of publications has no significant effect on women's rank attainment. For women scholars, this is a bleak statistic. Research by Foschi (1996) is a more damning indictment of implicit bias against women and their perceived productivity: they must outpace men in their publications to persuade tenure and promotion committees of their continued commitment to scholarly output. Mason, Wolfinger, and Goulden (2013, 48) similarly observe a need for careful interpretation of the relationship between gender and professional success, finding that women are "21 percent less likely to get tenure than their male colleagues" but that this effect appears unrelated to marital or parental status.

Our survey participants' self-reported academic positions reflect the broader trends observed in the literature. More than a third of respondents in our survey (36 percent) are assistant professors and about a quarter of respondents (28 percent) are associate professors. Nearly one in five respondents (18 percent) are in a non-tenure-track position: adjunct (4 percent), visiting assistant professor (2 percent), research assistant professor (3 percent), postdoctoral fellow (3 percent), or instructor (6 percent). This contingent has few if any privileges or perquisites, such as access to family leave or extending a (nonexistent) tenure clock (Mason, Wolfinger, and Goulden 2013). The oversupply of PhDs on the job market in an academic system weighted heavily in favor of the highest-ranked programs (R. Oprisko 2012) has generated an academic purgatory for tenure-track hopefuls.

To compete with peers from top-ranked programs, scholars in non-tenure-track positions maintain a precarious balance of weighing time spent on perpetual job searching, research output, (often) greater teaching responsibilities, and the simultaneous demands of family formation. Furthermore, many non-tenure-track positions have comparatively lower salaries and fewer bargaining or negotiating options, meaning that families must make do with less. Only 13 percent of respondents attained full professor at the time they completed the survey. Two in five respondents (41 percent) have tenure, while three in five (59 percent) do not. Figure 1.2 illustrates our survey respondents' positions. With respect to institution type, two in five respondents (41 percent) work at research universities, and a quarter (26 percent) are at public institutions; only 8 percent work at private institutions.

Some of the factors that contribute to leaks in the academic pipeline are subtle, while others are overt (McMurtrie 2013; Voeten 2013). On the overt

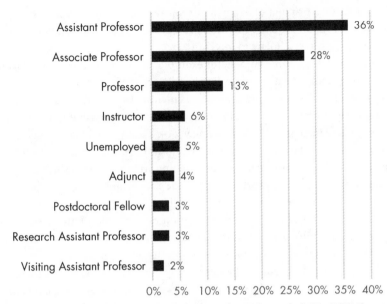

Figure 1.2. What is your current professional employment? (n = 274)

side, the academic probationary period often (but not always) coincides with the years in which early-career scholars are contemplating family commitments, including the decision to have children (Armenti 2004); depending on the level of support available, these competing demands can take a toll on academics of any gender. Those who face conflicts between family commitments and the job search or the tenure track may make the decision to accept lower-ranked positions, such as adjunct professorships or instructorships, or leave the profession entirely. In fact, some research suggests that this strategy is a promising one that helps women scholars "stay in the game"—although it does not measure the quality of life or the personal toll this process takes on women and families (Wolfinger, Mason, and Goulden 2009).

Mundane, seemingly inconsequential, daily decisions at home and on campus compound to create larger trends in the profession. One of the more subtle factors contributing to unequal advancement between women and men is the role of informal mentorship and networking. Connections between junior and senior scholars may occur in formal settings like conference panels or research talks, but they often happen in the conference bar or pub, during the department happy hour, or over dinner with university visitors. What begins as a simple conversation during a social outing can turn into a lasting and productive mentoring relationship. Invitations to informal

events may be a product of department norms and social networks, connections among senior scholars and their protégés, or sheer chance, but logistical
hurdles force some scholars to miss out.

Pregnant or nursing women, for example, are strongly discouraged from
consuming alcohol, with further disincentives from fatigue or health-related
issues. Parents of young children—fathers included—may be unable to attend
happy hours or late evening dinners because of daycare schedules or after-
school pickup responsibilities. What may look like an individual self-selecting
out of valuable networking and mentorship opportunities may in reality be
the result of health concerns or family commitments. The resulting gap in
mentorship can penalize early-career academics who then miss opportunities for coauthorships, participation in selective workshops or conference
panels, access to potential recommendation or evaluation letter writers, or
information on job openings. What begins as a simple social outing may thus
contribute—inadvertently or otherwise—to the leaky pipeline.

We want to shed light on the nuances, trade-offs, and decisions that lead
academic parents, especially women, to press on through or exit the pipeline.
The leaky pipeline metaphor encompasses a range of decisions, norms, and
dynamics that create barriers to success or place pressure on an individual
to leave the academic profession. Although the subtle and overt influences
are numerous and highly variable across different institutional settings (e.g.,
large research universities versus small liberal arts colleges), scholars have
discussed at length several factors that contribute to the broader gender gap
in academia. These include discrimination in hiring practices, flaws in student evaluations of teaching, unequal career benefits of taking parental leave,
struggles to contend with not only the "two-body problem" that couples face
but the three-or-more-body problem confronting families with children, and
gender gaps in citations (Wolfinger, Mason, and Goulden 2008).

It should go without saying that these factors affect parents and scholars
without children alike; our focus is on the ways different factors combine for
scholar parents, especially mothers. The results from our survey point toward
one central issue: all of the obstacles women scholars already face in academia
are amplified and intensified during the time of family formation and throughout the years spent raising children. Having children makes an already difficult
process all the more challenging. We turn now to these factors.

Bias, Bias, Everywhere

When we discuss bias, we refer to the decisions, assessments, or judgments that
individuals make in response to a person, place, situation, or idea. Bias can lead

to a favorable/positive or unfavorable/negative view (Staats 2013, 7). Implicit bias refers to the attitudes and preferences human beings unconsciously possess, that lead them to form positive or negative (rather than neutral) response to a person, situation, place, or idea (Morrow Jones and Box-Steffensmeier 2014; Staats 2013). It is important to understand that implicit bias shapes decision-making processes without the decision-maker's awareness or control. Explicit bias, on the other hand, is consciously held; this form of bias is often more clearly aligned with our stated morals and values (Morrow Jones and Box-Steffensmeier 2014). Our biases form through our experiences, including and perhaps especially those in childhood, through exposure to media and popular culture, and via the norms, traditions, and practices in our immediate communities and broader cultures. As universities begin or continue efforts to diversify their faculty and student populations, decision-makers must account for the role bias plays in hiring practices, student evaluations of teaching, and other day-to-day realities of academic life. Implicit bias, in particular, can be difficult to address because it is inadvertent and individuals are almost always unaware of such bias. Tools such as the Implicit Association Test can help illuminate the implicit biases we each hold, which is an important first step toward mitigating the potentially harmful effects of bias (Project Implicit n.d.). We emphasize the role of implicit bias in men's and women's divergent career paths exactly because these same inherent biases are amplified around issues of family formation. An increasing number of universities are requiring implicit bias training for faculty on search committees, as well as promotion and tenure committees, to work toward institutional reform of inequitable practices that disproportionately harm women and minorities (Applebaum 2019; Pritlove et al. 2019).

Parental Leave: Asking for It, Taking It, and Acknowledging Unequal Career Benefits

"I asked if I could have some time off and they said no," a survey respondent reported. Once someone decides to expand their family, what types of support are available—whether for pregnancy and childbirth, fostering, or adoption? How have colleges and universities evolved in their positions on parental leave? More than a quarter (29 percent) of our survey respondents report that their department's or university's parental leave policy has changed over time, while just less than a quarter (22 percent) report that it has not. Most striking, however, is that almost *half* (49 percent) report that *they are not sure whether the policy has changed*. This represents a gaping policy chasm for departments and universities: faculty, staff, and students must be able to access and understand family leave policies if these policies are to be equitably and universally applied. Put differently, administrators, including deans and department or unit heads, must ensure that these policies are clearly communicated and equitably applied. Faculty understanding comes from clearly articulated, easily accessible, and consistently applied policies and practices.

Our survey responses indicate that this is not always the case: two-thirds of respondents (63 percent) report that their institution's family leave policies are consistent across departments, yet a *quarter* (23 percent) say they are not, and another 14 percent say they are unsure. This changes at the department level, however. Slightly more than half (56 percent) say that family leave policies are consistently applied across individuals in their department, whereas a fifth (18 percent) say they are not. A quarter (25 percent) of respondents report that they are unsure whether these policies are applied consistently across individuals in their department.

Figures 1.3 and 1.4 illustrate the similarities and differences in leave policies between respondents' institutions and departments. Generally speaking, our survey respondents offer some hope for those seeking improvements in support for families: when asked how university or department leave policies have changed over time, nearly half of respondents (49 percent) report that leave policies at their institution have improved (broadly speaking). Figure 1.5 offers an illustration of the range of responses to our question about policy change over time. It is worth noting that in many institutions, parents must use their accrued sick leave because there is no national, universal paid parental leave in the United States, and not all institutions have adopted such policies independently, inherently penalizing women. Men accrue their sick leave over time, while women use it to cover postpartum leave.

Parental leave is neither sick leave nor a "baby vacation," as some have called it. However, when departments and institutions require parents to use sick leave or vacation time, they reinforce the perception that welcoming a child is "time off." While there is obvious progress with respect to institutions' adopting family leave policies, the proportion of respondents who are unsure about departmental and university family leave policies is troubling. Administrators need to make policies and procedures related to family leave more transparent. Given the department-specific and often idiosyncratic nature of tenure and promotion decisions that determine the success or failure of an academic career, departments especially need to be clear about the policies and expectations for pre-tenure family formation.

Lack of transparency in departmental and university policies has dire implications for the outcome of family leave negotiations. We pause here to

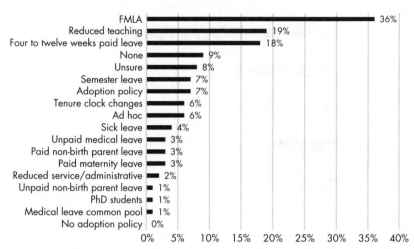

Figure 1.3. What is your institution's parental/maternity/family leave policy? (n = 222)

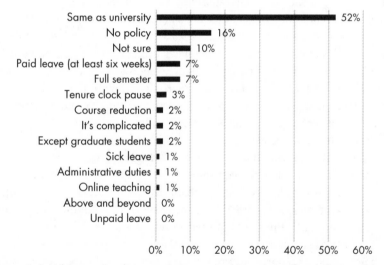

Figure 1.4. What is your department's parental/maternity/family leave policy? (n = 218)

reflect that family leave requires negotiation; it is not universally applied nor universally granted. Further, most of our survey respondents noted simultaneous family and work responsibilities during their official family leave time. The process of negotiation itself is time-consuming and energy-consuming: *What should I negotiate for? How much can I ask for? What did everyone else get?* Two

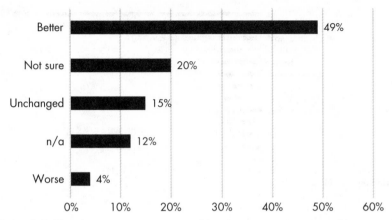

Figure 1.5. How has your university and/or department's parental leave policy changed over time? (n = 82)

things are true: a one-size-fits-all approach will not meet everyone's individual needs, and accommodating family leave should not be idiosyncratic, personality driven, or dependent on a supervisor's willingness to negotiate. Similarly, it should not depend on a faculty member's success at communicating their need for time off to care for a child. Many women may hesitate to negotiate aggressively for fear of retribution or reprisals at tenure decision time for having taken maternity leave, a well-founded concern affirmed by scientific studies of gender and negotiations (Bowles, Babcock, and Lai 2007).

In theory, family leave policies are designed to accommodate and alleviate the dual responsibilities of career and family. As we emphasized earlier, parental leave is not the equivalent of sick leave or vacation time. It is certainly not research leave or a sabbatical. Parental leave is an essential and basic accommodation for parents recovering from childbirth and new parents adjusting to the needs of their growing families. In practice, however, parental leave is viewed as time off and often counts against women in their pursuit of tenure and promotion if institutional support for family leave is inadequate. Some new mothers avoid taking leave because of the fear of stigma, criticism that they are not serious about their careers, or the presumption that they are leveraging their biology for personal and professional gain. Meghann Foye (2016) codified the widespread opinion of maternity leave as time off or vacation in her book *Meternity*. She taps into a widely held belief that reinforces the motherhood or parenthood penalty: that women are abusing the system and capitalizing on childbirth and the perceived perquisites that come with it, like extra time to publish or to relax, when the research demonstrates that in actuality the opposite is true (Antecol, Bedard, and Stearns 2018; Wolfers 2017).

Furthermore, part-time, visiting, or adjunct faculty members, faculty members at institutions without paid leave, and graduate students may be ineligible for official leave or unable to take leave because the financial burden of doing so unpaid is insurmountable (Wolfinger 2013). For parents who do take leave, the benefits are less than equal. A parent who has just given birth must balance their own physical recovery, emotional health, and a newborn child's needs. A parent who has welcomed a child but who has not given birth does not have the additional challenges of physical recovery or the psychological and emotional effects of postpartum hormone fluctuations but may be similarly sleep-deprived, stressed, and adapting to the realities of life with a new family member. For instance, many of our vignette contributors are adoptive parents whose adjustment periods are not widely visible or understood by colleagues.

Extant research does not affirm the notion that women "use" childbearing to their advantage; in fact quite the opposite is true. Scholarship has identified that in academia, children have negative effects on women's chances of success in the profession while nearly universally benefiting men's careers (Mason, Wolfinger, and Goulden 2013; Wolfinger 2013). One reason for the disparity in effects of family leave relates to the demands on each parent's time. If a parent is not recovering from childbirth or learning to breastfeed, that parent has more capacity to continue—at least to some extent—research, other ongoing projects, or an academic job search. In addition, recent research shows that after universities adopt paid parental leave, the probability that a man gets tenure increases by 19 percent, while a woman's chances fall by 22 percent (Antecol, Bedard, and Stearns 2018). Figure 1.6 illustrates how our survey respondents reported spending their parental leave time in response to the question, "What were your professional responsibilities after birth/adoption/family status change?"

In the chapter "Women Don't Ask," Babcock (in Bowles, Babcock, and Lai, 2007) notes that at least some of the disparity between men and women in academia results from women not asking for better or more accommodations, for salary raises, or for more than they were offered. Women are praised for their compliance, whereas men are rewarded for their ambition through quantifiable and career-impacting metrics like letters of recommendation and teaching evaluations (Dion 2008; Trix and Psenka 2003).

For respondents to our survey who did negotiate family leave, a third (33 percent) negotiated for reduced teaching, a third (33 percent) for an altered schedule, 7 percent for tenure clock changes, and 10 percent for official leave.

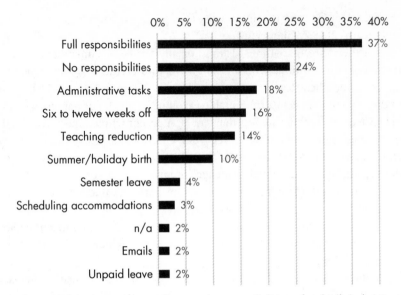

Figure 1.6. What were your professional responsibilities after birth/adoption/ family status change? (n = 209)

Yet 15 percent of respondents said that their chairs, deans, or other administrators *refused* to negotiate with them. One respondent said, "I tried, but ran into a lot of brick walls. I spoke with the division head and with the vice-president/provost, and the latter insisted that maternity leave was only for women giving birth (which was treated as an illness!) and did not include adoptive parents. This was at my previous institution, a public liberal arts university." Another said, "I tried—there's no sick leave; the chair was female without children and was not sympathetic, so I did not get leave." Another respondent raised several issues: "For my first child, I was a graduate student and so did not negotiate any leave. For my second and third children (twins), I was a faculty member and *attempted* to negotiate leave, but was not granted leave. The policy stated that I had to be the 'primary caregiver'—my wife was at the time a self-employed preschool director teaching courses in our home. Our institution said that because my wife would be physically in the walls of our house, I could not claim status as a 'primary caregiver' for the purposes of leave." Many respondents to our survey from outside the United States expressed disbelief that family leave required negotiation; institutions outside the United States often have universal—even national—family leave policies that apply equitably across all individuals with little or no negotiation required.

The opacity of family leave policies and the physical and emotional demands of family formation may encourage early-career women scholars to make decisions about their departmental contributions that are deleterious to their careers. Supervisors may also use service assignments to compensate for inadequate family leave policies—or in place of implementing policies already on the books (Crawford and Windsor 2019). Women may prioritize service assignments that can be accomplished by multitasking family and work responsibilities and thereby engender goodwill in their departments (Murdie 2017) rather than declining the service assignments and prioritizing publications that will improve their chances of earning tenure and promotion. Discrepancies in service expectations (both self-imposed and institutionally reinforced) are not limited to tasks performed during leave time. In general, women tend to take on internal and lower-esteemed service assignments that do not raise their profile at their institution or in the profession.

With our survey respondents' answers in mind, we recommend a number of approaches at the administration, department, and individual faculty levels that represent best practices for embracing parents on campus.

Best Practices for Embracing Parents on Campus
What university administrators can do:

- Communicate family leave policies clearly to department chairs and faculty.
- Change or amend tenure-clock policies capped at two children.
- Offer diversity training for tenure and promotion committees and department chairs to reduce the effects of implicit bias.
- Determine policies for non-tenure-track faculty similar to stopping the tenure clock.
- Provide health insurance and Family and Medical Leave Act accommodations to graduate student parents.

What department chairs and unit heads can do:

- Negotiate with your faculty.
- Do not tolerate, promote, or ignore anti-family hostility among department members.
- Do not tell your faculty or graduate students when (or when not to) start families.
- Provide a semester of research leave for parents who have given birth after they return from maternity leave.

What faculty can do:

- Don't settle for off-the-books solutions that don't benefit your career.
- Know your department's and institution's tenure and promotion requirements.
- Stop the tenure clock.
- Know your institution's family leave policies.
- Don't feel guilty or like a failure if you leave academia. While some situations are personal, there are endemic structural impediments that are sometimes insurmountable.

Note

1. In addition to proceeding cautiously in the interpretation of factors leading women to exit academia, some scholars disagree with the focus on the leaky pipeline entirely. For instance, in their research on women in science, technology, engineering, and mathematics (STEM) fields, Miller and Wai (2015) take issue with the leaky pipeline metaphor, contending that gender gaps in the bachelor's-to-PhD pipeline in STEM narrowed in the 1990s and that the metaphor fails to describe demographics in these fields today. The authors also make the case that discussion of the leaky pipeline places an undue burden on women who decide to pursue interests and employment outside of STEM fields.

2 Thesis Baby

Getting Student Parents the Support They Need

"As early as undergraduate, I was privy to the establishment rule that women must wait for children until after tenure," one survey respondent reported. The path to tenure begins in graduate school. Since the ultimate goal is to make the profession more inclusive of women and families, we must examine and change the norms, rules, and practices that dictate who succeeds and who fails, who gets the best jobs after graduation, and who drops out of the job search. Importantly, we must consider what happens when graduate students have the audacity to have personal lives. Consider the advice that young women scholars are given: remove your wedding band before a job interview; never disclose a pregnancy, spouse, or family; and portray a neutral life free from complications. "Neutral," of course, means that women should conform to masculine norms.[1] Cisgender men can never be pregnant on the job market, never need to pump milk or nurse a child, and are generally perceived as free of attachments, save the supportive spouse who cares for all the domestic work on the home front. Furthermore, *having a child while in graduate school is unthinkable*.

Life and career changes often happen at the same time. Optimal child-bearing years roughly coincide with the rigors of the job market. Early-career scholars need support to progress in their graduate programs through major life changes, like family formation. This is especially important given that the graduate school years traditionally span the twenties and early thirties, the years in which long-term partnerships and parenting may become personal priorities. In the United States, most doctoral programs last at least five years, so it is almost inevitable that life will intervene in some way at some point. Whether life gets in the way of academic success or becomes the inspiration for it, the path to a successful academic career should not be left to individuals alone. The broader system of mentors, faculty, university administrators, and professional associations have important roles to play in creating equitable policies and support structures that empower student parents to succeed (Leeds et al. 2014).

Given the importance of mentorship, we have written this chapter as much for the people who work with graduate students as for those student parents themselves. Here, we focus in particular on a graduate student's decision to have children in graduate school or to start graduate school with children in tow. While this chapter cannot provide an exhaustive account of the complex considerations and challenges that graduate student parents face before, during, and after PhD programs, we highlight the potential benefits and challenges of graduate school parenthood and offer suggestions for student parents and those who support them.

It is important to note that there is an element of survivorship bias with respect to the graduate school experience in our survey sample: because of the avenues we used to distribute the survey, we missed those who left graduate school—or never started—in whole or in part because of the bias or challenges they faced as parents. However, many people did mention that they considered not starting graduate school, taking time off, or dropping out entirely because of the challenges they faced juggling graduate school and parenthood. Our survey respondents and vignette contributors offer us a wealth of insights and suggestions for best practices, information that is incredibly valuable as we consider how best to reduce bias against student parents, but this advice comes too late for those who have already suffered the consequences of systemic bias and have chosen or been forced to leave the profession. Our hope is that by learning from those who have stayed, this work will be useful to those yet to begin their studies and careers as well as those who mentor and advise undergraduate and graduate students.

It Is Perfectly OK to Have a Thesis Baby . . .

Because we are all subtly or overtly led in graduate school (and earlier) to believe that having children before tenure is a career killer, we continue to accept bias against parents. We assume they cannot be serious scholars. We believe the pregnant job candidate will surely change their mind about work once the baby is born. We assume the colleague with children will not have enough time to commit to a collaborative research project, departmental service, student mentorship, or adequate research output. We accept that the male model of academia is the standard by which everyone should be judged and that diverging from it sends the signal that your career is not your first priority.

Our goal here is not to advise anyone on the ideal timing of family formation. In fact, our point is that *nobody* should tell you when the right time is to start a family. Instead, we underscore the importance of embracing student parents and dismantling the systemic obstacles they face along the path from graduate school to tenure. We must dispense with the conventional wisdom that it is unwise to have children before tenure. Few graduate programs have health insurance, and graduate students' stipends often provide meager financial resources for one person, let alone a family. Childcare alone is cost-prohibitive, and many graduate students live far from family and support systems that may help offset this expense—a theme that continues on, unresolved, through the process of tenure-track employment.

A survey respondent with a tenure-track position offers an illustrative example of the prevalence of this advice from senior scholars:

> I have been told on countless occasions that having children before tenure is a death knell to my career. I have been told this by faculty, (former) mentors, and graduate students. One story that stands out particularly is when I had a one-on-one discussion with the top female in my sub-sub-field as she visited our campus. As a reward (of sorts) I was given the duty of escorting her to the airport. When I learned her children were the same age as mine, I commented on the coincidence. She took the opportunity to tell me that children do not belong before tenure, that I would surely miss out on countless opportunities, and implied heavily that it would affect my career opportunities. At first I took this as a harbinger of career death; now I know that my story needs to be told to help kill this misconception (and discrimination).

A generous read of this interaction is that the senior mentor continues to harbor unhappy memories about the struggles she faced as an academic parent, including the sacrifices she had to make. Her advice mirrors what she was likely told by her mentors—almost certainly men. And this interaction also raises the issue that not all senior women colleagues are willing allies in the struggle against the patriarchal academy. They have internalized masculine academic biases and continue to distribute shockingly poor advice about family formation expectations. Women can be some of the most steadfast stalwarts of patriarchal norms in academia. Conversely, many survey respondents noted how their men mentors provided insightful advice about growing families.

We are happy to report that only 10 percent of our survey respondents had tenure before they became parents, demonstrating that even if this is the advice commonly given, a large majority refuses to follow it. Most of our survey respondents identify as women as well. What if, instead of perpetuating the advice to delay having children for what will be more than a decade in even the smoothest and most privileged of career trajectories (about six years for the PhD and another six on the tenure track), we accepted our prospective and current colleagues and students as they are? What if we *dared* to consider the benefits of the "thesis baby," or attending graduate school with child(ren) in tow?

Recent research suggests that parents do not actually suffer a career-long drop in productivity or efficiency. On the contrary, a 2014 study by the Federal Reserve Bank of Saint Louis observed that academic women with children were more productive in the long term than their women colleagues without children. Still, widespread gender bias leaves women in general, regardless of parental status, at a disadvantage with respect to tenure and promotion. Further, parents of any gender with two or more children outpaced their colleagues with one child or no children. Let this sink in a minute: *women with children are more productive in the long-term than their women colleagues without children.* This is not what the pervasive gender bias in academia leads us to believe. This does not square with the mythology that women are too distracted by childbearing to be successful academics. If we begin with this notion that children are not, on average, career-killers, then we are free to examine the *benefits* as well as the challenges of family formation and parenthood in graduate school.

Graduate school has the potential to be an excellent time to grow a family, as some survey respondents observe. A grad student's schedule is generally flexible, especially after coursework is complete, allowing student parents to coordinate childcare with classes, teaching or research assistantships, and dissertation research and writing. A large number of our survey respondents who welcomed their children during graduate school noted that schedule flexibility made up for any lack of official accommodations or family leave policies for students. Our respondents' experiences ranged from being hired by a professor but never receiving any task assignments to an official policy of "working it out" with one's supervisor. Truly flexible schedules allow parents to take time to recover from childbirth, bond with a new baby, and figure out life as a larger family.

However, official policies and accommodations prevent student parents from having to rely on the mercy of an individual faculty member. Individual departments or academic units often provide generous accommodations to individual student parents. This is not the ideal scenario, however. One of the themes of this book is that solutions should not rely on individual generosity or specific circumstances. Idiosyncratic accommodations can be revoked. They should instead be institutionalized, regularized, and publicized so that *all* student parents may benefit from them.

While the graduate school schedule may be flexible, the childcare schedule can be rigid—and expensive. Perhaps counterintuitively, the inflexibility of parenting logistics can be helpful. The perils of unstructured time vanish when you are paying daycare or a sitter and have a finite number of hours to complete all of the day's work-related tasks. Procrastination is simply too expensive, and this financial constraint can encourage greater work efficiency. Perfectionism, too, falls by the wayside when you have only a certain amount of time to devote to the journal article or dissertation chapter and competing demands are always on your mind. We can both personally attest to these truths, having been cured of perfectionism and procrastination by the five lovely children between us.

The downside to having finite time and financial resources is the stress that accompanies these constraints. As other scholars have noted, short-term stress can incentivize task completion; long-term, acute, chronic stress can decrease productivity and, more importantly, decrease overall health and well-being. The key is to balance work efficiency with respite and maintain realistic goals. We also emphasize that it is important to generalize the work lessons of adjusting expectations regarding procrastination and perfection beyond the work environment—good enough is good enough, at home and at work. As the saying goes, perfect is the enemy of good.

To highlight two normative points that Amanda Murdie makes clear in her vignette, the stress of "having it all" in graduate school can make you more empathetic to the experiences of your colleagues and students. Moreover—and closer to home—scholars' children can have such interesting childhoods, gaining fieldwork experience, learning conference behavior, and demystifying the work-life balance from an early age! Of course, these observations presume that student parents have sufficient mentorship, resources, and support, none of which are guaranteed.

. . . But There Are Difficulties Built In to the System That We Must Address

Academia is slow to change, and student parents face a range of challenges, many of which stem from a system that equates "student" with a single, childless, relatively privileged young person (often a man) whose health, finances, and social relationships do not interfere with making progress toward the

Bias and Family Formation in Academia

Dr. Amanda Murdie
Department Head, Department of International Affairs
Thomas P. and M. Jean Lauth Public Affairs Professor
School of Public and International Affairs
University of Georgia

I married at nineteen and had both of my children before I started my PhD program. I don't think I'd recommend that path to anyone; I was constantly tired, broke, and on the verge of divorce. However, if I had to do it over again, I probably wouldn't change a thing.

I graduated high school from a small religious town in Kansas. My parents are wonderful, and they no doubt wanted a traditional midwestern life for me. Perhaps because of this, even though I had done well as a high school student and had a full tuition scholarship to attend a state school, I thought one of the main goals of college was to find a spouse. When I met my husband (who, somewhat surprisingly, is still my husband) at eighteen and married at nineteen, I don't think anyone was that surprised. I continued going to college for my bachelor's degree like nothing had changed. My parents had encouraged me to be an elementary school teacher; it was my husband who encouraged me to continue taking courses in international relations and comparative politics, a subject area that fascinated me.

At the end of my junior year of college, I found out I was pregnant. Although we were both very young, we were excited. I don't remember much of what my career goals were at that time. I knew I wanted to work with college students, but I think I wanted to be an academic advisor. At the start of my senior year of college, I wrote to my professors and explained that I would be having a baby in November but that I would be back for finals. I kept my 4.0 average that semester. However, a new baby was extremely challenging. My husband was working almost nonstop at that time. No one had explained to me how exhausted and broken new mothers often feel. I bounced back in the next semester, but I remember some very dark early days of motherhood.

In my last semester of my senior year in college, the professors who supervised my honors thesis recommend I stay on and get a master's degree. They told me that some students were funded, receiving both a stipend and a tuition waiver. At the time, this sounded too good to be true! I signed up, mainly because I thought this would be a great way to work part-time with a baby.

I loved my master's classes. This was where I first was exposed to social science research. I convinced my husband that the next step for us should be me getting a PhD. Despite our rather traditional upbring-ings, he's always been supportive of me and my career goals. I started researching all I could on PhD programs and academia. I even started reading the *Chronicle of Higher Education* on a regular basis. I knew this was what I wanted, even if I still had only a vague idea of the workload it entailed. At this point, we decided to have another baby. My think-ing was that I could probably have a child now and start a PhD with two children or I'd miss my chance to have kids close together in age. I was nine months pregnant when I took the GRE and applied to PhD programs.

One of my only negative experiences as a student with children came as I was preparing for my second child. As a master's student, my assistantship duties involved both administering a lecture series and teaching a course. I was due in late December, and my plan was to have the baby and then come back to classes and assistantship duties in mid-January, when the spring semester started. I had worked very hard to ensure everything was planned and ready for the spring. Even though I was very visibly pregnant, one of my supervisors must have missed it. As the fall semester ended, I told him that I would have everything done before delivering. He looked at my belly and finally must have noticed that I was pregnant! He marched me to the depart-ment head's office and basically asked something like, "What are we going to do about this?" I stood there dumbfounded. The department head was in a meeting at that time with another professor; I remember both looking at me with disgust. The head, probably not fully aware of what he was saying, told me we'd have to talk about how any absence would affect my stipend. His words hurt. Instead of asking me about my plans for returning or—gasp!—congratulating me on the child, he assumed I'd miss work. There was no care for me as a person or a stu-dent, just shock that a graduate student would even think about hav-ing a baby. When I went home that evening, I was so stressed about the situation and the lack of support I had felt that I ended up asking my OB/GYN to induce me early, just so I could ensure that I didn't miss a day of work. Even now, the situation stings.

I chose my PhD program because the graduate coordinator, hav-ing read my personal statement, invited my entire family to visit for a recruitment weekend. The program was incredibly supportive, and my advisors never questioned my commitment to my work or to my family. Nonetheless, a PhD at a top program is vastly different than a master's program at a non-PhD-granting institution. The first year was incredibly rough. My husband was working nights and weekends so that we didn't have to pay for childcare. We rarely saw each other and were constantly stressed about money. I learned I couldn't possibly excel at all aspects of my life. The next few years were a constant merry-go-round of feeling guilty about whichever part of my life was falling apart at that time.

Despite this, or perhaps because of this, I did do well in the program. And my children thrived. In 2008 I was in my fourth year of the PhD program and had just finished my prospectus. The economy crashed. Thankfully, my wonderful advisors ended up recommending I go on the job market early, before the job market dried up. I received three tenure-track job offers that year, including one at my alma mater. It was the best offer of the bunch, and, even though we didn't really want to go back to Kansas (especially given my memories of the department), we ended up returning. We spent three years there before moving on to greener pastures.

Fast-forward a decade. My girls are now fourteen and sixteen. They are fabulous teenagers, spunky and socially conscious. My oldest started encouraging us to march for social causes while still in elementary school. For the annual Pride parade, the girls dyed the dog's hair rainbow colors. I'm sure they would have been great people if I hadn't chosen this path; however, I think their lives have been enriched by our shared experiences.

My marriage is also strong. I've learned that my husband can adapt (and help me adapt) to whatever situation we find ourselves in. We've lived in cities, in suburbs, and even ran a working farm for three years, where I milked a goat twice a day. When we saw discrimination happening in our local school district a few years ago, we helped organize a parental response. We're stronger people together now than I think we would have been if I'd stayed in Kansas as an elementary school teacher.

And, finally, I've done well with my career. I'm an endowed full professor and department head of a fabulous department. I'm the editor-in-chief of a major journal. I've won awards for my research and been lucky enough to brief policymakers and advocates in many different countries. I've helped dozens of students get their doctorates, including some who had children while doing so. I love what I do. Looking back, higher education made all the difference in my life. I still have periods and situations where the stress of "having it all" becomes too much. These periods pass, though, and the job's high points—together with a rich family life—have more than made up for the low points.

At the end of the day, I don't think there is a perfect time to have a family. There are many downsides to having children so early. However, there are also some benefits. The whole experience made me wickedly efficient and empathetic to those around me. I can contemplate administrative roles without worrying about how it would affect young children. I'm very close to my kids and excited for our future. And, more importantly, especially for my husband and I, I feel like we've accomplished something pretty great; if we can make it through that, we can make it through anything. It was a team effort to get me through the PhD. And, thanks to that PhD, I get to help others accomplish their career goals.

degree. When a student must navigate pregnancy, the postpartum recovery phase, breastfeeding and lactation, miscarriage, or the sleepless nights, frequent illnesses, and childcare gaps that complicate daily life as a parent, that student needs flexibility and accommodation. The trouble is, these are not guaranteed. Accommodation is often idiosyncratic and dependent on individual departments' norms and values. Moreover, graduate student status is still conceptualized as indentured servitude, marked by underpaid, overworked, and underappreciated labor. Not only are these characteristics detrimental to *all* students' health and well-being, they are especially prohibitive for student parents, whose concerns extend to their dependent children.

Accommodation needs are rarely well timed or easily anticipated. When professors design course syllabi, they do so with content, literature, and learning objectives in mind, carefully plotting the course across fifteen weeks and accounting for university breaks—but not for local school closures and flu season. When professors create late assignment and class absence policies they are mindful of fairness—but fail to anticipate all-night emergency room visits with sick children. Our default image of the ideal student is the person whose first priority is their coursework, and as a result many of our course and campus policies fail to provide the flexibility that student parents require to succeed. Scholar parents and student parents can't *not* take care of their children. This does not mean they are not serious scholars as well. Academia—at least within the United States—has perpetuated a false dichotomy that pits family priorities against work priorities. In other countries, employers require that employees disable their work emails during evenings and weekends. Other countries offer much more generous family leave and general vacation policies.

To manage competing demands, some scholar parents recommended that when you're at work, *be at work*, and when you are at home, *be at home*. In academia, it is quite easy to fall into a destructive pattern of work-life fluidity, where work spills over into nonwork time (e.g., evenings and weekends). This is true for parents and nonparents alike. The efficiency and time management skills that scholar parents and student parents must implement include having identifiable goals for each work period and minimizing nonwork distractions such as social media during those times. Whitney Pirtle observes in her vignette that her son made her work harder and focus during the time she had to work. In writing about her determination to succeed in her doctoral program despite the obstacles she faced as a new parent, a woman of color, and someone who grew up poor, Pirtle concludes—powerfully—that "women will continue to birth babies and PhDs, but an inclusive academia will be kinder to both processes."

As Whitney Pirtle's experience reminds us, the logistical difficulties and isolation of parenting as a student are compounded by other marginalizing factors, like race and socioeconomic status. One survey respondent mentioned that as an international student, she was largely ignored unless the department needed a token diversity participant. She flew under the radar until she published an article in a prominent journal, at which point departmental "mentors" began to seek her out. Racial, gender, ethnic, regional, socioeconomic, religious, and other biases infiltrate the job market and hiring process, affect a candidate's career trajectory, and shape the campus environment (Bertrand and Mullainathan 2003; Duffy 2013; Moss-Racusin et al. 2012; Romero 2017; Stewart and Valian 2018). Morrow Jones and Box-Steffensmeier (2014) acknowledge the realities of implicit gender bias in faculty hires:

> One sees the name at the top of the CV and a frame of reference or context is established that one is not even aware of. Then, for example, if one sees a coauthored article on the CV the frame of reference for the male applicant might lead one to comments such as: "interesting topic," "good journal." The frame of reference for the female applicant might instead lead one to think something like "I wonder if the coauthor is her advisor?" ... Note that there is nothing wrong with any of those points—all are relevant to the search, but the positive ones came out in the context of the male applicant and the questioning one came out in the context of the female applicant.

Although our survey respondents noted that schedule flexibility was a key benefit of having a child in graduate school, we identify a pervasive and persistent need for universal, equitable, and clearly communicated parental

Birthing a Baby and a PhD

Dr. Whitney Pirtle
Assistant Professor
University of California–Merced

I can barely remember my anniversary or my second child's birthday, but I remember vividly the day I found out I was pregnant with my first child: December 1, 2009. After two failed pregnancy tests I decided to go to the student health center on campus this day. I wasn't sure what exactly was going on, but I thought for sure I wasn't pregnant. After insisting on a pregnancy test the nurse assistant came back in the examination room and asked, "Are you trying to get pregnant?"

In my head, I thought: "Of course not! I am here, at an elite private institution on my way to obtaining a PhD. But I am not *supposed* to be here, as a woman of color who grew up poor with two parents who dropped out of college—my mother after she became pregnant at twenty." I had handled every obstacle thrown at me so far and I was not about to become sidetracked. I was well on my way to achieving my dreams to become one of the less than 3 percent of Black women faculty in the academy.[2] And, I just celebrated my twenty-third birthday two weeks prior. With all of these thoughts running through my mind all I was able to do was shake my head and let out an assured "no."

"Well, you are!" was her response.

I nodded in silent agreement, scheduled a follow-up appointment, sent my boyfriend a text to call me when he could (he was teaching at a middle school), and sent an email to my writing partner to cancel our meeting. I walked to the parking lot in a daze, thinking about this life-changing news, and also my growing to-do list. My writing partner called to check in after seeing my email and as soon as I answered I finally lost it. "How am I going to do this?" I cried.

My friend assured me that I would be OK. My partner gave me the same assurance, pledging his support. My mom was committed to helping see me through. But I think it was my undergraduate mentor who said the words I really needed to hear in an email: "Women have been birthing PhDs and babies forever. You will have both, and be great at both!" And then my mind was set. I wouldn't change any of my plans, I would only add to them.

I did remain 100 percent undeterred. I had my son in the summer after my second year of graduate school. Thankfully, neither of us had any complications. My university had a six-week leave policy, which meant I pushed back all departmental deadlines by six weeks and didn't have to show up the first week of classes. I got special permission to be ten minutes late to a grad seminar because I needed the time between my teaching assistant class responsibilities and my own grad class to pump. I had learned this after I leaked during class my first week back. My office mates understood my need to kick them out of our joint offices on occasion. Professors allowed me to bring my kid to meetings when childcare fell through, and nearly all of my grad school friends offered to babysit if I needed. I asked to be relieved from a teaching assistant position that was inflexible and opted to put a pause on some additional research opportunities. I missed conferences that year but showed up to nearly all departmental events. I passed my master's and then my exams.

I continued as if business was normal. But in many ways, it was not. At the time of my son's birth, there was no other graduate student parent in my program. So, compared to my grad student peers, the fact that I was awakened every two hours at night to nurse a baby was abnormal. That I had to rush from commitments to get home to my child set me apart. That I refused to make being an academic my main identity, let alone priority, meant I was different.

I learned that for some, it signaled I was not committed (Pirtle 2017). I was not selected for some research positions that I had been invited to before. I wasn't asked to join in collaborations that my peers were, despite my interests being more tightly aligned. I was told I wasn't working hard enough. I was either implicitly or explicitly excluded from happy hour events, barring me from socializing opportunities as well.

Yet, despite this perception by others, when I look back, I was as committed or more than most. I continued as business as normal, but it was not. I had to work twice as hard as most. Factor in these intersecting systems of race *and* class *and* gender (Collins 2016), I worked exceptionally hard to not only survive but to thrive. In fact, I was a successful case. I won a coveted internal fellowship my dissertation year, finished in six years, and earned a tenure-track position at a research university.

In many ways, my child is to thank for that. He made me work harder. I had to be dedicated in the time I had. He also made me separate my work from my life. Attending to him was so much more important and fulfilling. Rejection still stung, but I was keeping a child alive. I was going to be alright.

I am still not sure, though, how the stress of having to do it all while being perceived as not doing enough might have negatively impacted my mental and physical health. I worked so hard that I honestly don't know if I even stopped to process what it means to be an academic parent. I mean, the second person I told about my pregnancy was a friend, yes, but I told her specifically at that moment because I had writing on my mind. What was my determination costing me?

I planned to have my second child. I conceived in my first year on the tenure track, timing to have the birth one week after my classes ended the following fall semester. As I have written about elsewhere, though, the pregnancy was not as seamless. I had a threatened miscarriage, sending me to the emergency room one night in a major scare. One doctor advised me against my planned research trip abroad (but I went anyway), and I had to be induced toward the end of the pregnancy. As I have written about elsewhere (Pirtle 2018), it is hard for me not to speculate that the weathering, or additional wear and tear on my body from gendered racism that has been found to impact Black women's pregnancy health as they age (Geronimus 1992), wasn't a factor here. Thankfully, my second was also born without complications. But I vowed then to take full advantage of my university's parental leave policy—allowing me not to teach for a year—and a leave I did have!

I bonded with my youngest and was able to pick up my oldest from kindergarten most days. I cooked and cleaned and watched TV and went to library reading time and MOPS [Mothers of Pre-Schoolers] events. I did the things I wanted to do as a new mother and felt no guilt about them. In fact, my mental and physical health probably improved during this time. And I finally had time to reflect back on my earlier experiences, thinking, as sociologists do, about what sort of culture and system changes need to happen to make sure parents are supported.

What is needed is an understanding of motherhood as status, a status that is an asset for the individual and the university, but one that needs to be better protected and uplifted.[3] Some of the changes are seemingly straightforward, like increasing private lactation rooms, subsidizing on-site childcare. Some might be harder, like addressing implicit biases. Others require systemic change, like mandating parental leave. Brilliant women will continue to birth babies and PhDs, but an inclusive academia will be kinder to both processes.

leave policies for graduate students—and for faculty. While the United States lags behind in this policy area, campuses should extend and use parental leave accommodations to ensure that student parents, *especially* birth parents, have the support they need to stay in the program even as they work through a major life change. Without universal, equitable, and clearly communicated leave policies, decisions about progress through the graduate program, paid assistantships, student health benefits, excused absences from classes, and late coursework fall to individual departments and faculty members. When policies are absent or unenforced, students who are better connected to the faculty or simply more comfortable asking for accommodations are more likely to get them. Students who are marginalized in or newer to the department or simply uncomfortable negotiating accommodations will inevitably get less support. Equitable policies ensure equal opportunities for success, and fair parental leave policies are a strong starting point.

A second point stems from the limited income that is endemic to the graduate student experience: children are expensive, and graduate students get by on limited income. While doctoral students are often given a tuition waiver and living stipend in exchange for research and teaching duties, few students are financially comfortable during graduate school. Still, student parents must find ways to pay for healthcare, childcare, food, clothing, rent or mortgage, and other basic necessities on top of their typical student expenses (books, conference travel, and the never-ending need for coffee). The fact that many academics live far from their extended family support networks compounds the usual expenses of parenthood, especially if on top of daily childcare a family must also have an on-call babysitter available for evening meetings, classes, or events. Tolerance for families varies widely in academia in the United States. Some universities provide on-campus childcare for faculty and students. Some campuses have policies that forbid children in the workplace. There is no standard for family-friendliness across US universities and no ground floor for basic provisions for all student parents.

Healthcare costs also occupy or threaten to jeopardize a household budget. While comprehensive student health insurance is a good starting point for graduate student support, universities should prioritize family health insurance plans available for student parents. Universities invest a tremendous amount of money in graduate students; it behooves them to foster an environment where student parents can thrive and succeed and remain in academia. Student-parent dropouts threaten the department's graduation rate—a metric increasingly used at the university level for funding allocation. Having graduate students successfully matriculate and find employment is another university-level metric that contributes to the university's prestige. Investment in graduate student and family health care and childcare will go a long way to improving departmental and university metrics that affect accreditation and funding streams.

Professional expenses present an additional hurdle for young families, especially those with single parents. Academic conferences often require participants to pay for registration months in advance. Conference-goers also need to book flights and lodging well in advance, paying at least a portion of those costs up front. Even if graduate students have access to travel funding, the reimbursement arrives *after* the conference, sometimes many weeks later. Travel funding rarely covers fees for babysitters or (for those with progressive professional associations) on-site childcare centers at conference venues; university or state guidelines may not permit childcare costs as reimbursable expenses. Without significant reserves of discretionary income, conference travel and research travel may be out of reach for graduate student parents.

The third and final difficulty we address here (but certainly not the only other difficulty facing student parents) is the job market and its potential hazards for parents, especially for pregnant candidates. One survey respondent recalled, "I was pregnant while on the job market for the first time. I was early enough that it did not show, but I was so nauseous I could hardly stand the trips. I also did a job interview when I was late along in pregnancy and I do not think people took me seriously." Pregnancy is a highly variable condition: some pregnancies are physically and medically uncomplicated; others are quite difficult and require more accommodations, such as mandated bed rest. A pregnant graduate student on bed rest fundamentally cannot participate in on-campus job market interviews.

Graduate students on the academic job market are often advised to keep their family situations private, which may be reasonable advice if the potential employer's family-friendliness and campus or department norms are yet unknown. The picture for parents on the job market is not entirely bleak: in her research on graduate student parents, Kulp (2019) finds that parents "were more likely to attain tenure-track jobs early on within the first 2 years post-PhD compared to men and women without children," but scholars without children "were more likely to attain jobs at research institutions." Mentorship and support are crucial determinants of success on the job market. Having a network of mentors who provide backchannel information about departmental dynamics, patterns, priorities, and personalities can help job candidates make informed decisions about revealing family characteristics.

To complicate the situation, prospective employers in the United States are barred from discriminating on the basis of pregnancy or fertility (Scott 2013), so search committees generally avoid asking candidates about their marital or family status. This "don't ask, don't tell" approach, however, prevents the job seeker from learning essential information about schools, daycares, department norms on children in the workplace, or spousal hires. For the search committee, this practice is harmful because many accommodations are easier to make earlier in the process, but this is when job seekers are most guarded about their information.

To overcome this information gap between what search committees are allowed to ask and what candidates are hesitant to reveal, some departments retain a real estate agent to provide context about community-level amenities and features. The real estate agent also is a neutral third party who can field questions related to availability and cost of childcare and housing markets without the concern of revealing private information to the hiring committee. A real estate agent can provide valuable information to the job candidate about the hospitability of the larger community without compromising bargaining power during employment negotiations. Ultimately, changing the norms around academics and families will help both job seekers and search committees, but this is a long process and one that requires a good deal of (possibly unfounded) trust.

Implicit bias infects the job market for student parents, especially mothers. Subtle aspects of family formation are embedded in search committees' unconscious estimations. When reading the CV of an applicant who appears to be a man, it is doubtful a hiring committee would wonder if he intends to have children pre-tenure and, if so, whether he will request special accommodations, upset the department's distribution of service or teaching assignments, or suffer a decline in productivity. A man applicant's CV fresh out of graduate school would likely not include gaps or absences or reflect a longer time to degree completion. A woman graduate student job applicant with children—especially if the children were born during her graduate school years—does not have the equivalent of "stopping the tenure clock," and the length of time in graduate school, perhaps marked by stops and starts, may raise eyebrows and questions.

The hiring committee is not the only avenue through which implicit bias can derail a qualified candidate's prospects: implicit gender bias has insidious effects on recommendation letters. Letter writers tend to describe women in communal terms and focus on their positive personality traits; when writing for men they tend to focus on a candidate's individual characteristics, innovative work, and intellectual achievements (Madera, Hebl, and Martin 2009). Both men and women write highly gendered letters of recommendation; women are not immune to this bias. Thus, our implicit biases are at work even as we advocate for highly qualified, well-regarded women students, colleagues, and mentees.

Implicit bias training can and should address the subtle, pervasive, and gendered ways that recommendation letters mischaracterize women's competence and undermine their chances of success. Members of hiring, admissions, tenure and promotion, or award committees—who may be implicitly waffling about whether a woman candidate is a good fit for the position, promotion, or award—should read recommendation letters with an eye toward identifying gendered language that highlights men's accomplishments and downplays women's achievements.

These three key obstacles—inadequate, unarticulated, and uneven leave policies; limited income; and bias in the job search—are issues of access. As Nancy Rower's vignette makes clear, academia was not designed for student parents, and failure to adapt as faculty, departments, and campuses will lead talented scholars to exit the profession. Without sufficient accommodations and support (both formal and informal) parents have a difficult time keeping pace with nonparent graduate students to excel in their doctoral programs. As Erin Olsen-Telles details in her vignette, even when mentors, the department, and the university are supportive, parenting in graduate school can be a Herculean feat, and student parents must be prepared to be flexible, adjust personal goals as needed, and treat themselves with grace.

Ensuring Student Parents' Success

How can graduate student parents succeed and stay on course? A recurring observation in our survey responses is that individual faculty members have a strong influence on the success or failure of graduate student parents and expecting parents. For example, one respondent described pregnancy accommodations this way: "A kind professor hired me as an RA and never made me do anything for him." All student parents would want to have such accommodations, and we commend this professor's kindness and generosity, but this cannot be the status quo. In fact, ad-hoc accommodations could backfire and lead to accusations of misuse of funds or of students gaming the system unfairly since solutions like this one are not always feasible or advisable.

Individual-level fixes will not solve the systemic problems that keep parents, especially mothers, from succeeding in academia. Accommodations for pregnancy, adoption, illness, and childcare must be transparent and equitably applied. Students should not have to rely on the generosity of a faculty member who may have the resources at just the right time to fund de facto parental leave. Professors should not have to use research funds to compensate for insufficient university support for students. Still, each of us can take on efforts to create systemic change through our individual roles in the academy. While individual accommodations or fixes will not address systemic inequities, we do call on academic men to participate actively in mentorship of junior women and men and to work alongside academic women in the effort to create an academic culture that supports women, parents, and families.

Investing in the Human Capital of Our Scholars

Lt. Col. Nancy Rower, USAF (Ret.)

People are the greatest investment for any organization or institution. Investment in human capital includes wages, education and training, potential of advancement, and other, less obvious investments, such as professional development opportunities, morale, creating a positive institutional culture and allowing compassionate leave to take care of emergencies for a dependent.

Academic institutions repeatedly failed me over eight years as they neglected to recognize both my ability and potential as well as the investment they placed in me, for no other reason than that I simply did not fit the demographics. I was a single parent. I was rare. I had a responsibility that made me an anomaly, and the institutions could not adapt to it. I was forced to choose between my daughter or a grade in a class. I was forced to choose between my daughter's health or my career. I chose my daughter.

I chose academia purposefully and thoughtfully. The defining event of my life was a deployment to the Kosovo-Albanian border in 1999 as a captain in the United States Air Force. I witnessed the human cost of war. Refugees crossing the border with nothing but a bag of belongings, some carrying children. The aged, the wounded, the pregnant, the children, the traumatized, the sexually assaulted, a grandfather dying of cancer being pushed in a wheelbarrow over the mountainous Balkans by his grandchildren. One family that crossed into Albania had left one of their four children behind in Kosovo. A border guard demanded payment from the family, and when their payment was insufficient, a border guard pointed to the nineteen-year-old daughter and said that they would take her. Pain that I will never forget. There is no hell on Earth like a refugee camp.

It was then, that spring of 1999, at the Kosovo-Albanian border, that I knew I would dedicate my life to do anything in my power to reduce the suffering from war and conflict. I believed political science was the academic discipline best suited to educate people on the complexities and atrocities of international conflict, to educate the future generation to make foreign policy choices and develop military strategy with an understanding of the human cost of war. This was not a career to me; it was my mission in life.

I had an undergraduate and a master's degree in computer science. I was determined to be a political scientist. I went back to school completing a master's in international relations. My goal was to earn a PhD and become a professor of political science at a military academy. I knew that I would teach the best and the brightest, just like the students at Harvard or Yale. Unlike students of Ivy League universities, I knew they all would enter the profession of war.

I was achieving my mission. I was a lieutenant colonel with twenty years of service serving as an instructor at a military academy when the air force selected me to pursue a PhD. Selecting an officer to pursue a degree at a civilian university is an investment that the air force makes for a select few. The air force loses the officer for three years at a cost of more than $60,000 in tuition, in addition to, in my case, a lieutenant colonel salary and housing allowance. The total financial investment was $495,000. Only the very best are selected. I had significant postgraduate degrees and education: an MS in computer science from Boston University, an MS in international relations from Troy State, and graduate credit in strategic studies from Air University. I was named Instructor of the Year by the dean of faculty and staff in my first year as an instructor.

I have great respect for many of the professors at my civilian university and the leadership at my military academy. It was those people who I turned to when I was placed under unreasonable demands and impossible situations where I was forced to choose between my daughter's health or my grade, or my daughter's safety or my career. It was their ability to see the investment in people, their support, and, at times, their intervention that allowed me to continue my ten-year career in academia. I will be forever grateful for these people.

I entered a PhD program at forty-one years old and as a single parent of a two-year-old. I did not fit the demographics of my colleagues. The majority were unmarried, in their twenties, and did not have children. There is an institutional desire that the student body comprise people who are dedicated to their studies and without competing responsibilities. PhD classes were held in the evening. Additional lectures were also held in the evening. I understood the rationale for evening classes: PhD aspirants often have jobs. The expectation that I would attend the evening non-credit meetings and lectures was not reasonable to me. I needed to spend time with my child. I already had babysitters for three to four evenings per week as I attended required evening classes. Because of this, several faculty members did not consider me a serious student.

In one class the syllabus stated that a late project would receive a grade of zero. The day of my project presentation, the daycare at the Jewish Community Center called me to pick up my daughter immediately, as they suspected pink eye. I took my daughter to the pediatrician, who was concerned that it was a corneal tear and sent me to an ophthalmologist. I could not attend class. The professor told me that I would receive a zero for the project since it was not me who had the medical emergency. "It is not fair to the other students!" was a statement I heard from the handful of professors who could not adapt to the reality of an older student with a child.

During my years in the PhD program, a few women asked me about being a parent while pursuing a PhD. They wanted children and were uncertain if they could manage parenting and defending a dissertation. My responses were always the same:

1. I am not walking on thin ice; I am jumping on it.
2. If I fail, it will be the PhD program and not my daughter.
3. Your years to have children are limited; your career options are endless.

The institutional desire to have members free of competing responsibilities was not limited to this university. It is most prevalent in institutions that predominantly comprise people who are available any day and at any time. People who do not fit the demographics stand out.

After three years and four months in the PhD program (the maximum amount of time allowed by the air force), I returned to the military academy. My department was over 90 percent men. Of the few women, none had children. As far as I know, I was the first single-parent officer to teach for this department. The challenges I would face over the following years became immediately evident to me after a blizzard that delayed public schools. The department asked me if I could send my daughter to live with someone else. After all, it snows a lot in Colorado. Having another instructor substitute for my class was not permitted. Having no choice during a blizzard where my babysitter could not make it, I took my seven-year-old to work. I put a movie on in my office as I taught in the classroom next door. Another officer found her in my office and reported me to the base police to arrest me for child abuse (it is illegal on a military installation to leave a child under the age of twelve alone).

There was no tolerance for being late due to blizzards and school delays. Yet another officer was permitted to work from home or have a substitute for his classes when it snowed because he had an expensive sports car not meant for icy conditions. No tolerance for a sick child, no tolerance to leave early if my child became ill at school, no permission granted to take leave to care for my daughter after she spent all night in the emergency room. On that occasion, I sent her to school, where a sympathetic teacher allowed her to sleep in the corner.

At an end-of-year party, the department presented a slideshow of humorous events, which included a slide of the instructor who frequently stayed home with his sports car when it snowed. It was a well-known department joke that at the slightest flurry, he would work from home. Everyone laughed. It was not funny to me at all. I was fighting for my career and against allegations of child abuse over three major blizzards. I saved that slideshow as documentation.

I received multiple letters of reprimand that threatened my career. I hired lawyers and would spend the next year documenting every incident, fighting for my career, and counter-threatening legal action against my department for creating a hostile work environment. I struggled and was diagnosed with major depression and anxiety. The dean removed me from the department, and I served the remainder of my active-duty service commitment on his staff. I am forever grateful for his compassion and intervention.

I retired at fifty with no desire to continue with my academic career. I am living a new dream with my daughter on an island in the Gulf of Thailand. I still enjoy building and educating others: I teach English part-time at a yoga and wellness resort.

Based on my personal experience, I offer some recommendations:

- Institutions need to invest in their scholars and faculty.
- Human capital cannot be purchased. It is developed over many years and it is difficult to replace.
- Institutionalize a compassionate leave policy for parents.
- Develop syllabi and grading standards that account for dependents and emergencies.
- Accommodating parents is not giving them a perk; it is retaining talent and the institution's investment.
- Colleagues can lend support. Everyone, eventually, will need support.
- Parents who find themselves discriminated against need to document every instance, every discrepancy and every double-standard. Document. Document. Document! Your notes may save your career.
- Reach out to supportive leaders.
- If necessary, hire a lawyer sooner rather than later. Know your legal options.
- Problems will pass.
- Never miss an opportunity to tell your children how much you love them.

Thesis Baby

Erin Olsen-Telles

I had goals: to finish my master's and PhD in under five years, to publish while in graduate school, to find an amazing tenure-track job at a liberal arts institution, to have a solid career. I never imagined the turn my life would take when I had children, or the choices I would make. I had personal career goals. I still do. I have to remind myself that I still have them, that despite progressing more slowly than I had planned, I will finish my dissertation, that while my goals may have evolved over time, while my life has changed, I still belong in academia.

My husband and I found out we were expecting halfway through my second year of graduate school. I had planned to have children while in graduate school, but not quite so early on. My first trimester, which coincided with the spring semester of my second year of graduate school, went off without a hitch. I did have extensive morning sickness, but thanks to a steady diet of Zofran and coconut water, I was able to attend class with no one the wiser to my pregnancy. I was terrified to announce my pregnancy, though. While it was not uncommon for men graduate students in my department to have children, for women graduate students, it was very rare. Surprisingly, the year I was pregnant, another woman graduate student in my department was also pregnant. We were the first two women in several years though to have babies while working on our PhDs. I was happy and relieved to not be the only woman graduate student breaking with tradition, but I quickly learned why it is uncommon for women graduate students to choose to become parents: it's really hard!

Fortunately, my department was incredibly supportive and accommodating, allowing me to TA an online class the semester I was due and the following three semesters as well. Though my department was very accommodating, I learned right away that graduate students have little to no options for parental leave (at least in my state). I was grateful to be offered the online course and to not have to pause my studies for a semester or longer, but that also meant that I worked up until the day I was admitted to the hospital to give birth, and I was back to grading papers three days after my daughter was born. Additionally, I took my two- or three-week-old daughter (it's a blur now) with me to a graduate seminar (with my professor's permission of course) so I could finish the class and show her off to the department. Having a baby while in graduate school meant that I had no maternity leave. I had no time to just be a mother and learn how to be a new mother while allowing my body to heal from childbirth. I had papers to grade, papers to write, books and articles to read, and exams to study for, plus a tiny infant who depended on me for literally everything.

I thought I could do it all. I thought I could stay at home with my child full-time, exclusively breastfeed, cloth diaper, make homemade organic baby food, and keep pace with my peers in academia. I was wrong. Middle-of-the-night nursing sessions meant I was sleep-deprived. Working around the sleep schedule of an infant meant that my work was frequently interrupted. I often read academic journal articles to my baby instead of baby books. I baby-wore her in a carrier all hours of the day so that I could work and care for her at the same time. I tried to do it all, and frequently felt like I was failing at all of it, but I kept working at it.

My spouse. Pregnancy was not the only factor that altered my graduate school progress, however. My husband is in the medical field, a demanding and inflexible profession, at least for the training years. We knew we would have to make compromises. The month we found out we were expecting was the same month he submitted his rank list for medical residency. His compromise was to rank at the top of his list residency programs in the same city and state as my graduate school. My compromise was to move with him for residency, as opposed to living separately while I finished my PhD. Luckily, we stayed in state, allowing me to commute. This, however, was just the beginning of the compromises I would make. I quickly learned that in medical residency, hours are long and schedules are largely inflexible, so when our daughter arrived, I became the primary caregiver.

Daycare. As I am sure is the case with most first-time parents, the parent I thought I would be was not exactly the parent I ended up being. I thought I would be OK with putting my daughter in daycare relatively early on and diving full-time back into my studies. I wasn't. I chose to not put my daughter into daycare regularly until she was eleven months old. That was not the wisest decision as far as my graduate studies were concerned. But as a parent, that was what felt right to me. Part of it was personal. I often wished I could be that parent who embraced sending her two- or three-month-old baby to daycare, but I could not. I wanted to be home with my baby, exclusively breastfeed, make my own organic baby food, and for me, it was worth falling behind in my graduate studies (for a while). I acknowledge I was in a privileged position, though. While I was making sacrifices to stay at home with her, I was lucky to even have the choice to do so, a choice many parents do not have.

But while I told myself at the time that I *wanted* to be home with my daughter, I now acknowledge that other parts of that decision were related to fear and finances. I did want to be with my child (though I relished my "adult time" at school), but as a new parent, I was also afraid. Would she love the daycare provider more than me? Would she be well cared for? Could I trust my precious child with strangers? At some point I just had to get over it and find a highly recommended daycare that I was comfortable with. That came at a price, though. While my husband and I were doing fine between his residency salary and my graduate stipend, a thousand dollars a month in daycare expenses was a tough pill to swallow. So, with these justifications in mind, I convinced myself to work from home with my daughter, piecing together care for her (family, friends, drop-in daycare) the one day a week I had class. Finally, almost a year after she was born, I acknowledged that the arrangement was not working well for either of us. I could not focus any significant amount of time on my own work and was unhappy with myself over my limited progress. Likewise, in my attempt to work from home and care for her at the same time, I could not provide my crawling, curious daughter with the level of interaction she desired. When she was eleven months, I enrolled her in daycare two days a week. I instantly felt the relief of that decision and wished I had embraced daycare sooner. I finally had some time to pursue my own goals and regain the sense of self I had lost in the early fog of motherhood.

When she started daycare, we dealt with separation anxiety. It broke my heart a little each time she burst into tears when I dropped her off in the morning, but her providers assured me the tears stopped and she was happily playing within five minutes of my departure. It took me another year to be comfortable with the idea of full-time daycare, but that too provided additional relief and freedom, not to mention greater progress on my dissertation prospectus and eventually dissertation.

Lactation. Breastfeeding is certainly not a must, but for those who choose to do so, a pumping-friendly university is so important. I was lucky that my university had multiple lactation lounges across campus. I was not aware of these the first time I brought my daughter to campus, however, so I stumbled through the awkward conversation of asking the two colleagues I shared an office with (one of whom was a man and neither of whom had children) if I could have some uninterrupted time in the office to feed my baby. Finding out that there was a lactation lounge in my building felt like I had won the lottery. Granted, it was not fancy: a small room with a relatively comfortable chair, a sink, counter space, and a hospital-grade, closed-system breast pump.

But it met my needs. It also helped me to feel that I belonged. The university cared enough to provide me and other lactating employees and students with a space to comfortably provide food for our babies. We were important. Our babies were important. Our feeding choice was important. That was a hugely empowering realization.

Finishing my dissertation and the job market. I am still finishing my dissertation. Another move for my husband's medical fellowship, a second child, and a breast cancer diagnosis all added additional pauses to my progress. Fortunately, I had no issue finding an adjunct teaching position while I continued work on my dissertation. I may not be finishing my dissertation on the same timeline as most of my peers or on my department's typical timeline, but I am finishing it. My children will only be young once, and I have had the luxury to attempt having the best of both worlds. It has come at a cost, but for me, it has been worth it.

If you do decide to have a baby while in graduate school, consider the following:

1. Try your best to time your baby's arrival for summer break (easier said than done). I do not recommend having a child mid-semester. Given that graduate students do not have the same family leave protections as actual employees in many, if not most, US states, summer break would allow you to actually take the much-needed time off to bond with your baby, heal from childbirth if you're the one who gave birth, and figure out parenting.

2. Since pregnancy timing doesn't always go as planned, should you find yourself having a baby during the semester, be sure to advocate for yourself. Let your department know early enough along that they can assign you an online teaching or research assistant position so that you don't have to pause your studies (unless you want to). Make a plan with your advisor and any other faculty members you will be working with that semester. Plans can change, so the more flexibility you can build into your schedule the semester baby is set to arrive, the better.

3. Breastfeeding and pumping, while convenient once you get the hang of them, can be quite challenging and time-consuming, especially at first. If you plan to breastfeed and pump, be sure to get a quality pump through your insurance and invest in a hands-free breastmilk pumping bra. I took and passed my thirty-six-hour, take-home international politics qualifying

exam when my daughter was living exclusively on breastmilk, but every time I took a break from the exam to pump, I sorely regretted not having a hands-free pumping bra. It's a thing. Buy it. Additionally, find out where your university's lactation lounge is. If they don't have one, ask your department or human resources to find you a private space (that isn't a bathroom) where you can pump. Graduate students may not be covered under the Fair Labor Standards Act, which mandates that an employer provide time and space to pump, so understand that there is some legal gray area as to whether your university has to provide you with these, but that doesn't mean you shouldn't advocate for yourself.

4. Embrace childcare. It is important to find a care provider you are truly comfortable with and can afford (check with your university and other programs for childcare subsidies, discounted providers, etc.), but find that provider. It is OK to be afraid to leave your child. Give yourself time to get comfortable with the decision. Your child will thrive from the peer interaction and you will have much-needed time to breathe, converse with adults, and work on your very important dissertation.

5. Prepare to get sick (a lot) that first year of daycare. It seemed like both my children were sick constantly once they started daycare. It didn't matter what age they started, as soon as they were in regular contact with other children and were exposed to all those new germs, they were constantly getting sick and bringing it home with them, which meant my husband and I caught the small human viruses as well. On a positive note, we very rarely have sick days now. Our children's immune systems are in tip-top shape!

6. You may find that your love of research spills over into parenting (or not). When pregnant with my first, I found myself compelled to research everything, from all aspects of childbirth and breastfeeding, to baby gear safety standards and testing, to the "best" baby products on the market. At one point, I could rattle off car-seat use best practice in detail, complete with the scientific justification for why specific car seat types should be used for certain ages and which car seats (brands and models) were most recommended for which age. Other friends in academia who had children after me chose to skip all this research and instead ask me when they had a question about car seats. If you can find a trusted friend who has already acquired a wealth of knowledge on many things baby, save yourself the

> time and avoid the baby research rabbit hole. While a general understanding is certainly a good idea, many parents do a great job safely raising their children without all the time spent on research, time that could be devoted to your dissertation.
>
> 7. And finally, give yourself a lot of grace. Sometimes you will feel like you have it all together, but a lot of the time you won't. Sometimes you will feel like a horrible parent. Sometimes you will feel like your dissertation is a hot mess and will never be completed. Take a deep breath. Enjoy some baby snuggles. And keep working. You will get there.

A recent publication by the National Academy of Sciences related to sexual harassment of women encourages universities to go beyond "legal compliance to promote a change in culture." Similarly, a 2017 best practices document from Baruch College, City University of New York, outlines tactics for improving diversity and overcoming implicit bias against minority scholars through culture change on campus. Their suggestions include launching campus climate assessments and retention studies, providing detailed institutional diversity plans, engaging campus-wide efforts to promote diversity, integrating Equal Opportunity offices or administrators in faculty and staff searches, implementing cluster hiring of minority faculty and staff members to establish cohorts of underrepresented scholars, inviting visiting scholar or exchange programs, maintaining updated multicultural resource directories, providing accessible funding opportunities for promoting diversity and investment in the work of minority scholars, fostering mentorship opportunities, and extending leadership opportunities for underrepresented scholars (Romero 2017). The effort to change both culture and policy is applicable to family formation and the work requires an all-hands-on-deck approach involving administrators, faculty, and students.

Along these lines, we present change-making ideas for the top of the university hierarchy as well as for professors and students.

Best Practices for Supporting Graduate Student Parents
What university administrators can do:

- Establish and communicate clear and universal parental leave protections for full-time graduate students.
- Ensure compliance with existing policies, such as Title IX protections.

- Foster family-friendly norms through formal and informal on-campus programs and resources.
- Create and maintain funding programs to help graduate students cover professional costs, such as conference and research travel, and necessary childcare related to these activities.
- Establish on-campus childcare facilities that graduate students can access at subsidized rates or provide childcare subsidies that students can use to offset the cost of off-campus childcare.
- Establish or maintain affordable comprehensive health insurance programs for graduate students and their dependents.
- Establish student-accessible lactation rooms or spaces on campus.

What faculty can do:

- View and treat graduate students as colleagues, granting them the same consideration and respect you would grant any other department colleague.
- Offer flexibility in course or research completion or teaching duties to the extent possible.
- Support graduate students in their efforts to gain access to resources, including funding costs related to conference and research travel, and work with administrators to create and enforce policies that support student parents.
- Be transparent about your own story—show that it can be done.
- Serve as a mentor in both formal and informal capacities.
- Work to counter the culture of hierarchy and grad student vulnerability—student parents, especially pregnant and lactating parents, may not ask for what they need since they do not feel secure enough to make requests for accommodations.

What student parents can do:

- Make a plan for your day, week, month, semester, and year, but be ready for anything to happen.
- Learn to work more efficiently than your nonparent peers, be impeccable with your time management, and move beyond perfectionism.
- Do not wait until close to the deadline to finish your work—childhood illnesses and childcare emergencies have an uncanny way of coinciding with deadlines and important events.

- Work with other graduate students to negotiate systemic changes like healthcare, leave policies, lactation rooms for students, and childcare on campus.
- Ask for help wherever you can get it—family, neighbors, friends, cohort members, your partner or coparent.
- To the extent you are able, preserve your evenings and weekends for non-academic time.

This list is not exhaustive. As with all of our suggestions throughout the book, the key takeaway is that administrators, faculty, and professional associations should think beyond the bare minimum policies and protections—to the extent that they exist—and look to create more comprehensive support networks for early-career parent-scholars and change the academic culture for student parents and scholar parents. The takeaway for student parents is that the problems they face as graduate students persist at the junior faculty level, albeit offset somewhat by higher salaries, greater status, and employment stability. The payoff—retaining talented scholars and fostering diverse perspectives—is well worth the investment. Graduate student parents, for their part, should strive to succeed and seek out the protections and support that exist, resting in the knowledge that there are many, many current and former student parents out there. Success is attainable.

Notes

1. This advice and the assumptions that underpin it are indicative of overall gender-based discrimination. Willis and Jahanbani (2019) write succinctly about graduate student experiences with misogyny.
2. See National Science Foundation data found at https://ncses.nsf.gov/pubs/nsf19301/data.
3. See more of Whitney Pirtle's ideas at https://www.insidehighered.com/advice/2017/03/03/higher-ed-must-do-more-help-grad-students-babies-essay.

3 How to Scale the Ladders while Sidestepping the Chutes

On Parenting without the Security of Tenure

We begin this chapter with two observations: first, it is not uncommon for early-career scholars to receive advice to delay having children until after earning tenure; second, the majority of our survey respondents welcomed children into their families through birth, adoption, or becoming the partner of a parent *before* earning tenure. Life, the conventional wisdom, and ubiquitous advice, it seems, are out of sync. These observations beg the question: What happens when someone becomes a parent before they have the privilege and job security of tenure? What about parents who never even have the prospect of tenure? The short answer to both questions: stress. Starting a family while on the tenure clock or in a non-tenure-track position, as an increasing number of academics are, means having at least two full-time jobs: working and parenting. Pre-tenure academic parents and those in contingent positions such as graduate students, instructors, visiting assistant professors, and adjuncts trying to publish, teach, and serve to meet departmental and disciplinary expectations also contend with the fog of sleep deprivation just when their brains need to be thinking most clearly. Contingent faculty may aspire to a tenure-track position and undertake the process of family formation amid much higher teaching loads, much lower salaries, and much less institutional support than tenure-track faculty. They are also trying to keep pace with their tenure-track peers and compete in an increasingly tight job market. Stress can manifest in many ways, some of which we address in chapter 6, "Sick and Tired."

As the vignettes in this chapter suggest, the goals of having children and achieving tenure are not incompatible, given a combination of support, persistence, and sheer luck. But sometimes those goals *are* incompatible—resulting in an exit from the tenure track or academia altogether or the decision to delay parenthood for the sake of professional survival. Sometimes a contingent or non-tenure-track position is the answer to the two-body problem in dual-academic households; in this scenario, one partner accepts precarious employment in order to keep the family physically together. Because our survey and the goals of this book address people still in the profession, we acknowledge there is a survivorship bias. However, the stories of challenges that academic parents face make it very clear why people leave the profession. The solutions to the precarity of Academic Chutes and Ladders (or the so-called leaky pipeline) cannot come solely from individual accommodation "hacks" and strategies to attempt to "have it all" but must also include systemic reforms.

All campuses—and the profession as a whole—must do more to foster the inclusion and success of pre-tenure and non-tenure-track scholar parents. It behooves us to support academic parents because the skills and efficiency they learn while balancing young children and a new career serve them—and the profession—well over time. Balancing work and family *is* professional behavior. Although much of the focus here is on the professional chutes that women scholars encounter, the discussion stemming from this chapter and the rest of the book must include academics of all genders, especially men. Men have been largely left out of the conversation, whereas women have been encouraged to "lean in." Men have a responsibility for repairing problems with gender equity, and they need mentorship as well to become better, more vocal advocates and allies for women colleagues.

Fixing the System: Best Practices for Improving Support for Early-Career Scholar Parents

Non-tenure-track positions and the tenure track are rife with challenges for women, especially mothers, and parents who take on both visible academic work, invisible care work at home, and unseen service work on campus without the job security that comes with tenure. The average six-year probationary period for tenure-track faculty requires scholar parents to navigate the persistent and competing demands of teaching, research, and service alongside the persistent and competing demands of children and family. Graduate school, the academic job search, postdoctoral fellowships, visiting professorships, and other contingent appointments also coincide with the years in which individuals and their partners contemplate adding children to their family.

Avoiding the Chutes on the Path to Tenure

Early-career scholar parents of all genders benefit from both formal and informal support systems as they navigate the tenure track with children in tow. Existing research that highlights the gender gap in faculty ranks suggests that women scholar parents are especially vulnerable to the career-altering chutes. Women comprise slightly less than half (44 percent) of all faculty on the tenure track, but only slightly more than a quarter (28 percent) of tenured faculty. In other words, the profession loses one in three women down the tenure-track chutes, and only two in three climb the tenure ladder. While the tenure track offers significantly more security and benefits than contingent positions, tenure is far from guaranteed. We asked our respondents who welcomed a child or children while on the tenure track to tell us how childbearing or family formation affected their progression toward tenure. While the responses ranged from "there was no effect" to "I left the tenure track," many respondents recounted stress, guilt, fear, strained relationships, and a sense of just barely getting by.

Some respondents indicated uncertainty about outcomes, as illustrated in this response: "I don't know yet, but I think the answer is going to be: it's not going to help. I get a year additional on my tenure clock, but I've been told by people at lots of institutions that this is typically not respected (that is, you are expected to have published more than someone who didn't take the extra year)." In other words, stopping the tenure clock is not viewed as a pause in productivity but rather a "bonus" year during which parents, especially women, are expected to show evidence of *more* productivity rather than offset that they accomplished less professionally due to the rigors and time devoted to childbearing and family formation. This perverse outcome may originate from the misuse of family leave policies by men in the profession. Women are penalized for *not* using the tenure clock stop for increasing their research output, while men are not penalized for misusing it for that very same reason!

Parental leave actually exacerbates gender inequality in departments. As Antecol and colleagues (2018) find, when departments adopt gender-neutral tenure-clock-pausing policies, women achieve tenure less often and men achieve tenure more often. For women, this outcome is not puzzling because of ample "anecdata" evidence: men misuse parental leave to accomplish more research with a break from teaching, and in some cases go on the job market to "move up" from their current position. For women, FMLA is restricted to the time immediately following birth or adoption (except for circumstances when administrators make special exceptions). In some cases reported in our survey and recounted in the vignettes, men have been granted parental leave in subsequent semesters following a child's birth. The burden of proof that men are not misusing parental leave should be on them, and on their supervisors, to close the gap between inequitable outcomes for men and women on the tenure track. One survey respondent noted that her department offered a teaching-free semester upon return to work, followed by a semester research sabbatical. Policies like this have real potential to level the playing field.

Furthermore, some institutions have capped the number of times a tenure clock can be stopped (twice) for the purposes of family formation. As one survey respondent wrote, "I was the only woman with kids. Some of my male colleagues had children, but they were older. The department has since changed. When I became pregnant with my fourth child I was ridiculed by faculty and graduate students. The graduate students told one faculty member that they were taking up a collection to pay for my birth control. Another faculty member told me that my choice to have another child was immoral because of the environmental impact it would have. Another faculty member told me that he had never seen me not pregnant and that I should be careful not to have too many distractions during my probationary period." Thus, having kids pre-tenure is considered ill advised, but having too many kids overall invites even more judgment.

Others reflected on the stress and fear of combining parenthood and the tenure track, as these three brief responses show: "It was scary as hell but I made it"; "increased my sense of guilt"; "more stress and fear." Another set of responses reveals the isolation scholar parents often feel and the personal costs they bear. One respondent observed the difficulty of relating to colleagues without children: "I did not have any sense in any of the three tenure-track positions I've held that there was any consideration for family formation impacting work. I kept working excessive hours to fulfill research and teaching expectations. Colleagues who didn't have kids talked about binge-watching TV and reading for pleasure and I just couldn't relate." Another respondent offered a poignant reflection on the obstacles she has overcome and the changes she has undergone: "I had to go on the job market with a newborn, breastfeeding between interviews, et cetera. Overall it has made me much more productive, but at a tremendous personal cost. I hardly recognize myself these days, although of late it does seem to be getting better."

Having kids while on the tenure clock—or hoping to start in a tenure-track position—can put the precarious work-life balance in jeopardy. As we address in the next chapter, many academics work all of the time, including evenings and weekends, to alleviate the stress they feel in juggling work and family. Stress has negative consequences for health, productivity and efficiency, and relationships. Given geographic isolation, many academics live far from support systems and must make it work by themselves. As another scholar noted, "The most important thing a university can do for a young academic family, aside from paid family leave, is to make available high-quality, affordable, childcare (especially infant care). No parent can excel in work if they are worried about their child."

The tenure outcomes some of our respondents reported when answering this question varied. Some respondents met their original goals of tenure and promotion: "It only pushed me to work smarter and with purpose—surpassing tenure expectations." Others revised their plans, as this respondent reports: "Ultimately, I left the tenure-track position in the fourth year to pursue other work and am still at the university in a staff scientist position. Children and the demands of trying to get tenure while teaching two classes ultimately forced me to abandon the pursuit." Still others flipped the question, observing that the tenure progress affected the family formation process. One responded that they "didn't dare have a child until post-tenure." Another noted that their "progression toward tenure severely impacted family formation—because I needed to get tenure as the sole wage earner." Yet another respondent was more specific about the conflicting demands of academia and parenthood: "I had one child. We couldn't risk having *another one*, because we don't have the time to allocate to both tenure (teaching, research) and to raising a baby."

Tenure-Track Adjacent: Adjuncts, Instructors, and Visiting Assistant Professors

And yet, as much of a balancing act as parenting on the tenure track is, it is still a privileged position in comparison with colleagues in adjunct, temporary, and permanent non-tenure-track positions. One respondent who was on the tenure track recalled when they welcomed a child: "I was offered the option of stopping my tenure clock but did not—I was well beyond my institution's tenure requirements on every measure, because I had to remain marketable while my spouse was on the market. It almost killed us."

Scholar parents, especially women who do not have the security of tenure, are professionally vulnerable. There is an oversupply of highly qualified candidates for tenure-track academic positions and a limited number of jobs they can fill. Consequently, many people opt for non-tenure-track employment, hoping to convert that temporary position into a full-time tenure-track position. Sometimes departments dangle that carrot of hope, sometimes with good intentions. However, as one senior scholar expressed, "Once a mistress, never a wife." In other words, it is very difficult, and very rare, to parlay a non-tenure-track position into a tenure-track one because the department perceives its colleague in that limited role as a non-tenure-track faculty member. Instructors and adjuncts increasingly carry departmental teaching loads, so it benefits the department more overall to keep them in underpaid, overworked positions. Simultaneous new parenthood in untenured positions can further pigeonhole a tenure-track hopeful scholar in the eyes of their department, which may view the colleague as having divided loyalties or lacking the chops to be a serious scholar. Thus, while family formation on the tenure track is hard, having kids while in a temporary or contingent position is even harder, exacerbated by perceptions that may not match reality.

We asked respondents who welcomed a child or children while in a non-tenure-track position to discuss how childbearing or family formation affected their or their department's expectations of academic productivity, career progress, or potential. The responses converged around a central theme: the expectations did not change. This translates into a rigid lack of accommodations and the threat of termination of employment. Contingent faculty have all the penalties but none of the perquisites that their tenure-track peers have. There is no tenure clock to stop. Time marches on, as do expectations. One respondent recalled, "I had my child while not in a tenure-track position. During my pregnancy other women warned me that my job would be in jeopardy after my child was born and I returned from FMLA protected leave time. They were correct. I was told I had to find a job at a time that was almost completely at the end of the academic hiring cycle. I quickly sent out applications and transitioned to a tenure-track job at another institution."

Another respondent shed light on terribly inflexible expectations: "When I was an adjunct there was absolutely no wiggle-room for childbearing. I was in that class ASAP. They forgave me for hosting the first two classes online, but there was no other support." Another respondent observed the limits of their department's "leeway" for new parents: "I think you get a little extra leeway for the first couple of months after return. But that leeway is associated with being able to ask a few more favors, get better forgiveness for minor sleep-deprived screw ups, less time in the office, and so on. And it definitely didn't extend to making sure your projects hit their deadlines, or that your papers got in, or that you're going to present your big project to sponsors. So leeway on the little things, not the big things." Non-tenure-track academics may have their workload offset more by departmental service, which also feeds into the perception that they are "taking care of the academic family" rather than pursuing more high-profile service opportunities on campus or in the profession at large—as those are reserved for "serious scholars." Many respondents indicated that they were offered online classes to extend their time from home.

What all of these responses highlight is the need for better support in recognition of our colleagues' humanity. We focus here on three themes central to parents in tenure-track and non-tenure-track positions: first, the importance of parental leave to care for and bond with children and (for parents who give birth) physically recover from pregnancy and childbirth; second, the importance of flexible accommodations beyond formal leave tied to the arrival of a new child; and third, the need for high-quality, reliable childcare starting with infancy. In exploring these best practices for improving support, we recognize that both formal leave policies and flexible accommodations will be more difficult for scholars in less secure positions to negotiate; that is exactly why we make the case for systemic change.

The Importance of Leave

Parental or family leave is a crucial formal support mechanism for new parents.[1] In chapter 1 we explored the range of parental leave policies and options reported by our survey respondents as well as the transparency of those policies and the extent to which family leave policies have changed over time. We were taken aback by the rate at which our respondents reported uncertainty about changes in parental leave policies over time (49 percent of respondents were unsure whether the policies had changed) and the consistency with which those policies are applied across the university (14 percent were unsure) and the department (25 percent were unsure). What this uncertainty suggests is that parental and family leave policies need to be more transparent and clearly communicated, and institutions must ensure that policies are universally applied. Inequity thrives in uncertainty. People can be taken advantage of in more profound and systematic ways when they do not know their rights. Not only do department and unit heads and deans need to communicate the policies better, but faculty ought to *demand* to know what the policies are.

We also asked our survey respondents to rate their satisfaction with their department or university's parental leave policies on a scale from "very dissatisfied" to "very satisfied," and the results are telling. Of those who responded, 40 percent selected "very dissatisfied," "dissatisfied," or "a little dissatisfied"; 36.9 percent selected "very satisfied," "satisfied," or "a little satisfied"; 9.7 percent selected "neutral"; and 13.4 percent selected "other." Clearly we have work to do. Given that 40 percent of our respondents indicated some degree

The Importance of Parental Leave

Sara McLaughlin Mitchell
F. Wendell Miller Professor of Political Science
University of Iowa

Parental leave issues have been important to me in my academic career, spurred in part by having a child in a university system with minimal leave policies. I got married in my second year as an assistant professor at Florida State University when I was close to thirty. Some women I knew in political science waited until they got tenure to have children, but I viewed this as a risky strategy. My skepticism was warranted because after a year of trying to get pregnant with no luck, I soon discovered that I needed fertility drugs to increase my chances of having a child. Every month when I got my period, I felt depressed. Having colleagues who were expecting children was difficult too. After eighteen months of trying to conceive and going on fertility drugs, I finally took a pregnancy test that was positive! I was so excited that I drove twenty minutes to where my husband worked to tell him. The joy of getting pregnant after a long infertility struggle was soon replaced by the realities of having a child while on the tenure track.

My daughter, Vivian, was born in 2001 when I was a fourth-year assistant professor on a tenure clock where my materials would be considered in my sixth year. At Florida State at the time, there were no parental leave policies for paid leave or tenure clock extension. I checked with the department chair and university administrators and was essentially told that I would need to use accrued sick leave to take time off under FMLA rules. To get eight weeks off, my doctor had to certify that I needed the extra two weeks of time at home. My chair was quite generous in helping me to arrange for help with my spring classes because I was due before the end of the semester. And my colleagues were supportive, bringing us dinners for more than a week after Vivian was born.

As the primary breadwinner for our family, though, I made the decision to put my daughter in daycare when she was eight weeks old because I had published only three articles (and none in top general journals) and I feared that tenure denial was a high likelihood. I came back to work after taking two months off to find a letter in my mailbox from the *Journal of Politics* saying that a revised and resubmitted paper had been rejected.[2] This was a devastating moment, but I knew that I had to find a way to succeed for my family. Four months later, I had two articles accepted at the *American Journal of Political Science*, and two years later, the department and university voted in favor of my promotion to associate professor with tenure. The vote was in my favor, but I had to sacrifice time with my child and put my own physical and mental needs in the background to get tenure.[3]

After having my child, I started to wonder whether the deal I had negotiated with the chair was the best I could have received at Florida State. I talked with a woman professor in the chemistry department and learned that she had an entire semester of teaching released by her department. I also talked with women in the political science discipline about what kind of parental leave policies they had at their universities. I soon realized we had very little comparative information about parental leave policies on campus or within the discipline. I embarked on a project to collect this data for universities housing the top thirty political science departments.[4] As one might imagine, getting this information online in the early 2000s was not easy. It was also difficult to determine if faculty and staff had similar or different policies. Staff policy manuals were often posted on university websites, while faculty policies (if distinct) were more difficult to locate. I collected information in 2003 on whether faculty had paid leave, whether they had to use accrued sick leave for parental leave, the amount of (unpaid) time that could be taken off, whether leave was possible for childbirth and adoption, and whether tenure clock extensions were granted (and the maximum number allowed). With assistance from my graduate students, I updated the data in 2011 to include information for the top fifty institutions and to provide website links to the pages where policies were posted. Since posting the original dataset, I have received dozens of emails from faculty in many disciplines asking questions about the data and wondering if I have updated the information (it is time!). Other scholars, such as Jessica Weeks at University of Wisconsin, Madison, are collecting similar information through crowdsourcing efforts.[5]

We know a lot more today about variation in parental leave policies, which is advantageous for job market candidates and institutions seeking to improve policies. Paid leave typically ranges from six weeks to six months, with six weeks being the mode.[6] Thirty percent of the top twenty-five political science departments provided paid leave in 2003, around the time I gave birth, while 90 percent provided paid leave by 2011. On the other hand, 64 percent of the top fifty programs required the use of accrued sick leave for paid leave, which obviously puts women faculty especially in a disadvantaged position if they suffer health problems. Most universities offer three to twelve months unpaid leave as an option for new parents. Getting release from teaching or having other modifications to faculty duties is almost universal today. FSU was unusual when I gave birth because 77 percent of the top twenty-five political science departments offered tenure clock extensions in 2003; among the top fifty programs in 2011, 90 percent offered tenure clock extensions. These policies typically set limits to two children total. Policies can apply differentially to childbirth and adoption, but this is rare. Some universities, such as Stanford and Columbia, provide financial assistance for faculty seeking to adopt children. There are also differences in terms of how parental leave policies apply to female and male faculty, although more universities today provide leave equally to all faculty. Examination of the data I compiled assured me that parental leave policies improved dramatically over time and that faculty in 2019 faced fewer hurdles to balancing their families and careers.

However, survey data collected in 2009 by the American Political Science Association (APSA) of 1,399 political science PhDs shows that women experience more parental "penalties" than their male peers (Mitchell and Hesli 2013). First, the survey shows that women are not bargaining more for parental resources even though women face greater physical consequences from having children and often take on greater second-shift roles for childcare. Women faculty were not significantly more likely than male faculty to request childcare financial assistance (0.9 percent vs. 0.6 percent) or special timing for the tenure track (11.2 percent vs. 9.4 percent) from their institutions. Second, the aggregate survey data shows significant differences in life outcomes for male and female faculty in political science. Women are significantly more likely to be single (14.7 percent vs. 9.7 percent) or separated (9.8 percent vs. 3.6 percent) than their male peers. Women faculty also have significantly fewer children than their male colleagues (60 percent vs. 71 percent with children), and women are more likely to be married to people who have fewer children (40 percent vs. 29 percent for men).[7] Third, women also report more dissatisfaction with their work-life balance than their male colleagues (37 percent of women dissatisfied vs. 18 percent of men) as well as greater dissatisfaction with their current positions (17 percent vs. 11 percent). Even though parental leave policies are becoming more generous, it is apparent that women have different experiences in our profession, with many choosing to exit the pipeline (Hesli, Lee, and Mitchell 2012).

Many factors contributed to my ability to get tenure in a system with minimal parental leave policies, including a supportive spouse, helpful colleagues, and assistance from extended family when I traveled to conferences. I will conclude with some general thoughts and advice for scholars today. First, you should learn more about parental leave policies before accepting a faculty position. The APSA crowdsourced data will provide better information than my dataset currently contains and will help academics make better choices if they want to have children. Second, my experience also shows that negotiating directly for parental leave can provide additional benefits, with some department chairs willing to go beyond institutional policies. It is useful to seek out senior allies to help you with these negotiations. Third, don't worry too much about when is the right time to have children. My experience suggests that waiting for the "right time" could backfire if you experience infertility problems. Fourth, while scholars in our profession disagree about whether parental leaves should be revealed to tenure letter writers, I personally think it is a good practice. It is a good idea to ask your department chair how this will be handled when requests for external letters are sent out for your tenure case.[8] Fifth, you might consider giving up some things financially (e.g., a nice house or an expensive wardrobe) to help pay for quality childcare. Without access to quality childcare as a junior faculty, I think I would not be here right now writing this chapter. Sixth, we must remember as faculty with children that we should not overburden our single faculty colleagues with extra service. It is not fair to ask them to take on more dinners with speakers or other evening events. Finally, while women in academia may never have it easy in terms of work-life balance, it is encouraging that universities are creating better working environments to support our endeavor for an optimal balance.

of dissatisfaction with their parental leave options, we suggest that institutions revisit their policies and their campus community members' needs.

Still, we take heart in the responses indicating that family leave policies have improved over time and the nearly 37 percent of respondents who indicate relative satisfaction with their family leave options. One of the most encouraging findings from our survey is that campus conditions are much better for women and families than they were thirty years ago. Progress has been made, but we still have quite a way to go. Sara Mitchell's vignette offers important insights into what parental leave looked like in the past, how leave options have evolved over time, and the implications of (lack of) access to parental leave.

The Importance of Flexibility

Support for scholar parents cannot start and end with a few weeks of parental leave upon the birth or adoption of a child. And yet this is the way the system is presently structured: FMLA starts when the child is born, neglecting the challenges of conception, adoption, and pregnancy prior to the child's arrival, and ignoring the turbulent early years when kids and parents are sick quite often. A powerful approach to mitigating the effects of Academic Chutes and Ladders for parents, especially mothers, involves informal support. One survey respondent's experiences with pregnancy loss and parenting underscore the need for support beyond formal leave policies: "I'm tenure track now. Having a child has not really affected my goals; however, I've gotten married while tenure track and I'm now trying to conceive and have had two miscarriages. The mental toll of these miscarriages, along with the physical toll of miscarrying and medical appointments has affected the time I have to work and my connection to my work. I'm beginning to worry how it might affect my tenure portfolio." Pregnancy, adoption, and miscarriage are processes that occur before the onset of parental leave but can nonetheless be physically, emotionally, and financially draining and logistically complex. Parental leave is not always sufficient to accommodate scholars balancing work alongside health and family struggles, which we address in depth in chapter 7, "Love, Loss, and Longing."

To compensate for insufficient formal accommodations, informal support is key. These efforts can and should vary by campus, department, and person but might include professional lifelines like mentorship (Leeds et al. 2014; Lundquist and Misra 2017), peer coverage for classes and meetings, collaborative research that allows scholars to tag-team work as each member of the research team is able, and campus and department policies that convey flexibility by allowing faculty to hold online class sessions or activities or bring children to campus as needed. Other scholars have suggested diversity and sensitivity training for supervisors, deans, and members of tenure and promotion committees to illuminate the accommodations that scholar parents may need (Winegar 2016).

Beyond these efforts, we cannot understate the importance of recognizing our colleagues as humans with lives outside of the classroom and office; when we begin with that recognition, compassionate policies and practices follow. For example, some faculty bristle at the occasions when their colleagues' children come to campus. Academic schedules often do not align with pre-kindergarten programs and grade school holidays and closures or even with regular school hours. In some cases, children may need to spend time in their parents' offices. We acknowledge that children can be—and often are—disruptive, a reality that is patently unfair to colleagues who expect that their work environment maintain professional decorum to foster the working and learning environment. Bringing children to work can potentially upset the work balance in a department. However, the occasion may arise when the only responsible thing to do is to bring a child to work. On the other hand, some universities have official policies that state that children are legally not allowed to be on campus. This puts academic parents in a bind, especially when departmental visibility is important and support systems are sparse. Anecdotally, scholars have noted that the children-at-work phenomenon is also highly gendered: men are seen as doting, involved parents, whereas women are seen as unprofessional.

Kathleen Hancock's vignette illustrates the importance of both formal and informal support systems, especially for women. At the nexus of formal leave policies and informal support efforts is the notion of "stopping the clock." Stopping the clock adds time to the tenure track to help parents (usually mothers in practice) make up for time spent caring for an infant instead of working on research and teaching. The use of these policies varies, as does their utility (for instance, do they help or harm the tenure deliberations?). Recall the survey respondent referenced at the outset of the chapter who related a departmental rumor that the tenure committee expected anyone who had stopped the clock to have published more in that "extra" time; obviously, this type of norm will create more harm for anyone who has opted to stop the clock.

In her vignette, Kathleen Hancock writes that she had not heard of stopping the clock policies; indeed, these policies are often not as consistently recognized and applied across departments and campuses, and the option to stop the clock may not even be formalized in campus policies. We suggest that the option be made available to all scholar parents who wish to use it, but that the expectations for contract renewal or tenure and promotion remain the same regardless of whether someone has stopped their clock. Simply put, the additional semester or year helps to level the playing field for new parents. It is not, in fact, *extra* time to publish or innovate courses and should not be recognized as such.

As we consider best practices for improving support for scholar parents, we should begin with (1) transparent, universally applied, and clearly communicated family leave policies; (2) flexibility beyond parental leave upon the birth or arrival of a child; and (3) high-quality, affordable, and accessible childcare on or near campus. Ultimately, each academic institution should work from these initial formal and informal support efforts and expand to initiatives that suit the needs of scholar parents on campus, including (but certainly not limited to) on-campus childcare options, considerations for days when the college or university and local school or daycare calendars are out of sync, clear policies and norms for stopping the tenure clock without

Supporting Our Professor-Moms

Kathleen J. Hancock
Associate Professor of Political Science
Colorado School of Mines

She was tinier than I expected. The video shows me mouthing to my husband behind the camera, "She's so little." At last, I was a mother. Not through the conventional means but by adopting a nine-month-old born in China. Why go all the way to China to adopt your daughter? Because that's where my daughter was born. I always liked that answer.

Motherhood challenges came fast. Less than twenty-four hours after holding my tiny girl, we were rushing her to the hospital, where she would stay for a week in the infectious diseases ward. It was measles. We had barely made it in time. With a minimal medical budget and measles running rampant in many orphanages, she would have died had we not arrived when we did. With another adoption agency, we would have been blocked from going, as it was at the height of SARS, a deadly virus sweeping Asia. But our daughter did not die. She recovered in a large hospital with loving doctors and nurses but also filth-covered walls and outdated medical care.

Adoptive mothers do not have a pregnancy, but we have our own difficult process that involves months of work and waiting. To adopt from China, you must undergo an extensive, often intrusive, investigation. Our tax records were scoured to ensure we had enough money to take care of our daughter; we did. We were asked if we had guns in the house; we lived in Texas, but we didn't. We underwent medical exams to ensure we would not soon die of illness, leaving our daughter "abandoned" again; we were deemed healthy.

The process took about four months. At last, the adoption agency sent our dossier to China, along with those of eight other families. We waited. And waited. Rumors spread. We would hear that week. We would not hear that week. The babies were sick. A baby died. A dossier group that went after us already heard; why hadn't we? Birth parents wait for their water to break; we waited for the phone to ring.

Then one day the phone call came that left me on my knees and in tears of joy. My husband was in San Francisco; I was in San Antonio. We celebrated over the phone. Our baby had been selected for us. Then came the emailed photo of a baby girl wrapped in layers and layers of red and blue, her little face above it all. We were in love.

I became a mom the summer after I became an assistant professor on the tenure track. I know people who had babies in graduate school and were told it was poor timing. I knew professors who advised women not to have babies until they were tenured. But I never asked myself about the timing. By the time I met my dream man, I knew it was going to be hit-or-miss if we got pregnant. We immediately started down the path of adoption. I knew I would already be an older mom. No point in waiting any longer.

On the job market, I had been open about my path to motherhood. I made clear I would be having a baby in my first or second year. No one raised any objections. One senior faculty member asked me inappropriate (illegal) questions about my marriage—"What makes you think your husband will follow you to Texas?"—and my gender—"We've already hired three women. How many more do we have to hire?" But everyone seemed perfectly fine and even happy for my impending motherhood.

My daughter came to us, and we to her, just as the spring semester ended. I felt lucky. I did not have to miss classes or take maternity leave or a leave of absence. I had the summer to play with her, bond with her, take her to doctors' appointments. To be her mommy. I tried to work on research and writing, but I was often tired or too busy being her mommy.

When the fall semester arrived, we hired a nanny to help most of the day so I could work on courses, publications, and service. Without family nearby and feeling the pressure of tenure, I viewed our nannies as a blessing. I later heard a department administrator say that I had it easy because I had a nanny and did not have to use daycare. I pondered that. I did feel we were fortunate to be able to afford a nanny, but it did not always feel easy. Nannies came and went. They had their own lives, and sometimes children, that resulted in missed days. I wanted my daughter cared for in specific ways so was in perpetual training. So many nannies rotated through the house, I wrote a paper called "The Nanny Go-Round." Still, I know I was lucky to have the support.

Like all professors with research obligations, I knew my publications would be the key to tenure, but they came slower than I had hoped. My PhD mentor asked me one day if I was going to have the tenure clock stopped—that is, get an extra year on my tenure clock to make up for the time parenting had taken from my research and writing productivity. I had never heard of such a thing. It was 2004. Although these policies were popping up at some universities, people did not talk about them. My friends in academia, my colleagues, and my administrators had never mentioned the idea. When I raised it with my department chair, he said he did not know about such a policy but he would check. Indeed, we did have a policy to stop the tenure clock for up to two years due to a variety of issues, including family or personal illness and becoming a parent.

As with many universities, especially at that time, the policy was unevenly enforced. First, you had to learn about it. Second, you had to write a letter to the chair, who decided whether or not to grant the extension. It was unclear why one parent would be granted an extension and not another. I do not recall exactly what I wrote, but I got the extension, as did my colleague and friend who had become an assistant professor and mother through adoption at the same time I did. We were not told why our applications were successful. We were happy to receive the extensions and did not question the process.

My husband and I decided to grow our family. Almost exactly two years after our first trip to China, we returned to meet and fall in love with our second daughter. As before, the investigation and paperwork were extensive. The rumors and waiting, agonizing. The joy unparalleled.

As before, I hoped I could do the work without needing extra help in the form of maternity leave or an extension on the clock. But having a second child was no easier or less time-consuming than having the first. The learning curve was less steep, but each child is unique, with different challenges and joys, and needs her own bonding time.

Just because you have children, your life does not otherwise remain static. While caring for our first daughter and with a second on the way, I was diagnosed with thyroid cancer. I had surgery to remove my thyroid and recovered very well; I have been in remission for nearly fifteen years.

As the tenure deadline neared, I once again had to acknowledge that my publications were not where I wanted them to be. Although my book, based on my dissertation but with two new empirically rich chapters and a new theory, was nearly finished and ready for submission to publishers, I was concerned it would not be published in time for the tenure review. Although our department did not have clear tenure guidelines, it was assumed that at least a book was required. To be safe, I decided to ask for a second yearlong extension.

Unfortunately, the policy still gave discretion to the department chair, a man with whom I had had conflicts since my arrival. In my first semester, he wrote me a lengthy email accusing me of "stealing" his honors student who had decided to switch from him to me as thesis advisor. He wrote a similarly scathing email to the student, who came to me in tears. He accused us of conspiring behind his back. When I tried to meet with him to discuss the situation, he told me, "You made your bed, now you lay in it." Our relationship never improved from there.

Despite my concerns that for personal reasons the new chair would not approve my extension, I figured that two children and cancer warranted a second extension and that if the chair denied me, surely the dean or provost would overrule him. I was wrong. The dean told me I had not made sufficient research progress to warrant an extension. This struck me as paradoxical: why would I need an extension if I was on track for the research? In the end, I was denied tenure despite having four peer-reviewed articles, one non-peer-reviewed article, and a book contract with a major academic publisher who wrote to the department saying he was asking only for minor revisions. My tenure decision was split at the department level, the chair and dean wrote against me, and the campus-wide committee unanimously supported me. The provost was new; he told me he decided unless it was unanimous at all levels, he was denying people tenure.

Happily, while I was up for tenure, I went on the job market and landed a great job at my current institution where I have thrived. I sent my resignation letter to the provost with a smile on my face.

One might think all is well that ends well, but the path had been difficult and fraught with uncertainty. I had been fortunate that another university took a chance on me. One should not have to rely so much on luck or struggle so much harder than others just because she wants to be both a mother and a scholar.

My experience led me to two take two steps to try and help others. First, I created a network called Mothers in International Relations. The acronym, MIR, means "peace" in Russian. As a scholar of the former Soviet Union, I rather liked that. I added 2006 to the Yahoo! Group title to always remind me of when the group was founded. There are currently more than ninety members, all women who are mothers or intend to be mothers. At the International Studies Association (ISA) annual conference, we had our first meeting over lunch. I recall asking everyone what they would like to do with our group. Should we do some research about women and children in our profession? Should we advocate for better childcare at the meetings? There was silence. One person finally offered, "Can we just share stories about our challenges? Can we just complain a bit?" And so we did. There were tales of beginning work at 2:00 a.m. when the baby had finally fallen asleep. Of colleagues telling women they should not have had children until after tenure. Of faculty meetings held at the end of the day, after daycare had closed. Of the challenges of nursing in the office or of pumping milk in bathroom stalls. For many of us, just knowing we were not alone was enough.

Second, and much more time-intensive, I codesigned, conducted, and analyzed a survey of the members of the ISA. The focus was on publication rates and what factors account for higher rates of publication during the tenure-track years. Given the importance of research for most institutions, whatever affects publication rates would also affect who gets tenure. Underlying the survey was the question of whether men and women performed differently on this metric. The ISA governing board made the unusual decision to send the survey to all members.

My motivation for the survey was my experience as a mother on the tenure track and my observations of who was getting tenured. I had applauded as women I knew announced they got tenure, many at prominent universities. The needle was finally moving. Women were moving up the ladder, from PhD student to tenured faculty member and later to full professor. While happy for these women, I began to notice a pattern. These successful women did not have children. I wondered if my challenging albeit ultimately successful path to tenure was more common with women who had children while on the tenure track. Assistant professors are faced with a host of challenges; having children is one more hurdle to tenure. While I have never met a mother-academic who regretted having her children, it seems obvious we made it harder on ourselves in terms of getting tenured.

In the survey, we asked about family-related issues that we suspected might affect publication rates: the number of children under five, the type of childcare used, the primary caregiver, extended family support, and stopping the tenure clock. We did indeed find significant differences (Hancock, Baum, and Breuning 2013, 2015). Some of our findings include

- Single women publish more than married women; for men, marriage does not affect publication rates.
- Compared to 51 percent of men, 62 percent of women reported they had no children under age five while assistant professors. This is most likely due to women deciding not to have children while on the tenure track.
- Men and women academics were nearly equally likely to have one child (20 percent and 18 percent, respectively), whereas more men than women reported larger families, with 29 percent of men having two or more children under age five, compared to 20 percent of women. This finding is consistent with Scott Long's (1990) research in which he found that American men in the sciences have more children than women in similar disciplines.
- Women report using childcare much more than men, presumably because more men rely on their women partners to take care of the children: 60 percent of women, compared to 32

percent of men, said their children were in childcare for thirty or more hours a week.

Few doubt that in most relationships women shoulder more child-care responsibility than men. As with most families, when it comes to day-to-day childcare; staying up with sick children; researching pre-schools, public schools, and colleges; overseeing homework; guiding nutrition; and dealing with personal dramas, I take the lead. Single mothers, of course, do it all. I have loved my dual role as mother and professor, but we must acknowledge that these joys and burdens take time and energy from professors who are simultaneously trying to earn tenure, a key to a long and successful career in academia.

As a community, we must support professors who want to be mothers. That support can come in the form of policies like an extended tenure clock, educating mothers on the policies available to them, not discriminating against those who take advantage of those policies, and providing feedback and support for each other. We can do better.

retribution, and equitable teaching and service burdens shared among all faculty. Some obstacles facing scholar parents, however, are rooted in entrenched professional norms that disproportionately affect women. We turn now to these issues.

Beyond the Babies: Service Roles and the Gender Gap in Citations

Two of the obstacles facing early-career scholar parents affect women more broadly and are not limited to academic mothers. These obstacles are generally less likely to affect an academic man's career trajectory, regardless of whether he has children. Here we look beyond the effects of motherhood to explore how unequal service burdens and the gender gap in citations threaten a woman's ability to earn tenure or to move from a non-tenure-track position into a tenure-track or tenured job.

"Taking Care of the Academic Family": Gender and Service Roles

Women contribute disproportionately to the profession by taking on more than their fair share of service assignments. Guarino and Borden's (2017) survey of faculty at more than 140 institutions of higher education and analysis of faculty annual review data on two midwestern campuses yielded the unsurprising finding that women faculty take on more service responsibilities than their men colleagues, even when controlling for department, field, faculty rank, race, and ethnicity. They also observed that women are more likely to take on internal service roles, whereas men are better represented in higher-profile roles with professional associations and editorial boards. Women, in short, are "taking care of the academic family" (Guarino and Borden 2017; Murdie 2017).

Responses from our survey align with these findings. Many participants noted that administrators compensated for inadequate family leave policies with reduced teaching and research responsibilities while maintaining service assignments. As one respondent said, "Mothers in my department get one semester off from teaching and are assigned service activities to 'compensate' for the four-week difference between the twelve weeks of FMLA and the sixteen-week semester. Fathers do not take leave. This varies by department, both in terms of amount of time off and amount of pay received during leave." The reallocation of effort may in fact work against women scholars in the long term, however, as the service assignments they take on tend to be of low prestige and internal to the department or university.

As Murdie (2017) observes, this is a discrepancy worth studying because those external service positions are the ones that "can lead to requests to apply for positions, attend invited conferences, be part of grant proposals, etc." And although internal service roles are key to the daily functioning of the university, they are "much less likely to get you noticed by your discipline peers" and thus may contribute to the leaky pipeline, as esteem within one's field (judged by letters of support in the tenure file) is a key requirement for tenure at many universities.

Given the implications of service burden discrepancies for pre-tenure faculty and those in contingent positions especially, how should individual faculty members respond when asked to take on service commitments? Bessette's piece on service discrepancies on the website Inside Higher Ed is illustrative:

> Part of it is that most of the time, I am saying yes to friends and colleagues, something that I feel is necessary in order to be a good community member. But I also feel like, in my contingent position, it is necessary to say yes, because I never know what opportunity will lead to a better position. There is also the gendered component: women in academia are more likely to take on "service" roles

within their departments and disciplines. I am no exception, and my department knows that whenever a committee needs representation from an Instructor that they can nominate me and I will accept the position. Research also shows that women aren't rewarded for these roles.

So should women "just say no"? Mitchell and Hesli's (2013) analysis of a 2009 American Political Science Association survey suggests that women are asked more frequently than men to perform service tasks, that they agree to do so more frequently than men, and that these service roles occupied by women are "token" roles instead of major leadership positions that tend to boost one's standing on campus or in the discipline writ large. Time spent on service is time not spent on research and writing, which threatens the long-term job security of pre-tenure faculty in departments that require a certain number of publications for promotion and tenure (Bellas and Toutkoushian 1999; Mitchell and Hesli 2013, 357).

The discrepancy in service burdens is not limited to junior faculty. Since there are fewer women associate and full professors thanks to the leaky pipeline, or what we call the game of Academic Chutes and Ladders, there is a more limited pool of senior women available to fill service roles at the higher levels of the university. If universities strive for diversity in their task forces, committees, and other service positions, then the service burden on senior women will be higher than that of senior men (Mitchell and Hesli 2013, 357). Since white academics are more likely to hold positions within the higher academic ranks, the effects of service discrepancies related to gender are magnified for faculty of color (Bellas and Toutkoushian 1999, 367–68).

In short, women perform more service roles throughout their careers than do men, whether or not they have children. Still, the solution is not as simple as telling tenure-track and contingent faculty to say no more often; this is an individual response that will not change collective expectations in the academy and could jeopardize one's prospects for tenure or a more permanent position.

Acknowledging the Scholar: The Gender Gap in Citations

Time spent on tasks other than research detracts from the ability to publish, but when women scholars publish their work, that research is generally less likely to receive recognition within the discipline. A persistent gender gap in citations favors white men scholars over women scholars and scholars from marginalized groups (Ainley, Danewid, and Yao 2017; Dayal, Schramm, and

Stark 2017; Maliniak, Powers, and Walter 2013). Maliniak, Powers, and Walter (2013) analyzed three thousand international relations journal articles published between 1980 and 2006 and found that articles written by men had an average of 4.8 more citations than articles written by women. In their examination of articles published in two international relations journals in 2005, Mitchell, Lange, and Brus (2013) observed that men authors and mixed-gender coauthor groups are less likely to cite woman-authored scholarship than women authors are. The citation gap may arise in part because of the underrepresentation of women authors in top journals, but the research on this point is mixed (Goddard et al. 2017; Teele and Thelen 2017). Researchers have also found that women are less likely than men to cite *themselves*, thus compounding the effects of gender bias in citation practices ("Promotion and Self-Promotion" 2013; Maliniak, Powers, and Walter 2013).

More than just a measure of popularity, the citation count is an indicator of influence in one's discipline. For scholars to stay in academia, especially at research universities, they must not only publish their work but also gain esteem among their peers on the basis of their scholarship. A low citation can adversely affect one's odds of achieving tenure and promotion, especially to the rank of full or distinguished professor. Maliniak, Powers, and Walter (2013, 90) cite a full professor who observed the impact of the social science citation index and Google Scholar citation counts on departmental discussions; the professor makes reference to the increased importance of citation metrics in recent years as that information has become available.

Beyond the effects of the gender gap in citations on an individual scholar's career, there are also ramifications for the classroom and the next generation of scholars. The same implicit biases that drive the gender gap in citations—and also, presumably, the decreased tendency to cite scholars from marginalized racial groups and the Global South—are at work when faculty members compile course syllabi. Colgan (2015) analyzed graduate international relations course syllabi and found that women authors were underrepresented relative to men authors but that women faculty members were more likely than their men colleagues to include women-authored work on a course syllabus.

The scholarly works that undergraduate and graduate students study is also similarly biased in favor of men scholars (Sumner 2018). Sumner built the Gender Bias Assessment Tool, a web-based platform for scholars to analyze their syllabi and provide quantitative metrics for determining whether the course material skews heavily toward men or represents a balance. Since students and faculty alike have called in recent years for the decolonization of curricula and better representation of voices from the Global South and scholars of color, as well as coverage of issues related to gender and race

(Sabaratnam 2017; Yao and Delatolla 2017), tools like Sumner's offer scholars the opportunity to gauge the inclusiveness of their classrooms. Those inclusive curricula, in turn, could stand to ease the citation gaps as students rise through the academic ranks, as well as prove pedagogically important in shaping the next generations of academics and their views on the scholars and topics central to their disciplines.

Concluding Thoughts

As we consider the need for better, more transparent, clearly communicated, and universally applied parental leave policies, informal support systems, equitable service burdens, and recognition of women's scholarship, the obstacles facing parents—especially women—on the tenure track are daunting. As a result of the COVID-19 pandemic, some academic institutions have issued across-the-board tenure clock extensions for pre-tenure faculty. While this is a well-intentioned policy, it does not address the additional burden on and insecurity of non-tenure-track faculty and will likely exacerbate existing publication gaps between academics with and without children (Windsor and Crawford 2020). Academic caregivers—both men and women—are simultaneously balancing their jobs, running homeschooling programs, and holding down the second shift (Hochschild and Machung 2012). Academic journals have already recorded gendered patterns in manuscript submissions, with women submitting far fewer than men in the early months of 2020 (Flaherty 2020; Minello 2020). The academic community will likely be reeling from the effects of the pandemic for many years, as academic parents work to recoup work productivity time lost to caregiving. Now more than ever, departments and administrators should consider how one-size-fits-all policies will disproportionately benefit some academics and penalize others.

An empowering takeaway from this discussion, however, is the notion that all of these obstacles can crumble if we thoughtfully and collectively chip away at them. Informal support for colleagues is something everyone reading this book can undertake; the approach will differ but the intention is the same. Each of us can make an effort to read, cite, and teach scholarship by women and nonbinary authors. Faculty with job security can start conversations about sharing the service burden more equitably in the department and across campus. Tenured faculty and administrators can similarly examine and advocate for ways to improve parent leave policies and options for stopping the clock. We all have a role to play in keeping talented scholars from falling down the academic chutes so they can persist in climbing the ladders.

Best Practices for Supporting Untenured Parents

What university administrators can do:

- Advocate for excellent childcare policies and facilities on campus.
- Make tenure and promotion expectations clear.
- Have a visible and consistent tenure clock policy for families.
- Make policies consistent across tenure-track and non-tenure-track faculty.
- Grade yourselves. Ask faculty in anonymous annual reviews about family formation policies (or annual survey of the department or university) and publish the results of the survey.
- Comply with accreditation standards that mandate gender equity policies be upheld.

What department chairs and unit heads can do:

- Check individual and departmental-level biases against non-tenure-track faculty.
- Make tenure and promotion expectations clear.
- Check gendered biases against extending the tenure clock.
- Do not discourage your women students (or assistant professors) from starting families.
- Apply departmental and university policies equitably across individuals, including non-tenure track faculty.
- Make parental leave expectations and oversight clear for men to curb misuse.

What faculty can do:

- Know your department's and university's tenure clock extension policy.
- Put everything in writing, and get everything in writing.
- For tenure-track faculty: stop the tenure clock.
- For non-tenure-track faculty: maintain and foster your connections in the broader discipline, seek mentorship, and strategically coauthor when possible.

- For men: use parental leave for the intended purpose and actively advocate for women colleagues—especially those who are pre-tenure or in non-tenure-track positions.

Notes

1. Family leave, broadly, permits time off to care for a new baby or a family member in need of medical or mental health care. The application and importance of family leave beyond care for an infant is outside of the scope of this work, and it merits a discussion in greater depths than we can explore here. It is important to recognize, however, that caregiving does not end when a parent no longer has an infant in the home; aging family members, family members experiencing mental health crises, and acute and chronic health conditions all throw off the ever-precarious work-life balance and require greater recognition and flexibility than what is currently available.
2. This was quite surprising because the editor at the time did not give out many revise-and-resubmits and thus conversion to publication was highly likely. However, an editorial change occurred and the new editor sent the paper to all new reviewers and then rejected it.
3. Like many mothers, Mitchell experienced baby blues after her child was born and those feelings lasted for several weeks. She also gave birth via C-section, which made physical recovery more difficult.
4. This information can be found on Mitchell's website at http://saramitchell.org/ParentalBenefits.xls.
5. See http://web.apsanet.org/cswp/data-on-parental-leave-policies/.
6. The information Mitchell is discussing in this paragraph comes from her dataset in 2011. Policies have most certainly become more generous by 2020.
7. On the other hand, among respondents that have children, women are significantly more likely to have children under the age of eighteen than men peers.
8. In some countries, such as Canada, listing parental leaves on CVs is a common practice. This helps to treat leaves as part of the standard academic record.

4 The Elusive Work-Life Balance

Daily Challenges in Academic Parenting

The consensus among academic parents, especially mothers, is that the work-life balance is a myth. There is no balance—there is only juggling, managing, falling short, regrouping, and hopefully succeeding. In keeping with the theme of the book, we explore how lower-order and higher-order processes affect the work-life myth. In family-friendly institutions where policies are implemented equitably, parents report that balancing the dual demands of career and children is easier. While the work-life myth is biased in that any parent who flouts gender norms and expectations likely suffers negative consequences in their careers, the emphasis on balancing career and family demands is directed primarily toward women. Some of the lower-order processes involved in managing the simultaneous demands of career and family include individualistic prescriptions directed at women (rather than academic institutions), "leaning in" in ill-advised ways, gendered time-management challenges, carrying the unpaid mental and emotional labor for the family, and succumbing to the myth of "having it all." To remain in academia, parents must find a way to manage the simultaneous demands of career and family even given the challenges of geographic isolation and inequitable gendered expectations of parents. Advice abounds, but much of it is not grounded in best practice and disproportionately amplifies women's burdens.

Leaning In . . .

A substantial part of the work-life myth is the fallacy that having it all is a static goal and that leaning in will get you there. "Lean in" is a set of strategies and career and life suggestions to keep women advancing in their careers while simultaneously becoming mothers (Sandberg 2013). Its chief architect, Sheryl Sandberg, gained a rapid following in 2013 with advice about "women,

91

work, and the will to lead." *Lean In* (the book) started a movement, gaining acolytes who hosted book clubs and mentoring groups to generate visibility for issues facing mothers in the workplace. To effectively lean in, women are encouraged not to "check out" before they become parents but rather to continue working long and hard, taking on projects and assignments to demonstrate their commitment to their career. In other words, to ensure they would not become redundant or stagnant, women should plan for and sustain their career future by consolidating their essential roles in their organization before taking maternity leave. Women who are "gone before they are gone" risk irrelevancy (Sandberg 2013).

Lean In quickly generated substantial backlash for its failure to account for the roles of class, family status, socioeconomics, and lack of institutional responsibility (hooks 2013). The well-intentioned paradigm fell quickly into disfavor amid cries of sexism, classism, and elitism. Single parents have no choice but to lean in. Parents in low-paying jobs (like adjunct professors or graduate students) have no choice but to lean in. Most importantly, individuals are responsible for leaning in, while institutions bear little responsibility for protecting women and their careers when they choose to become parents, including complying with legal mandates and accommodations. Men, and colleagues without children, also have little responsibility for ensuring a favorable environment for leaning in and succeeding. Recent research from Duke University found that "lean in"–type messages increase the perception that women are responsible for gender disparities and inequality (Kim, Fitzsimons, and Kay 2018). Lean in absolves everyone except women from resolving gendered inequalities.

It also amplifies the challenges that non-neurotypical people face. Being a woman and being a parent in academia involves juggling many things at once. It demands the ability to multitask, prioritize, and delegate. For non-neurotypical people these coping skills may not be available. Non-neurotypical people and those with chronic health conditions like depression—which can be exacerbated during the postpartum phase as we discuss in chapter 6, "Sick and Tired"—may experience daily life and major life changes differently, with different coping mechanisms at their disposal. *Lean In*'s one-size-fits-all approach to gender parity ignores these realities.

To underscore this, Ruth Whippman's (2019) *New York Times* opinion editorial emphasizes how leaning in puts the burden on women to do more, be different, and adopt more masculine strategies in order to succeed—in spite of well-documented research that demonstrates how women are penalized professionally for doing these very things. Whippman advocates instead that men "lean out" or "lean back" and writes that systemic change depends on their efforts to create space for women. As she points out, women are encouraged to "power pose" in the bathroom before presentations, but men are not similarly encouraged to "capitulation pose." The road to gender equality in academia—as in the broader workplace and society—seems to be a one-way street.

In 2018 the American Political Science Association hosted a hackathon to generate ideas for how men could more actively support women in the profession. In late 2019 the journal *PS: Political Science and Politics* issued a call for papers addressing this issue as well. The discipline is becoming increasingly aware of the role that men need to play in addressing gender inequality. Rather than leaning out or back, men need to lean in *more* in their roles as mentors, advocates, and allies for their women colleagues. Newly tenured men colleagues can play an essential role in changing departmental and institutional culture because they occupy a middle ground and are able to speak with job security to issues of entrenched sexism and bias while setting a positive example for pre-tenure men.

. . . Without Faceplanting

If leaning in is wrong, is there a better approach? The pursuit of fulfilling both work and career commitments can lead women and parents to make irrational decisions that are time-consuming and ill advised for advancing through the tenure and promotion process. For example, as compensation for inadequate family leave policies, departments often offer service assignments to women. While these service assignments might keep them covered by health insurance during their maternity leave, they do not foster short-term goals of maternity leave as genuine time away from work to forge a bond with a new family member or longer-term goals of being research productive as service assignments are often low-prestige internal tasks that do not raise the scholar's profile in the discipline or within the university. Thus, when women lean in, they should do so strategically.

Furthermore, even when women lean in and speak up, they do not get what they bargain for, as Artz and colleagues (2018) find in "Do Women Ask?" The long-standing and prevalent perspective is that wage gaps and other rank disparities are due to gendered norms that inhibit women from directly asking their supervisors or employers for pay raises. Artz and colleagues find that on the contrary, women *do ask* but *do not get* what they ask for. The responsibility falls on women to improve their position and salary—as does the blame when they fail to achieve their objectives. Rather than viewing this as systemic bias against women, society and the academy view this as an indicator of the shortcomings of women scholars both in their work and in their ability to bargain on their own behalf.

So, not only is leaning in an activity that reinforces women's responsibility for creating systemic change; it is also a strategy steeped in privilege. It's possible to lean in if you have adequate economic resources and social support. Rather, it's *only* possible to lean in if you have those things—and many academics, especially those in graduate school or in contingent, non-tenure-track positions, do not. Academic parents are often uprooted and live far from their families and social support systems. Well-intentioned family and friends often suggest "getting a job closer to home" without understanding the geographic inflexibility of academia. With a tight academic job market and ample competition, job availability in desirable locations is scarce. For dual-academic career spouses, the options are even more limited. Similarly, accessible, affordable, and desirable childcare is elusive and often the only option available to academic parents. And a growing number of first-generation academics come from working-class backgrounds, meaning they have additional financial demands, including substantial student loan debt, that constrain their budgets.

Shifting Balances, Structuring Time

The time and task allocation between parenting and working is dynamic. There is not a universal static formula with a winning combination. Children require different amounts of hands-on attention at different developmental points, and the ebb and workflow of academic commitments changes during the semester and over the course of a career. Conference presentations, grant proposals, and submitting final grades impose firm deadlines. In-class teaching occupies a regular schedule, but one of the benefits of academia is that in many cases, it affords generous flex time. Course prep can be done in the evenings and weekends or over holidays and is not confined to a fixed office space.

Seltzer (2015) provides a comprehensive treatment of strategies for better time management in academia. For example, she recommends limiting class prep time, setting limits for social media and email, disconnecting from electronics, being fully present at both work and at home, knowing your department's and university's expectations for tenure, and strategizing negotiating at work. She also provides advice on "soft skills" like nonverbal communication and navigating contentious meetings, as well as networking and mentorship priorities that can provide support to women academics throughout their careers.

The anonymous assistant professor author of the second vignette in this chapter describes this situation well: academics do have tremendous flexibility in our work schedules, yet this can be both a benefit and a hazard, as a seamless continuum between work and home life may foster unhealthy habits. If you can work all the time whenever you want, you don't have to be efficient. Inefficiency is a luxury. For parents with limited bandwidth, efficiency is an important trait to foster. Many successful academics also consider healthy work and home life boundaries essential: work when you are at work, and be home when you are at home. Deciding to keep regular hours and not to work evenings and weekends may be tantamount to professional sacrilege for academics, but parenthood may have optimistically perverse consequences by increasing efficiency.

One scholar advises a "chipping" method to maintain progress and momentum in research and teaching: she advises junior scholars to use every ounce of time available during their workday to be maximally efficient. If you have fifteen minutes before office hours, chip away at emails. If you have thirty minutes in between classes, grade a few papers. Fifteen minutes here and there add up to hours, and these short blocks of time are useful for clearing "administrivia" tasks from your to-do list. It is a myth that you can't do substantive work unless you have an uninterrupted block of several hours, what another scholar calls the "tyranny of unstructured time." It is remarkably easy to waste several hours rather than convert them into productive uses of time. One way to address this is external accountability, such as the writing bootcamps Courtney Burns describes in her vignette.

As an academic parent, all time feels precious. Making the most of your time at work and with family, while often in an imperfect equilibrium, is possible. For women in academia, protecting our time is paramount, including wisely choosing service assignments, limiting the number of new course preps, and managing time with students. This includes student mentorship as well as student advocacy. Regarding the latter, the mental health crisis among university students is a growing problem, and students often feel safe sharing intimate details of their lives with women professors. This is both an honor and a burden: most professors are not trained mental health professionals, and the best help we can give our students is to refer them to appropriate university or community services. In doing this, we give students access to resources to address their needs, and we also protect our time. For student advocacy, women often dedicate more time than their men counterparts to providing public goods for the department, including student mentorship. Courtney Burns's experience also highlights gendered differences in mentorship priorities.

In a different way, the second vignette contributor describes how she protects her time: additional income via her spouse's work promotion is dedicated to outsourcing domestic labor, such as dog-walking, housekeeping, and the like. Our survey respondents consistently recommended this strategy: outsource what you can. This presumes a degree of financial flexibility and resources that many academics do not have, but perhaps the underlying concept is about prioritizing the most important things and fighting the right battles. Kids need to be fed, but every meal does not have to be haute cuisine. Squalor is unhealthy, but weekly baseboard polishing is unnecessary (unless, of course, this takes you to your happy place).

Survey respondents also mentioned how late afternoon or early evening faculty or committee meetings impinge on their carefully balanced childcare schedule. As one respondent relates (with frustration), "Many other faculty have children. The department is accommodating and perhaps too much so in some cases. While I think a work-life balance is important, I am frustrated by colleagues that simply can never spend afternoons or evenings on professional activities (grad classes, campus visitors, faculty meetings, working group meetings, etc.). I do appreciate that faculty, including myself, can bring children to the office when necessary." Finding childcare—especially at nonstandard hours (generally outside of 7:00 a.m. to 6:00 p.m.) can be difficult and expensive. Another respondent—straddling the line between empathy and pragmatism—wrote this: "I remember one colleague having to bring her young son with her to faculty meetings because the chair had chastised her for missing faculty meetings due to childcare issues." Still, other departments are thoughtful in their accommodations: "My department also has flexible working, meaning that they aim to schedule meetings between ten and three to permit school pickups, and they have protected one day a week when my son frequently has medical appointments to ensure I don't have to teach then."

It is important to note that academic parents leave their day job and head home to their evening jobs. As many parents know, the evening routine often teeters precariously between controlled chaos and unhinged pandemonium. When academic parents finish teaching, service, and afternoon or evening meetings, their workdays are not over. Rather, they are headed home to their next job to make dinner, bathe kids, supervise homework, get everyone to bed, and prepare for the next day—or what we like to call "wash, rinse, repeat."

Departmental change accommodating academic parents is possible, if slow, however: "When we arrived, there were no babies or really young children in the department. Most of the faculty were either childless or their

The Elusive Work-Life Balance

Anonymous Woman Assistant Professor

In preparing this contribution, I've puzzled for some time over the notion of work-life balance. Having been asked to reflect on my own experience, I've struggled with what that means exactly. Do I have balance? What? No, of course not. Does that imply my life is im-balanced? That doesn't seem quite right either. It is a false dichotomy, to create an either/or distinction between the two. The notion that one could divorce or bifurcate one's intellectual life from one's personal life seems impossible, and not in fact desirable. The stark reality of my life is that I'm simply too busy doing *both* of those things, *all of the time*, to worry very much about the trade-offs.

Of course one's perspective is largely dependent on where one stands. I am an assistant professor who will be promoted to associate in the coming months. I suppose this means I have cleared the tenure bar, but my day-to-day life is so full of the mundane joys and responsibilities of work and family that I have not really celebrated, nor has that accomplishment really set in yet. Like many accomplishments in the academy, it has been rather anticlimactic. My position is in a top-fifty department in my discipline, which is an R1 public research university. I teach two classes each semester, and do not teach in the summer so I can focus on research. Though I am a popular teacher, the vast majority of my tenure evaluation hinged on my research productivity and the publication of noted scholarship in high-impact peer-reviewed journals. I have no administrative or formal advising responsibilities, though I am a mentor to many students.

My husband and I coparent one precocious three-year-old and two dogs. My husband is also a midcareer professional whose position requires extensive travel; he is often gone from home, sometimes for multiple weeks at a time, and also works long hours. We do not have any extended family in the area. My child has been in private home care since she was four months old and is usually there between 7:30 and 5:30, Monday through Friday. While the childcare arrangements are excellent in many respects, this implies that in addition to the full-time job I maintain as a tenure-track faculty member I am often the sole responsible adult for myself, a three-year-old, and two "fur children." My life is full. It is a delicate ecosystem, the contents of which usually fall squarely on my shoulders when something goes awry. And while I have had days that are, without exaggeration, full of attending to other creatures' excrement and body fluids, those days are thankfully the exception, not the rule.

To be clear: I do not confuse my situation with single-parenthood, which is different in substance and in kind. I am also not oblivious to the socioeconomic privilege that greatly facilitates many contours of my life. We are a dual-income household; I have the unwavering emotional and financial support of my spouse even in his absences. With his promotion to his current position, we acknowledged that we would spend a considerable proportion of his new income on family "supporters": additional and backup childcare, dog-walkers, house-cleaners, and the like. These people are very much part of my family; their contribution to our well-being is immeasurable. But the fact of our reality is that many of the conveniences of our lives are made possible by our socioeconomic status: we buy many aspects of the balance and quality of our lives.

The best piece of family planning advice I've ever heard had nothing to do with children but was rather to be sure to pick a *partner*. In this respect I am lucky: my husband takes full and equal responsibility for childcare and parenting in every opportunity he can. Still, it was striking for me to realize how exceptional this is, even in 2018. I know of many female friends and acquaintances with young children, doctors, lawyers, women with advanced degrees and PhDs, who still bear the large part of the responsibility for childrearing in their homes. Despite what survey evidence suggests about changing norms regarding the division of labor among millennials, from my vantage there is still considerable gender disparity in many second-shift activities and childcare. In my professional life, there are many parents in my department, some of whom have young children at the moment. Nearly all of them have (or had) a stay-at-home parent (or a mostly stay-at-home parent) to attend to children and family life. Most of the mothers I know who work outside of the home at all work on a part-time basis.

People used to ask if I had made or maintain friendships with other working mothers. This is a well-meaning but laughable conjecture: for the other working mothers I know, we have no spare time between us to do things that foster friendships. The one exception to this rule is when I see my academic friends at conferences, which of course implies we are (and usually are at least partially relieved to be) attending without our children. I am immensely fortunate to have meaningful friendships from a variety of settings, none of whom have young children, all of whom enjoy (or at minimum tolerate) my child.

Many child-centric activities where friendships might be forged (playgroups, story hours, activity classes, and many preschools) are scheduled to begin and end between the hours of 9 a.m. and 5 p.m. It is astonishing the extent to which these economies of child-raising are constructed around the assumption that at least one of the child's parents is available for midday activities and pickups. Again, traditional nuclear family structures, as well as socioeconomic class, quickly cut into consideration. For families to attend many child-centric developmental opportunities—most of which are free and open to the public—at least one parent must be available between the hours of 9 a.m. and 5 p.m. This presumes either two parents at home with one of them not working, the support of extended family, parent(s) performing salaried work outside of the normal workday hours, or some alternative arrangement.

I am of course cognizant of and thankful for the many flexibilities my life as an academic affords me. I can work while my daughter naps or sleeps, and I can work from home. I create and regulate my own schedule; I report to no one save my coauthors and editors (and sometimes students). But how this works in practice is subject to gross misunderstandings; very few people—well-meaning though they may be—fully understand the realities of my daily schedule. Unsurprisingly, most non-academics assume that my work stops when I leave the classroom. Clearly, that's impossible, as I teach only six hours a week but work closer to fifty to sixty in an average week. But many of my academic colleagues, even those with children, have virtually no idea what the rest of my non-professional life looks like. Despite repeated conversations about my childcare arrangements, I am certain that most of colleagues assume that if I am not in my office, I am at home with my child. If only! To be clear, there is no amount of working from home that gets done while my child is with me.

A constant to all forms of womanhood, independent of one's decisions or choices, is judgment. With respect to parenthood and work-life balance, if you leave your children in the care of others to prioritize your own work, you will be judged. If you make professional sacrifices so you can spend more time with your children, you will be judged. If you are a woman who decides motherhood is not really your thing, you will be judged. If you have no professional ambitions but rather regard motherhood as a full-time job, you will be judged. I manage any sort of judgment of my situation, from myself or others, by my unwavering conviction that everything is as it should be. I have become a better scholar (and a far better teacher if I'm honest) since becoming a mother. I think bigger, I'm a better risk taker, I am more efficient, and I am more selective in my commitments. I am a better mother *because of*, not in spite of, my professional work. I do not spend time wringing my hands about the decisions I've made. And fundamentally, I don't have extra time or energy for hand-wringing or self-doubt in this regard.

As to the question of self-care, my biggest indulgence is a good night's sleep. Moving beyond that into what other manifestations of self-care might look like would usually involve paying a babysitter in addition to the regular childcare where my child already spends a considerable amount of time and taking even more time away from my family. I would love to spend a few hours a week at the gym, but that seems indulgent when I have two dogs at home who would greatly enjoy and benefit from some additional time outside. I simply don't have (or rather, I don't make) time for that at this point in my life. That is not to say that I never will again, but I have resigned myself to the fact that while there might be seasons of my life where I'm consistently hitting personal bests at the gym, this is not one of those times.

The best piece of advice I have in the realm of self-care for academic parents (or any academic, or any parent for that matter) is this: be gentle with yourself. Forget outdated and unobtainable notions of balance, or the idea that you could or should "have it all." You can have it all, whatever that means to you. But, outside of the exceptionally wealthy, you can't have it all, and to have it all requires a considerable amount of work and sacrifice. I am extremely fortunate to have been able to work at all of this, without any major health or financial crises. It is, objectively speaking, a lot to manage a career, a personal life, a family. But it is also, as far as I am concerned, extremely rich and rewarding on multiple levels.

children were adults or nearly adults. Most people in the department were also from this area so had relied heavily on extended family for childcare when their children were younger. It was a nightmare scenario for new parents in the department. I remember the hostility I faced from older (and mostly now retired) faculty when I brought a baby to department events because we had no local family and finding a babysitter for an infant was impossible. A colleague and I had babies at about the same time twice, and since then there have been quite a few babies born. Now the department is much more family-friendly. I have worked really hard to make it easier for new colleagues than it was for me."

A survey by Guarino and Borden (2017) illuminates how women contribute disproportionately to the profession in service assignments. They surveyed faculty at more than 140 institutions of higher education and analyzed faculty annual review data on two midwestern campuses, yielding the unsurprising but important finding that women faculty take on more service responsibilities than their men colleagues, even when controlling for department, field, faculty rank, race, and ethnicity. Furthermore, women are more likely to take on internal service roles, whereas men are better represented in roles with professional associations and editorial boards; women, in short, are "taking care of the academic family" (Guarino and Borden 2017; Murdie 2017). Responses from our survey concur with these perspectives, as many participants noted that administrators compensated for inadequate family leave policies with reduced teaching and research responsibilities while maintaining service assignments. As one respondent said, "Mothers in my department get one semester off from teaching and are assigned service activities to 'compensate' for the four-week difference between the twelve weeks of FMLA and the sixteen-week semester. Fathers do not take leave. This varies by department, both in terms of amount of time off and amount of pay received during leave." This reallocation of effort may in fact work against women scholars in the long term, however, as the service assignments tend to be of low prestige and internal to the department or university. In short, as we discussed in chapter 3, women perform more service roles throughout their careers than do men, whether or not they have children.

Does Having It All Equal Happiness?

Leaning in does not necessarily guarantee satisfaction or success in life or at work, however. Anne-Marie Slaughter's (2015) frank discussion of her own career decisions raises questions about how academics, and academic parents, define success. She questions the traditional narrative arc of a successful career; a prevalent meme in academia is "full before forty," meaning achieving the rank of full professor before one's fortieth birthday as a measure of worth. Nonlinear career trajectories, especially those that include childrearing, would seldom help advance women's careers to meet this goal.

Related, Slaughter ponders how marrying the right person—making good partnering decisions—as well as getting the timing "right" for when to have children affect academic success. Women academics are usually cautioned to delay having children until after tenure, but doing this jeopardizes the biologically constrained childbearing timeline. Adoptive parents also face tremendous uncertainty in their journey to become parents, with at least as much unpredictability as academic mothers who give birth and also with much less institutional and collegial support. Academic success is also viewed as a measure of commitment, and those who don't succeed are presumed to lack commitment. This rugged individualism approach singles out academic parents—mothers especially—as uncommitted to their careers since childrearing is a full-time job itself. As an institution, the ivory tower unfairly penalizes women and their career advancement because policies related to family formation do not exist, are not upheld, or are upheld inequitably. All the while, women are expected to achieve and succeed.

Happiness is often difficult to achieve and sustain in toxic work environments. Because of gendered expectations about women's roles as being positive, compliant, and congenial, women doubly suffer the negative health consequences of faking happiness while also being truly unhappy with their treatment at work (Colligan and Higgins 2006). Many of our survey respondents shared stories of low-grade and open hostility they experienced at work. One respondent wrote, "My chair (who had changed from the first one I approached before adopting) was clearly hostile to women and mothers and to adoption. He once said to me in a meeting, 'Your father must be very disappointed that you could not bring him a child of his own blood.' Wow!"

Some women try the fake it until you make it approach, but research consistently shows that feigning happiness and excitement is detrimental to health and well-being (Duke 2006; Lennard, Scott, and Johnson 2019). Lennard and colleagues (2019) distinguish between surface acting and deep acting, finding that surface acting—shallow-faking positive emotions—actually leads to more negative emotions. Further, surface acting is a form of emotional labor, which women already undertake more than men. One survey respondent's experience reflects this point:

> At the time I began at my current institution, I would describe the overall climate as hostile to women with children. I opted not to disclose that I had a child. I was regularly asked during my first year by senior male colleagues about parental status when discussing the merits of or feedback on a project on which I was currently working. Male colleagues who knew I was a parent made a point to announce that surely they worked harder than I did because I was a mother.

A common impediment to having it all is resolving the two-body problem—a dual-academic partnership household. When the two-body problem results in prolonged family separation, it leaves one parent in the position of sole caregiver of the child(ren) most of the time. This parent faces all of the day-to-day logistics of parenting—snow days, sick days, and conflicts between meetings and daycare or school pickup—on their own, all while navigating teaching, research, and service expectations and the stress of a long-distance partnership. While some departments and universities are taking steps toward spousal accommodation, the overall outlook for partners seeking jobs at the same institution is bleak. Some universities have formal accommodation policies, which represents progress. However, there are still many variables to consider: is it preferable (or not) for both academics to be in the same department—or the same college? The anecdotal evidence is mixed. In some cases it is easier to negotiate a partnership hire in the same department; in others, having a partner in a different department can complicate the process. The additional tenure-track line for a spousal hire is not universally viewed as a bonus; in many cases, the department feels that it is saddled with a faculty not of their choosing. There are further complications—as our next anonymous vignette contributor highlights—when partners are at very different points in their careers.

Mental Overload

As the biological sex tasked with bearing children, women and their bodies have unique temporally constrained reproductive demands as compared to men. However, the tasks associated with parenting—a.k.a. the "mental load" or "emotional labor"—such as remembering dentist appointments, arranging childcare, and doing housework, are not inherently gendered. In families where housework and the mental load are shared relatively equitably between parents and partners, women succeed more in their careers. As this chapter's second anonymous vignette contributor reflects about the push-and-pull of work and life responsibilities, "It is a delicate ecosystem, the contents of which usually fall squarely on my shoulders when something goes awry."

Some academic parents refer to their role as parents as taking the second shift after their workday ends. Women often take the third shift, as they are most often the ones responsible for managing household details like scheduling children's appointments and activities, orchestrating childcare, and keeping track of family commitments. Recent research on this invisible, uncompensated labor undertaken largely by women seeks to "illuminate the extent of an unequal distribution of household management" (Ciciolla and Luthar 2019). Gendered expectations run deep, and even the most supportive partners—women included—have internalized biased norms. As one survey respondent wrote, "If both people aim to do 80 percent it might end up fair. And babysitting is cheaper than divorce."

Commentary on the Two-or-More-Body Problem

Anonymous Senior Assistant Professor

As I pack my son's suitcase for the winter break, I ponder what I will tell him about where we are going. "We are going home"? No, probably not, because his home is where I teach. We are going to where my spouse teaches. Then my mind delves into a discussion of the meaning of home, belonging, and attachment only to realize that my son is thirteen months old. Eventually, I come up with an answer, "we are going to the dogs' home," and my son likes this answer very much.

I am a well-published senior assistant professor at an R1 institution. My spouse is a well-published full professor at an R2 institution and the founding editor of a successful journal. We have a son and four dogs. And our life is plagued by the two-body problem (TBP). We teach at different institutions and haven't been able to score a spousal hire despite our strong research and teaching records. Lines for spousal hires in the humanities and social sciences are simply not on the priority list of university administrators. And even if they were, as one administrator put it, my spouse is simply "too senior to place. If the roles were reversed, things would have been easier."

Many families are tormented by the TBP. Yet the TBP is not one of the most discussed issues in academia. This is partly because of the leaky pipeline. When couples cannot find jobs at the same institution, often the woman leaves academia, especially if children are involved. Those who decide to stick it out in academia tend to settle for adjunct, non-tenure-track, or staff positions to make sure their family is under one roof. Several women I know who felt they had no choice but to settle for such positions for the well-being of their family did so grudgingly, knowing full well that they were overqualified.

My family is still fighting the fight. I am publishing in top journals, hitting the job market, and continuing to request a spousal hire for my partner. As I write this essay, we are in the midst of all the stress, uncertainty, financial trouble, and emotional pain that comes with the TBP.

Writing this essay most likely will not be cathartic for me. But I hope this essay will shed light on what the TBP really involves, offer other suffering couples a sense of solidarity, and encourage administrators to take spousal hires more seriously.

Six months after his birth, my son and I moved to the college town where I currently teach and settled into our rental apartment. So I started my journey of solo parenting, with no family or relatives around. Out of respect to single parents, I refer to my experience as solo parenting. In our case the TBP means that I will be shouldering all the visible and invisible burdens of solo parenting. What I found most challenging is the lack of a support system. I don't have a single person I can ask for help where I teach. I have great colleagues, but they are my colleagues, not my friends. And because I had been traveling to the place where my spouse teaches at every single opportunity I had before our son was born, I have thus far missed out on the opportunity to make friends. This means that getting sick, exhausted, or throwing my back out became luxuries I cannot afford. I am never on the bench. I am never off. It's scary to be never on the bench. I had a nanny for a few months who helped with childcare. No matter how good they are, having a nanny is not the same as having your partner around. It is hard to explain why I feel a strong sense of relief when we go to the dogs' home or when my spouse visits us. But I do. It is not because I do less physical work. I have made it through teething, night feedings, illness, and sleep training all by myself. I have built up good stamina. I don't mind the physical work anymore. But when my partner is with us, I do feel a sense of relief because I feel less alone and less on edge. I feel supported.

I should also add that being 100 percent dependent on the nanny was also unnerving. The nanny at the end of the day is a stranger, a paid employee. She can give her two weeks' notice and quit at any time. She is not obligated to care about the emergencies in my life.

The TBP also put an unimaginable financial burden on us. Both my spouse and I teach at public institutions. We do not make much money. Almost all of my spouse's salary goes to paying the mortgage and maintaining our house. With the money I make, I am simply not able to afford childcare after paying for rent, utilities, health insurance, and living expenses. So we asked my family to pay for childcare for a year. We have been extremely fortunate that they were able to do so. But taking so much money from them was not easy. It hurt our pride. It made us feel obligated to give in to some of their requests that did not align with our parenting philosophy.

As senior positions are far and few between in social sciences and humanities in the North American academic job market, I, as the assistant professor, have been on the market. Being on the market while solo parenting an infant involves so many things that I have felt were overwhelming. Some mothers agonize over taking their breastfed baby to campus interviews. I agonized over whether I should take my breast pump and request pumping breaks. If I don't request pumping breaks, my breasts will leak long before the search committee drops me off at my hotel for the night. Since I did not have anyone with whom I could leave my baby, a campus interview also meant that my spouse had to arrange his teaching schedule and drive eight to ten hours to stay with our son while I was away and drive back for his next class.

A campus interview also meant a few days of emotional turmoil for our son. My son and I moved away when he was six months old. When I got the invitation for a campus interview, he was nine months old. Even though my husband had visited us a few times, by the time he was nine months old, my son saw him as a stranger. Actually, when my husband visited the first time, our son screamed and cried the moment I opened the door. This was the peak of separation anxiety for our son. So a fly-out meant traumatizing an otherwise happy child and messing up his sleep schedule. Please take a moment to imagine the stress and preparation involved in getting ready for a campus interview. Now factor in the challenges created by the TBP. We are confronted with similar problems each time I go to a conference or travel to give a talk.

The uncertainty created by the TBP about how and where our family will live is excruciating for several reasons. Should we wait it out for one more year and hope that my R1 will create a senior spousal line? Should we apply for jobs outside of North America? Should I quit academia and apply for jobs in the industry? Questions abound.

What bothered me and continues to keep me up at night is childcare. Getting your child into daycare is, unfortunately in my opinion, a competitive and unequal process in the United States. Given the uncertainty about our living circumstances, we had to hedge our bets to make sure our son got a spot at a daycare. We paid several nonrefundable application fees, got on waitlists at schools in my college town and in his, and tried to come to terms with the fact that our son will likely change schools a few times as a toddler.

Moving your child back and forth also means having two pediatricians and trying to explain your family situation to doctors and caregivers who look at you with disbelief, pity, or judgment.

Inevitably, both my spouse and I worry about the impact living apart and traveling back and forth for breaks will have on our child. We have the good fortune of having a very adjustable child. Most adults would envy his ability to adjust, I would say. So far, he hasn't minded sleeping in a different crib every few months. But we still worry. We worry that we are not providing a good enough family life for him. We worry that we are not providing the structure and stability he needs. We worry that he and my husband are not bonding as much as they should. Maybe all these are good reasons for mama to quit her job. Maybe they aren't. I do not know. But this mama, for one, is still fighting and keeping her fingers crossed.

The TBP also entails a lot of begging. Begging to administrators of all kind, to senior faculty who can write letters of recommendations for job applications, and to colleagues. I have been fortunate to have a very sympathetic department chair and dean. My institution does not have maternity leave. However, my department chair gave me an informal one by rearranging my teaching schedule. My dean also made it possible for me to teach a few online courses so that my son and I can spend more time at home with my husband. I have also had the privilege of having supportive senior colleagues who encourage me to apply for jobs and provide strong letters. Sadly, we have also been burned by some administrators and colleagues. We have been lied to, belittled, and made fun of. It is hard to beg whether you have leverage or not. Begging is just hard. It is even harder to turn a deaf ear to condescension and contempt because you need those people to fix your TBP.

I also hate that this situation sometimes makes me envious of my colleagues who have their family in the same place. Looking at colleagues who come to work after dropping off their children at the childcare facility of our college in the morning and knowing that they will return at night to a home with their spouses and children seems to turn into an unobtainable dream for me and my family.

I know couples who eventually managed to unite their family under one roof. I also know couples who after twenty years are still living in two places and travel forth and back. At the root of the TBP lies a culture in academia that is centered exclusively on the individual scholar rather than on academic couples. If a university is confronted with hiring a couple, administrators often offer a subordinate position to the spouse of the individual they are hiring. Giving a low-paying position of adjunct, secretary, or librarian to a spouse with a PhD is, however, not spousal hiring. It should not be a surprise that scholars too fall in love and marry within their peer group. It would be in the best interest of universities to hire successful couples and offer them equal opportunities since happy academic couples will be more productive than unhappy scholars.

As I write this essay, my story does not have a happy ending. I do not know where I will be next year or if I will still be a professor. But while wresting with the TBP, I discovered strengths I didn't know I had and found pockets of empowerment in my personal and professional life. I managed to publish three articles in good journals and won a research award. I learned to be efficient. I learned to be grateful and extend empathy to those less fortunate than myself.

Ask for What You Need, Take What You Need

To manage the demands of work and home, women should ask for what they need. In her vignette, Courtney Burns writes about the accommodations she didn't receive because she didn't ask directly. This insight points to a host of problems we have identified in our exploration of gender and bias in academia. First, women don't ask, because when they do, their requests are often denied and they suffer reputational penalties for being pushy or seeming entitled (Mitchell and Hesli 2013; Tinsley et al. 2009). Second, policies are not automatically applied equitably across individuals in the same department. Women should not have to advocate for themselves—asking not just for what they need but what is rightfully protected by law: to have access to the same accommodations as their men colleagues. These policies should be automatically applied equitably and transparently. Having senior colleagues as advocates can provide reputational cover for junior scholars; these colleagues may not necessarily be in the same department or even at the same university, but they can offer advice and perspective on strategies for successful bargaining and negotiating.

Tending to the demands of young children and a pre-tenure career can mean burning the candle at both ends, with little in reserve remaining for self-care and relationship care. Activities that promote health and well-being are not indulgent: they are necessities. As the anonymous vignette contributor mentions, be gentle with yourself. Part of having it all means not necessarily having what you want but wanting what you've got (Crow 2002).

To Summarize

Much-beloved children can complicate the scholarly and academic lives of their parents. Imagine the solitude and suffering of the parents who ride the family formation roller coaster alone, judged by their work output and teaching quality, while suffering quite literally unspeakable losses and grief. Some colleagues might be sympathetic, but many would not be. Childbearing and childrearing are not viewed as collective responsibilities. In academia, there is often no village. As Nancy Folbre (1994) argues, children are public goods. Yet parental labor is unpaid, and furthermore parents pay a considerable amount to raise children (by some estimates, one-quarter of a million dollars until age eighteen). All children are future taxpayers, future contributors to the social public welfare, and future productive workers. However, in the earliest and toughest years, they are perceived singularly as their parents' private pride and joy. To be clear, there are some joys that parents experience

Asking for Help

Courtney Burns
Assistant Professor, Bucknell University

Note: The author has moved to a new university and her vignette reflects experiences at a previous institution.

The biggest running theme of my work-life balance narrative, the thing that took me three years and two babies to learn, is to ask for help and ask for accommodations. It took having two children and seeing a male colleague whose wife had two children in the same time to make me realize that I was not being a big enough advocate for myself. I have been frustrated with myself time and time again because, despite being a staunch feminist and advocate for others, I did not advocate for myself! For three years I felt overextended, taken advantage of, and angry. However, I never told my male chair. I only complained with my female colleagues and an APSA mentor I was paired with. Only one of my colleagues had kids, and all of the women in my department were junior faculty. My APSA mentor is at a major R1 institution and has children. After telling her about everything, her advice was to get out. Would my chair have been receptive to my requests or complaints? Honestly, I think it could have depended on the day.

In December 2015 I had my first child via emergency C-section. It was my first year as a tenure-track assistant professor, though my second year at the institution. Prior to having my child, my chair and the dean of the college agreed that they would allow me to teach one class online and my two other courses could be online for four weeks before they needed to start meeting in person. In other words, I was back on campus teaching in mid-February 2016 with an eight-week-old at home. The timing of my second child worked out better. My second child was due in early June but wound up arriving in late May 2018. I was able to teach online that summer, although my chair asked if I could teach an on-campus class in the June–July term. I told him no, one of the only times I really spoke up for myself. In early May before my second child was born, I asked for two weeks of FMLA leave at the start of the fall semester. My partner was taking the other ten weeks, and we are employed by the same university, so we had to split the time. However, my chair refused my request, justifying this refusal because a student had complained about a colleague of mine not being in class enough. The only thing we negotiated was that my classes would be capped at twenty-five instead of thirty. I felt good that I even asked for accommodations given that I would have an entire summer before returning to work. Then I learned about FMLA and online accommodations that a male colleague received for the birth of his second child in July 2018.

After my first child was born, I started attending writing boot camps on campus for faculty in order to get work done. I rarely graded or did research after the hours of 8 a.m.–5 p.m., Monday through Friday. I stopped attending as many conferences or brought someone along with me to help with childcare and paid their travel out of my pocket. I regularly taught a 3-3 with ninety to one hundred students each semester; I was one of the only faculty in my department who did not have a reason for a regular course release. I had some success. I had three publications come out in two years, I attended good conferences such as APSA, I interviewed and accepted a job offer at a better institution, and I have a lot of work in the pipeline. I oversaw successful honors student theses and took students to conferences. To say that I balanced my work-life would be true, for the most part.

However, it could have been better. I am regularly stressed about the amount of class prep, grading, or research I am not doing when I am home because of the amount that is required of me. Moreover, I learned from a male colleague that he received better accommodations for the birth of his children than I did. For his first child born in September 2016, he was able to teach entirely online. For the birth of his second child, in July 2018, he first was able to teach entirely online in fall 2018 from a foreign country with his family and is taking FMLA for spring 2019. With his time at home he was able to write a book and go up for tenure. He also turned down mentoring of honors students and did not take them to conferences.

While I plan on not having any more children, the thing I learned through my experience in negotiating with my chair and talking to colleagues is that you have to be an advocate for yourself. As a junior faculty member, I did not feel like I could ask for more. However, that is not true. In hindsight, I could have pressed my chair about the two weeks of FMLA. I had a summer to ask, but I did not. As soon as I found out about my male colleague, I could have asked my chair why he received better accommodations, but I did not. After having kids in academia, I have learned that it takes asking for help and rightfully standing up for yourself.

uniquely, like all of the first things children do. However, society provides few support systems and safety nets for parents, from family leave to childcare (James 2017).

Academic colleagues who are openly or covertly hostile to colleagues starting families may focus myopically on short-term inconveniences rather than long-term benefits. Some bristle at the notion of shouldering the shared burden of service assignments while colleagues are tending to young children. Single academics note that society—and the academy—levies a "singles tax" wherein they are expected to fill the gaps for academic parents, taking on service roles (often low prestige and within the department) for parents taking family leave. There is ample anecdotal evidence that points to single women academics taking on more of these roles than single men academics as well—another gendered disparity in academic roles. Some argue, with great sympathy from academic parents, that they may also have caregiving responsibilities, for aging parents or other family members with health concerns for example. These concerns too deserve attention yet are beyond the scope of this book.

What *is* within the scope of this book, however, is the reiteration of our policy recommendation that department- and college-level policies should be universally accessible and equitably applied. It is quite possible that the singles tax is applied inconsistently and inequitably, where the burden of service assignments or less-than-ideal teaching schedules falls more on single women faculty than on single men faculty. If a policy does not exist for how service assignments are allocated to accommodate other faculty's family leave, why not? The sense of injustice or unfairness may be assuaged with a formal policy at the departmental or college level. Who fills the gaps when parents take family leave is a matter of gender and equity as well and should be formalized rather than idiosyncratically or haphazardly or inequitably applied.

Broadly speaking, academia as a microcosm of society needs to do much better to tend to the family commitments its faculty bear. Academics are not gender-neutral automatons—we are people, with partners and spouses, with complicated pregnancies and complex postpartum phases, with sick children, early pickup times, late nights, and public holidays and inclement weather when childcare is unavailable. We have to be present for dinner times and bedtimes, for morning routines and special occasions. Departments should not foster hostility toward parents for trying to be excellent academics and attentive parents; departments and institutions should make it easier for academic parents to have impressive research and teaching records and fulfilling family lives.

Best Practices for Work-Life Balance
What university administrators can do:

- Establish and use clear, consistent messaging on your campus about supporting healthy work-life separation.

- Find ways to create, implement, or reinforce existing formal and informal efforts to support faculty and students who are working to build careers and families.
- Model healthy work-family separation. Remind faculty and students that they are not obligated to respond to work-related requests after usual business hours. Avoid sending requests after-hours.
- Do not schedule major events and encourage units or departments to avoid scheduling meetings and events during after-school pickup hours, when parents are less likely to have childcare coverage. Alternately, provide childcare at these events.
- If applicable, discuss your experiences as an academic parent in an effort to normalize parents.
- Make childcare accessible and affordable for academic parents and students.
- Recognize how holidays, misaligned university and childcare or school schedules, inclement weather days, and unforeseen events such as the COVID-19 pandemic present unique challenges and work-life disadvantages for academic parents.

What department chairs and unit heads can do:

- Establish and use clear, consistent messaging within your department about supporting healthy work-life separation.
- Find ways to create, implement, or reinforce existing formal and informal efforts to support faculty and students who are working to build careers and families.
- Model healthy work-life separation. Remind faculty and students that they are not obligated to respond to work-related requests after usual business hours. Avoid sending requests after-hours.
- Do not schedule department meetings or events during after-school pickup hours, when parents are less likely to have childcare coverage.
- If department events, like visits from invited speakers, include an evening portion, make an effort to include daytime alternative networking events, like small-group discussions with invited speakers.
- Give as much notice as possible for meetings and events to allow parents to find childcare coverage.
- If applicable, discuss your experiences as an academic parent in an effort to normalize parents.
- Ensure that women are not penalized for taking maternity leave, as it is not a "bonus year."

- Ensure that men use parental leave to actively parent, not use it for research.
- Play the long game with academic parents, realizing that the early years of family formation are more demanding.

What faculty can do:

- Recognize that everyone's reality is different and that the mileage you get from various approaches to manage conflicts between professional and family demands will vary.
- To the extent possible, work when you are at work and be at home when you are at home.
- Enlist professional associations for support and best practices for work-life challenges.
- Carve out and, to the extent possible, defend work-home boundaries (e.g., do not check your email at 11 p.m. or feel compelled to respond to after-hours requests).
- Seek help with the academic parenting load as often as possible and in whatever forms are available, feasible, and affordable.
- Strive to help friends, colleagues, and students who are struggling to make it all work.

5 Doctor, Parent

Recognizing the Range of Experiences

In this chapter we center the voices of five vignette contributors, each of whom writes from a different perspective on parenting in the academy. In presenting this range of experiences we hope to underscore the need for more comprehensive, inclusive support initiatives for academic parents of all genders and family structures. When colleges and universities have formal policies and programs in place for parental leave and support, they often focus on women who have recently given birth. Where support systems extend beyond parents who have recently given birth—for example, to extend equal leave opportunities to new fathers and partners or to adoptive parents—informal norms serve to limit the effectiveness of such policies and programs. Faculty may be formally or informally discouraged from taking family leave altogether, or colleagues and supervisors may fail to respect the new parent's leave time.

The paths to parenthood and the obstacles new parents encounter are diverse. We focus here on the lived experiences of five contributors as encapsulated in their four vignettes (three contributors submitted solo-authored vignettes, and two coauthored their reflection on coupled academic parenthood). In focusing on these scholar parents' realities, we hope to shed light on the need for systemic change to create a more welcoming profession for all parents and families, regardless of how and when they formed.

An Academic Dad's View

We focus primarily on academic mothers throughout this book. Our research is motivated by and contributes to the wealth of literature on the increased likelihood that an academic woman will leave the tenure track or the profession before she has a chance to advance through the faculty ranks. But, of course, academic mothers are not the only parents who struggle to balance work and family demands. They are not the only ones who need to negotiate for parental leave when the institutional cards are stacked against them. Other parents also bear the burden of entrenched gender norms related to parenting as a professional in the workplace.

Academic fathers and non-birth parents who take an active role in caring for infants and children are similarly disadvantaged by formal policies and informal norms that presume all or most care work is done by mothers. As Margaret Sallee's (2014) work discusses, academic fathers experience tension between over-the-top praise and admiration for doing basic parenting tasks and suspicion or doubt for taking parental leave or otherwise making time to care for children. Dads who take parental leave for its intended purpose—to care for and bond with a new child—will not be as productive as their men colleagues who take parental leave and use that time to advance their research, apply for grants or jobs, or otherwise devote time to academic work instead of childcare work. We wholeheartedly advocate for and encourage academic fathers to take parental leave for the birth or adoption of a child. We even more *strongly* emphasize the importance of using that leave to actually *parent* that child and care for one's partner (and oneself) and the rest of the family as everyone adjusts to the new status quo. If all parents ask for leave and use it as intended, that will go a long way toward normalizing and embracing parenthood in the academy.

Our vignette contributor in this section is one of only two men who felt comfortable sharing a snapshot of daily life as an academic dad. To be clear, we asked many academic fathers to write about their experiences, and many times were met with, "But what would I have to say?" David Andersen-Rodgers highlights the value of an academic career's flexibility and the unique opportunity his faculty position has given him to fully coparent with his spouse. From his point of view, much of the flexibility he has enjoyed as an academic parent derives from his faculty rank, age, and gender. While taking the perspective of an academic partner, this vignette also highlights our discussion in chapter 6, "Sick and Tired," about the academic consequences of dealing with successive illnesses. While his vignette strikes a humorous note, he effectively highlights the reforms campuses must pursue if they truly wish to be inclusive.

As Andersen-Rodgers describes, a secure faculty position with a flexible schedule lends itself to actively engaged parenting. After the demanding newborn phase and sleep-deprived first (or second, or third) year of parenting, the ability to be present is especially useful when a child needs to be picked up in the middle of the day because they have spiked a fever or come down with the stomach flu. For families with one flexible academic parent

Letter from an Academic Parent

David Andersen-Rodgers
Full Professor, Cal State–Sacramento

Dear Editors:

I'm sorry you have not received my vignette about parenting in the academy.

I thought there would be plenty of time once the semester ended, but then my youngest son came home with pink eye, then my other son got pink eye, and then my wife got pink eye, and then I got pink eye. Needless to say, little got done. Once the pink eye cleared up I was absolutely sure that I would find time to work on the vignette, but then my youngest started throwing up. The first day he was sick he slept quite a bit, and you might be thinking that that would have been a good day for me to sit down and write a bit about being a parent in academia; however, my older son's school was closed that day and he really wanted to work on his new LEGO set with me, and how could I say no to that? The next day my older son was back in school, and I was sure that I would get this done. The younger one was still sick, so he would probably still sleep, and I could crank the vignette out in no time. That's what I hoped, but as it turns out he was unable to sleep well in his crib but could sleep lying on me. So instead of writing the vignette, I was in bed. I did finish a book I had been wanting to read for the past decade, but that, of course, is of no help to you. As I sat there, half reclined, I thought that I'd probably be able to work on the vignette after my partner got home from work and the kids were in bed. I really just needed one night where I was not exhausted and could really plow through it and write that vignette, but it is actually quite surprising how exhausting it is to be abed all day, particularly when you are pretty sure you are going to be woken up at five the next morning.

Sicknesses do not last forever, of course, and once he was well he would be back in daycare and then I would be able to sit down and write this vignette. His daycare is on campus. It is a fantastic facility staffed with many students studying early child development and teachers who show genuine love and care for my children. Our campus has a large population of students with children, so faculty and staff can only get slots when there are spaces not taken by students. I am one of the lucky ones that was able to get my children into the center, whereas other faculty members must search for other options. Because the daycare caters to students, they have decided that the week before classes start they should close the center to train new staff, clean, and get everything ready for the upcoming semester. Unfortunately, this means that once I had a healthy kid, I did not have childcare, and about those naps . . .

The daycare did eventually open, and I had a full day before classes started to work on the vignette and my syllabi, answer emails that went unanswered, attend to some committee work that got put on the back-burner during finals week, socialize with colleagues, and so on. To be honest, the first hour after getting to my office and closing the door, I just kind of sat there, doing nothing, and taking in the silence.

I really cannot complain, though. In the last month my children really needed me, and while I fell behind on some obligations and commitments, unlike my spouse who does not work in academia, I did not need to take a sick day or call a boss in order to take care of them. This flexibility enables me to better share responsibilities with my spouse—responsibilities that traditionally would have fallen solely on her. More importantly it is deeply satisfying to be able to be there for my children. According to a recent Pew Survey, when people answered an open-ended question about what gives their life meaning, 69 percent of respondents said family as compared to 34 percent who said work (van Kessel et al. 2018).[1] Sometimes it feels as if academia pressures us to prioritize these two aspects of our lives differently, but for me, it is my family that gives me greater satisfaction, and they should come first. Which, unfortunately, is why my vignette is late.

This isn't to say that I haven't been thinking about what I want to include in the vignette. This last bout of sickness happened during a period when classes were more or less finished. If these things happen in the middle of the semester, when I am obligated to be in the classroom, it becomes more difficult to juggle my obligations to my family with my obligations to my employer. Overall, though, I am able to be a consistent presence in my children's life. But I also became a parent for the first time as a late-career academic. My first child was born just after I earned tenure; my second child was born shortly before I was promoted to full professor. I am also a man. If I were a woman and waited to have children until that point in my career, it would have likely been very difficult or very expensive. Probably both. It was via this experience of having children at an older age that I realized my gender afforded me certain career advantages as it pertains to choices about family formation. These advantages perpetuate the problems of diversity within the academy. While it is certainly not impossible to have both a family at a young age and a successful academic career, it is certainly a lot harder.

These gender disparities are also seen in our parental leave policies. At my university you can either take thirty days' parental leave or a course reduction, which brings your course load down to a single class. As a man lacking mammary glands I took the unit reduction, since thirty days' parental leave seemed too disruptive to the semester. Who would cover my classes? It was not until after a female colleague of mine announced her pregnancy that it became obviously clear how much this policy favors male parents. For her, a course reduction was unrealistic, but in order to take a complete semester off she had to dip into her accumulated sick leave. Because that sick leave can be cashed out at retirement, it means that women who have children and need a full semester off are put at not only a career disadvantage but a long-term financial disadvantage. This disadvantage will be compounded for a woman who wants to have multiple children.

So this is the conundrum: the relative flexibility with scheduling that my job allows has facilitated my ability to be an engaged parent in my children's lives. I wouldn't change this for the world. But I have also become more aware that much of that flexibility comes from the biological and social advantages of being a man. I was able to have children late and therefore was not juggling career and family during the periods (PhD, job market, and pre-tenure) that determine whether you can have a permanent place at the academic table. If we are going to open the academy to a more diverse faculty, finding ways to support *all* types of families is going to be essential. This, I hope, will be a key point in the vignette . . . once I get to it.

I'm really sorry this excuse is so long, I will get working on that vignette now. Ugh, I just got a call from the daycare . . .

and one parent with a more structured work schedule, this gift of time and availability is invaluable.

The Challenges Facing Dual-Academic Couples

What happens when a dual-academic couple welcomes a child? Sarah Shair-Rosenfield and Reed M. Wood reflect on their experiences as parents and partners who work in the same department, focusing on their university's parental leave policy and the importance of negotiating, managing expectations, and striving for flexibility. Dual-academic households face obstacles that arise, in part, from their institution's failure to consider this particular employee family structure; put another way, if an institution has never had to accommodate parental leave for two employees who share a child, then it will not have policies in place to do so.

Managing Parental Leave in a Dual-Academic Household

Sarah Shair-Rosenfield, Senior Lecturer,
Department of Government, University of Essex

Reed M. Wood, Reader, Department of Government,
University of Essex

Note: The authors have moved to a new institution and this vignette reflects their experiences at a previous university.

We are a dual-academic household where both partners work in the same department. While beneficial in a variety of ways, this situation also presented a number of challenges when it came to planning a family. When our daughter was born our university's official leave policy was six weeks of paid parental leave, which could be split between the parents if both were university employees. Such a policy presented a number of questions: Would we split the leave? Or if only one of us took it, who would stay home and who would work? Was it possible to *ask* for more time off or make alternative arrangements? And even if our department were willing to offer additional accommodation, how much leave could we reasonably expect? How do we ask for the leave we want or need? And more basically, what arrangements would actually be best for our family?

In thinking about how to approach these issues, we first identified two principal goals we wanted to achieve during the first several months following the birth of our daughter. It was particularly important for us to think through what our priorities would be during the initial window of new parenthood. We knew that our first objective was that we both have the opportunity to spend as much time as possible at home with our newborn. Work should wait; it's a long career after all. Second, we wanted to share the burdens of home life and childcare as equitably as possible. These were both things that we wanted to do as a function of how we wanted to work as a family unit but also to preserve and strengthen the foundation of our relationship as a couple.

These are goals that we imagine many (if not most) academic parents strive to achieve, and thus they seem rather obvious in some ways. Yet they pose unique challenges to dual-academic couples, especially those who work in the same academic unit. This is in large part because even where institutionalized rules and policies exist to help individual academics balance work and personal life when starting a family, those rules and policies often don't address the potential complexities of dual-academic situations or they may actually create or exacerbate asymmetries between the two partners (which typically favor fathers).

Many institutions and department heads—even those who are sympathetic and well-intentioned—do not have a sophisticated plan or developed set of procedures for helping members of a dual-academic household navigate life with a newborn. We therefore summarize three of the central lessons we learned from our own experience. Before delving into the details, we should stress that we were incredibly lucky to have a very supportive chair, an excellent and responsive staff, and sympathetic colleagues who assisted us and supported us throughout the process. We fully recognize that not everyone enjoys that type of support network in their workplace that we have had, and we are extremely grateful for and appreciative of ours.

Asking for what you need. Sometimes you just have no idea what might be possible until you ask for it. Sometimes you might not know that a better or more useful option exists until you ask for one thing and end up with something else. More often, however, the people that can potentially provide you things you need just haven't thought about them until you ask. That was our approach anyway. Why not just ask and see what you can get? Historically, dual-academic couples have been rare. That's changing. Rapidly. Yet, because partners who are in the same department and at similar points in their career trajectories are a recent phenomenon, many department heads and tenured faculty members may simply have never encountered the practical complications of simultaneously extending the benefits of parental leave to two faculty members. And in some cases certain faculty members may even wonder (perhaps out loud) why on Earth both of their colleagues needed to stay home with the baby. Isn't leave for one of them good enough?

As a case in point, our department has for some years had a norm of providing a full semester of teaching release to faculty members that took the six weeks of paid parental leave formally provided by the university. This arrangement occurs largely because the heads of academic units at our university are given discretion to make additional, more generous allowances if they deem it appropriate. As a result of this discretion and the fact that unit heads also determine teaching loads, our chair continued the trend of his predecessor in extending a full semester of teaching release to any faculty taking parental leave. Yet this did not equate to a full semester without responsibilities to the unit. The teaching release was balanced out by additional service assignments following the official leave period. For example, if you took the regular six-week leave to start the semester, you would subsequently have a nine-week period in which you did extra service to compensate for the time not spent in the classroom. And of course the research expectation remained unchanged—in this case, 40 percent of post-leave time was still intended to be devoted to research. (Rest assured, one can accomplish substantial amounts of research in the first few months of parenthood.)

Despite the frequency with which this informal policy was implemented in previous years, there was no precedent in our department for how this would apply to two faculty members simultaneously parenting the same newborn under a single leave period. To accomplish the two goals of ensuring sufficient time with our newborn and equal burden sharing of household labor and childcare, it was apparent (to us) that the non-pregnant parent should also receive some reasonable accommodation. Ideally, we both desired to receive something along the lines of what the childbearing parent would normally receive: we both wanted sufficient course reductions to allow us to stay home with our daughter. So that's what we asked for.

Managing expectations. While the department norm was arguably sufficient to meet our basic needs, we didn't believe that it met our goals. We therefore assumed it was better to ask for everything we felt would help us meet those goals; however, we were also realistic in our expectations. In our discussions with our chair we asked that we both be given full teaching releases for the semester of our daughter's birth, and we hoped that our additional service assignments would be flexible enough to allow us to remain at home with our newborn most days of the week. In effect, we asked for the unit to provide double the leave normally provided by the department. We knew this was asking a lot, but it's what we felt we needed.

Ultimately, we didn't get all that we asked for; however, we received leave that allowed us to achieve our primary goals of newborn face time and the equitable sharing of household burdens. In the end, the parent taking the official university leave got a full semester of teaching release and a flexible service assignment for the balance of the semester. The other parent received a single course release and taught a single online class scheduled for the first half of the semester. This teaching schedule allowed that parent to work from home for the first half of the semester and to have no teaching commitment during the second half. Service commitments for that parent were still relatively high, but they were organized so that the bulk of the workload fell in the second half of the semester. These accommodations, while not perfect, permitted us to spend most of the semester of our daughter's birth at home and provided us the flexibility to ensure that one parent was always able to be at home with the newborn. It also permitted us to (mostly) achieve the balance of household work burden sharing we had desired. In short, with such a flexible schedule there was little pressure for the stay-at-home parent to manage a disproportionate share of the childcare and other household responsibilities while the other went to the office.

Being flexible. Because our accommodations fell a little short of what we ideally wanted, we had to be flexible and resourceful in how we adjudicated between the ideal situation to meet our needs and the actual situation we ended up with. In this case, we were able to meet our primary goals without both being fully officially on leave at any point in time, though it took a bit of work to juggle schedules and the reality of caring for a newborn.

It also meant that equal burden sharing at home became something we could not necessarily always count in exactly equivalent hours and minutes over the course of every day. For example, just before and for weeks after our daughter was born, one of us was managing an online class with enrollment of 150 students. The online part was helpful—pre-leave course construction to handle much of the infrastructure of the entire course, no expectation of coming in to hold routine office hours, the ability to work at whatever time of day our daughter decided to sleep or be easily managed solo by the other person. But the reality was still that it required attention that only one of us was required to give, somewhat and temporarily reducing the equality of burden sharing while still maintaining newborn face time for both of us.

Likewise, later in the semester, when the official leave period ended, the administrative work we both were required to do did eat up time and increasingly brought us into the office and away from our daughter. Here, we were both proactive about avoiding scheduling conflicts as much as possible so that we rarely, if ever, had to both be in the office at the same time. We appreciated that the colleagues with whom we shared committee assignments accommodated our desire to avoid overlap of meeting times. It helped that a number of our colleagues went out of their way to schedule meetings with an eye toward our needs; we are sure it would have made asking for accommodations much more difficult or stressful if we would have always been the ones initiating such discussions. But we also felt it was our shared responsibility to inform our colleagues when we needed or didn't need atypical consideration for the schedules of two full-time faculty colleagues with a newborn at home.

In sum, starting a family in a dual-academic household presents a number of challenges, especially when both partners work in the same field of study and department, and particularly if one or both partners are pre-tenure. In those circumstances, it is really not possible to fully achieve the types of goals we had set—both of us getting significant time at home with our newborn and roughly equivalent sharing of household and childcare burdens—without either institutional policies mandating extensive parental leave for both partners or a supportive environment that helps you make the absence of extensive leaves work for you. Our experience taught us that you should always ask for what you need, but be prepared to temper expectations and get creative if what you get falls short of what you have asked for. And, perhaps more than anything, those of us who have made it through this process and kept to those goals almost certainly had academic departments made up of administrators, staff, and faculty colleagues who acknowledged and responded to the challenges we faced by supporting and helping us wherever and whenever they could. We hope everyone could be as lucky as we were in that regard.

Institutional policies that provide extensive parental leave for both parents are rare in the United States. As Shair-Rosenfield and Wood emphasize, however, extensive paid leave for both parents allows families to divide care work evenly and ensure that both parents have the support they need to return to work. A key obstacle to adequate support and paid leave for academic parents is the casualization of academic labor or an increase in the number of faculty who are in contingent positions with heavy teaching loads (Cardozo 2017; Fichtenbaum 2014). When a large portion of the faculty population holds precarious positions, often without the support of unions, it becomes exceedingly difficult to negotiate with university administration for more equitable policies and increased support.

To understand how such policies would function, we can look to other countries with state-level parental leave policies in place, like the United Kingdom. Lynsey Bunnefeld (2019) wrote about her and her spouse's experience with shared parental leave, a UK policy that allows eligible parents to share nearly a year of leave, thirty-seven weeks of which are paid. While there are stark policy differences between the United Kingdom and the United States (especially given the latter's lack of federal parental leave policies), one of Bunnefeld's takeaway points resonates broadly: the institution must adequately support both the parent on leave and the parent who has returned to work. Without this support, in the form of true recognition of and respect for leave time, the parent at home is left unable to fully separate from work and bond with the child and the parent who has returned to work is unable to do so effectively. What support looks like in practice is true peer coverage for colleagues who are on leave: covering classes or altering course rotations; taking over advising responsibilities and supervising student research; postponing or reassigning service roles; and providing formal and informal coverage for other department, campus, and professional association roles as needed.

Empathy and the Road to Academic Parenthood

The path to parenthood is not always direct or simple. A child's arrival does not always conform to the demands of the academic calendar. The stress, anticipation, and cost of a complicated pregnancy, fertility treatments, or adoption take a toll on parents working through those processes, but we rarely discuss these issues with colleagues, supervisors, and students. Sahar Shafqat and Krista E. Wiegand share two vignettes on their respective journeys to parenthood. Both professors' experiences underscore the importance of a more inclusive, empathetic approach to parental leave policies and informal support options.

Both Shafqat and Wiegand became parents with the security of tenure and the accompanying flexibility, two benefits of having a child or children later in one's career. Nevertheless, both families overcame a range of daunting obstacles on the path to parenthood, obstacles that demanded flexibility and formal and informal accommodations from their campuses and colleagues. As Shafqat observes, her colleagues' and college's support made it possible for her to request leave and to arrange courses and meetings to maximize time at home with her new baby. In addition to providing universal, transparent, and clearly communicated leave policies, the efforts that departments and colleagues make to accommodate new parents or soon-to-be parents are key to building an inclusive campus.

First Steps toward Support for All Parents

What each of these vignettes tells us is that support for academic parents extends beyond providing the bare minimum of leave for parents who give birth. Efforts to provide real support for scholar parents must account for the diversity of paths to parenthood. One logical place to start is with *universal*, transparent, and clearly communicated parental leave policies and (as importantly) campus and department norms that truly permit all parents to use leave time for the birth or adoption of a new child. When paid parental leave is truly universal, clearly communicated, and equitably applied, it protects

Journeying into Parenthood

Sahar Shafqat
Professor of Political Science
St. Mary's College of Maryland

In June of 2018, I became a parent when my wife gave birth to our child. I was incredibly lucky to have terrific support from my employer, which allowed me to take a semester off for parental leave (even though I was the non-birth parent). My department was fantastic in enthusiastically supporting the leave and happily accommodating my requests for a more baby-friendly teaching schedule upon my return. My codirector for the summer internship program that I run was also tremendously supportive by balancing the work in the summer to enable me to spend the first few weeks of my child's life uninterrupted.

Sounds great, right? In fact, it *has* been great, and that begs the question of why have I, a queer brown immigrant parent, been so lucky, when academia is notorious for not being supportive enough of parents in general and women and queer folks in particular? Had I hit some kind of parental jackpot without realizing it?

The reality, of course, is more complicated, and it has to do with the fact that I found myself becoming a parent in my forties, which was much, much later than I had ever imagined. It wasn't for lack of trying. When my wife and I met, we discussed children very early in our relationship. One of our moments of early connection was realizing that both of us were really committed to adoption as the path to parenthood. So it was clear that when we felt ready to expand our family, we would turn to adoption. We didn't even consider any other possibility, so certain were we about our values and our preferences at the time. We started with international adoption, since I am originally from Pakistan and it seemed natural and desirable for me to adopt from my home country. (We had actually waited a bit longer than we had wanted, because I had to be a US citizen to adopt.) But international adoption was a maze that was very difficult to navigate, and the rules kept changing, following the whims and contours of international relations. It turned out that adopting a child from Pakistan would be very, very difficult even in the best of circumstances. And we did not have the best of circumstances, since we were a same-sex couple whose relationship was not recognized by anyone in the equation of international adoption (not even the United States, since this was in Defense of Marriage Act days). So I would have to adopt as a single person, keep my relationship hidden, and somehow maintain the charade throughout the entire process, which was an intensive and random and long affair (it usually takes two to three years to adopt internationally). But although it was certainly hurtful to have to hide my relationship and my true self, it wasn't completely foreign either—and what queer person hasn't had to do that, in order to gain some measure of decency or respect or just acknowledgment from the world? Plenty of people I knew or knew of had done the same to adopt internationally, so it wasn't a strange or unfamiliar idea, even if it was thoroughly unfair.

But it turns out that adopting from Pakistan wasn't meant to be, because just as we had become ready to adopt, big changes in international adoption law meant that international adoption had become even more difficult. Added to this was the fact that Pakistan wasn't part of the international adoption regime (as is true of many Muslim-majority countries), which made adopting from there very difficult. We tried adopting from India—my wife is of Indian descent, and culturally and racially, it made sense to do so, but India was as hostile to same-sex parents as Pakistan was. But the kicker was a change to US law; in 2014 the US Supreme Court struck down DOMA, which meant that my marriage was finally recognized by the US federal government. And while this suddenly provided me many rights and privileges that I had been denied until then, it had the unintended consequence of making it impossible for me to adopt internationally.

So we turned to domestic adoption, which required learning a whole new set of rules and processes. I've heard some adoptive parents complain about the burdensome adoption requirements, including a home study, and there are many, many clearances to be obtained (although the same was true of international adoption as well): police clearance, FBI background check, state background check, child abuse clearances from every place we had lived in since we were eighteen (which is a *lot* of places, and it's amazing how happily one can forget graduate school apartment addresses). For some, especially for queer parents, the long, invasive, and convoluted process of obtaining clearances feels offensive especially compared to the lack of any such barriers for people who are able to have biological children. (Of course, there is the added assumption that one is ineligible for adoption if there is anything of question in one's background.) But the clearances never bothered me. For one, as an immigrant, I've gone through years and years of incredibly invasive clearances, and the thought of doing so all over again never fazed me in the slightest. But also, I was willing to do whatever it took to become a parent.

What was much more difficult than the home study, however, was the completely new terrain of domestic adoption, including finding an agency that would fit our needs. We were rejected by one agency on the grounds that they didn't think they could help us, before finding an agency that seemed to have a philosophy that matched closely with ours. Then there was the search for a birth parent. International adoption goes through several gatekeepers and is generally closed, meaning that neither birth parents nor adoptive parents know each other's identities. There is usually a long wait, but there is something of a queue, which means that one moves along the process until a child becomes available, and if one meets the requirements, the adoption placement process goes forward. But US domestic adoption is mostly open, which means that both birth and adoptive parents know each other. In a way, domestic adoption is a lot like dating; birth parents select adoptive parents, and if there is a match, the process moves ahead. This meant that we had to market ourselves to potential birth parents, but all I could think of was that, given societal prejudices, no birth parents would ever pick us, a South Asian Muslim-Hindu same-sex couple. Every month, our adoption agency would make available some basic background data on birth parents who had approached the agency; I remember my heart sinking as I would scan the lists to see more than one birth parent noting "no Muslims" and "no same-sex couples" about the kinds of adoptive parents they would consider. It all felt daunting and near-impossible, but I kept reminding myself that we just needed the one birth parent who was the right match for us. We also had no choice, so I took that leap of faith, which is so much a part of parenthood, and jumped right in. We poured all of our hard work into the process. It basically became a second full-time job, and we spent all of our nonworking hours on the project, assisted by many of our friends.

Home studies are only good for a year and must be renewed annually, which means that clearances must also be conducted annually, and these checks became an annual rite, a joyless tradition, and as the years began to multiply, we worried more and more about whether we would ever become parents. The lengthening weeks and months and years were punctuated by a few possibilities, but in every case, the prospective birth parent would eventually pick someone else. And yet we kept the faith, because that is what parents do.

And then came the fateful day when we got the devastating news, completely out of the blue, that our adoption agency had gone bankrupt and would shut down immediately. It was soon after the 2016 election, which had already turned our world upside down in a very real way, and now this news was just too much to bear. It was the first time that I truly questioned whether parenthood was in the cards for me, and we spent many, many months grieving and feeling so hopeless.

As shock gave way to grief and eventually to some kind of acceptance of what had happened to us, we struggled to figure out what we should do. Our home study social worker turned out to be a wonderful resource, guiding us to different options when we were feeling so lost. We eventually decided to go the independent route instead of trying to find another adoption agency, which meant doing all of the paperwork, marketing, and legal services ourselves (which is what we had essentially been doing anyway). And we began to open up the conversation about having biological children. The hard thing about having biological children is that there is a very real biological clock, and although we really, really, really still remained totally committed to adoption, we realized that we did not have another decade to continue exploring that path before perhaps considering the biological option.

So we now entered yet another world, this one full of fertility clinics and medical care (this world has, by the way, become surprisingly hip to the needs of same-sex couples). And while we thought, oh no, here we go again, maybe to have our hearts broken yet again, we took that leap of faith yet again, because that is what parents do. This world, too, was a rollercoaster of emotions and experiences, and we thought many times that perhaps the universe just didn't intend for us to become parents. Many times, we had to take a pause in the process to give ourselves space to heal and recover and to just simply be free of the journey, if only for a little bit. And then it happened.

So fast-forward to present day, when I am bleary-eyed because I didn't sleep enough last night (or the night before, or the one before), and yet I can never bring myself to ever truly complain about any of it—not the sleep deprivation, not the lack of a social life, not the absurd costs of childcare, not the anxiety that instantly accompanies becoming responsible for another life. There is nothing more precious or more wanted in my heart than my child.

I'm truly one of the lucky ones, and yet I find myself becoming a parent later than I would have ideally liked due to circumstances largely beyond my control. That has meant, however, that not only did I have a permanent academic job when I became a parent, and not only was I already tenured, but I had also achieved promotion to full professor. I had already done all the things and passed through all the stages that are usually constraints on academic parenthood. *Of course* I felt completely empowered to request parental leave, even though I was not the one who had given birth. *Of course* I felt completely empowered to request class schedules that were better suited to raising an infant. *Of course* I felt completely empowered to request phone calls and video chats instead of in-person meetings because I didn't want to spend time on campus away from my baby.

It's easier to think about how academia can help accommodate parents in very specific and tangible ways such as parental leave policies and class schedules and tenure clocks. But how do we think about how academic institutions can help with the larger social and legal forces that make parenthood so difficult for so many of us? What are academic institutions supposed to do when the barriers to parenthood don't necessarily lie within academic institutions but outside them? How can they support parents like me? I don't have any answers, but while I'm grateful for the support I continue to receive from my academic institution and colleagues, I can't help but think that there must be a way for journeys such as mine to be honored and to help inform the ways we collectively support parents.

everyone regardless of identity, family structure, socioeconomic status, or position within the academic hierarchy.

We asked our survey respondents how they negotiated parental leave if they are the partner of someone who gave birth. These qualitative responses—like those in the rest of the survey—are anonymous, and there is no way to track respondents' gender, so the only known common thread between all of the responses is that each respondent self-identified as the partner of someone who gave birth.[2] A few responses offer matter-of-fact indicators that parental leave is standard and expected. One respondent wrote, "I took leave, it's in our faculty manual so there wasn't much to negotiate." Another responded, "It is part of the union contract." A third described the process this way: "It was straightforward. I told my chair we were having a kid; the departmental admin directed me to the appropriate paperwork; submitted to vice provost; approved." These are positive signs of universally applied, transparent, and clearly communicated parental leave options.

More troubling, however, are the many responses that indicate persistent gendered expectations that parental leave is realistically only for women who give birth. Many of these responses are also matter-of-fact: "I was told no"; "I didn't take leave"; "Option wasn't available at the time." Some point to the institutional constraints and expectations complicating leave for parents who do not give birth. One respondent recalled the limited leave "options" available in graduate school: "There was no negotiation. I was told that I could take unpaid medical leave or I could use a semester of non-service funding, but that this would count toward my graduation

Supporting Adoptive Parents

Krista E. Wiegand
University of Tennessee

Imagine this scenario: your due date is in December, after the end of the semester, but your baby is born in October, in the middle of the semester. You're teaching three courses, advising theses, fully engaged in research, and all of a sudden, without notice, you have to scramble to deal with being a new mom and continuing to work. This happened to me, but not exactly in the same way. For me, I had no idea when my baby would arrive—through adoption. Unlike with childbirth, prospective adoptive parents do not have the nine months to plan and prepare, and worst of all, no knowledge of when that day might come when you get a call from the adoption agency. The adoption process is tedious, expensive, and highly unpredictable. Regardless of whether the adoption is open (the birth mother chooses the adoptive parents) or closed (the agency makes the match), domestic or international, the process is full of intrusions like getting background checks with the FBI and the state (getting fingerprints at the county jail), having social workers come to your house to inspect it and to make sure you and your partner are suitable to be parents, and having to provide information about your private lives, all of which is shared with potential birth parents. Worst is the long wait and the uncertainty of when a match will be made, not by prospective adoptive parents but by the birth parent, the adoption agency, or an international government.

Everyone loves adoption stories—the match, the cute baby, the image of how the baby was "saved" from a young mother who couldn't care for her child. The reality is that adoption is one of the most difficult processes to experience in one's life. My husband and I spent two and a half years waiting for our son. During this time, friends and colleagues announced they were pregnant, gave birth, and their babies were toddlers all before we were matched with our son. Because most domestic adoptions today are open, that means that the birth parent, typically the birth mother, selects prospective parents and the agency then makes the match. Therefore, we had to essentially wait for a birth mother to come across our website or glossy brochure and hope that she chose us. We have the most wonderful son, and every day I look at him and think how lucky my husband and I were to be chosen as his parents. Yet that two and half years waiting time was agonizing, stressful, anxiety ridden, and frustrating—all while I worked in my stressful and anxiety-ridden career as a professor.

I was working full-time as a tenured associate professor in a political science department at a regional state school with a high teaching load and in the middle of multiple research projects during the process. The adoption was like a dark cloud that constantly followed me. It was hard to concentrate; it was tempting to daydream about names, baby clothes, and what it was like being a mom. It was awkward to talk about with my colleagues and students. Nobody really knows how to talk to prospective adoptive parents. There is no baby bump to see, there is no special treatment for soon-to-be moms, talking about infertility and miscarriages is taboo, and everyone keeps asking, "have you heard anything about the adoption yet?" when there is no news at all. Everyone loves congratulating an expecting mother, but not so much an expecting adoptive mother. I was fortunate that in my department, the women faculty and staff gave me a baby shower after we took our son home. But before that, it was hard to think about celebrating.

Only a few of my colleagues, including the chair of my department, knew about our adoption plan before our son came home. I couldn't talk about the failed match when we had a birth mother fly to stay with us for a weekend to get to know us, only to change her mind halfway through the visit. I had to agree to work on projects or attend conferences way in advance, not knowing whether I would need to rush anywhere in the United States at a moment's notice. I had to think about whether I should take a risk and be out of the country when we got the call, ultimately deciding to continue teaching my study abroad programs in the summers.

When we got "the call" (it was actually an email from our son's birth mother), it wasn't what we had expected. We had been expecting a newborn, but our soon-to-be son was already eleven months old and walking. We had to babyproof the house for a walking baby with only three weeks of notice. We had to give away the newborn diapers and formula previously purchased, return the bassinet, and get a crib, high chair, stroller, car seats, and clothes all in a very short time.

We had to make several long-distance trips to meet our soon-to-be son, spend time with him and his birth mother, and make the family transition as easy as possible for him. This was in the middle of October, just when the semester was getting busy. Luckily the chair of my department was willing to work with me in figuring out how to deal with my fall courses and how to get my spring semester courses covered. I announced to my students that I had a "family issue" come up and would have to be out of town for an unknown number of weeks. That put some of them on edge, not knowing when I would be back before the end of the semester or what would happen to their grades or credit hours. I could not tell my students or colleagues what was happening in case the match fell through or one or both of the birth parents changed their minds. Because our son was born in another state, we had to travel there and stay for three weeks while the legal processes of the birth parents' signing off on the adoption, transferring a child across state lines, and securing permission from Native American tribes in case our son was part Cherokee all took place. This meant that I had to quickly put together recordings and presentations of lectures that I posted online for my students. Despite the emotional roller coaster of meeting my son and jumping through the legal hoops that adoption entails, I had to continue teaching, answering emails, and advising students. The only thing I put on hold, for about a month, was my research.

Because my son was already eleven months old when he came home with us and it was very important to integrate him into our family, our adoption agency required that my husband or I be with him every day for at least the first three months. This meant on days I did not teach, I stayed at home, still working, but taking care of my new son. On days I did teach, this meant that my husband had to take off from his job, delaying work for him and his clients. I had to finish out the semester, and then I would take off the spring semester. Having an eleven-month-old thrust into our lives was tough. We had little time to learn about the development stage of our son, and we had only a general idea of his life before meeting us.

I arranged to take the spring semester off, but because I lived in a state without family leave for state employees, I had to use my entire bank of sick leave to take twelve weeks off, the maximum time allowed by the Family Medical Leave Act. Because the semester is longer than twelve weeks, I had no salary for five weeks. Even though I was not teaching, I still had research projects to work on, including a fellowship I received at a research center on the other side of the country. So off I went with my mother and fifteen-month-old son for part of that semester, while my husband stayed at his job away from his new son. Because I was already tenured, there was no stopping the tenure clock for me. I was at a place in my career where I was just starting to get my stride. I had just published two books and was aiming to publish in higher-ranked journals, write with well-known colleagues, apply for research grants, and make a name for myself as much as I could. What this meant is that my FMLA semester off was not really a semester off but just a teaching release. Back at home, we had not been able to put our name on the waiting list for the best daycare centers, so I would take our son to the YMCA for mother's morning out and spend four hours at the gym on my laptop scrambling to get some writing done.

I know all new parents have a difficult time with newborns, but I was unable to relate. My new son was almost a year old, and my friends with one-year-olds had known their babies since they were born. My adoptive parent friends all had adopted newborns too, so my husband and I felt we had nowhere to turn for advice. Eventually we got the hang of things, and we became a regular family with "normal" stresses.

Unless they were friends with me on Facebook when I announced the adoption, colleagues in my field probably do not even know my son is adopted. I don't talk about it, not because it's a secret but because I'm a mother, just like any other working mother, dealing with balancing work and family. The fact that my son is adopted mattered a lot during the process because it took so much time, cost so much money, and made work difficult, but today it doesn't matter at all. We are a family, and like every family, we deal with school, sports, behavior, sickness, stress, and time constraints. Because international travel is so important to my husband and me, my son has become an international traveler as well. By age six, he had already been to twenty-seven countries. He spent a semester at sea on a ship traveling around the world and a semester in Southeast Asia while I did field research. He is the best thing that ever happened to me, but he is also the toughest thing I ever did. Getting tenure was much less stressful than adopting a child. I was fortunate to have an empathetic chair of my department, and I was relieved that FMLA considered adoption significant enough reason to take leave.

Like with every field, there are many academic parents that do not take the typical steps to creating a family. It might be surprising to learn how many academics themselves are adopted or have adopted children. When asked for advice, I am always happy to share my experience because I want others to know how hard it can be, and I don't want others to go through some of the painful experiences that I had. For any prospective adoptive parent, here are some tips for you. First, make sure you talk to the chair or head of your department as soon as you start the adoption process and notify them that you will likely need to take immediate leave sometime, even in the middle of the semester. Second, find a support group of adoptive parents or close friends or family who you can count on to vent to about the never-ending hassles of the adoption process. Third, don't hold off on your research or other academic work as if you're waiting for "any day"; go on and make commitments that are important for your academic career. Fourth, try not to be envious of your friends or colleagues with babies; you don't always know their stories and how difficult their personal lives or work actually are. Last, take advantage of the pre-child stage and write as much as you can since you'll want to focus on your child after he or she is adopted.

Now, advice for anyone with colleagues or friends who are adoptive parents. First, it's not helpful to ask colleagues without children why they don't have children. Second, don't call the birth parents the "real" parents or ask why anyone would ever give up a child. You don't know their stories and wouldn't probe why parents decided to get pregnant. Third, if you have colleagues in your departments going through the adoption process and you know about it, offer to be available to cover lectures or meetings while they have to travel. Fourth, be empathetic to the prospective adoptive parent in your department or at a conference. Know that they are likely very stressed and could use some empathy and support, especially in an academic environment that is often competitive and challenging on its own!

'clock' and I would be expected to fulfill normal research obligations during this time." Another recounted the effects of the tenure track: "Not much negotiation, one fewer course was recommended—partly due to lower enrollments at the time. Did not feel comfortable to negotiate a leave in the first year of tenure track."

We also asked respondents whether others in their institution or department take leave when their partners give birth. Here, responses were split between variations of simple "yes," "no," and "don't know" responses. As in response to the question about negotiating leave after a partner gave birth, a few responses indicate that parental leave is equitable and clearly communicated: "Yes—our parental leave policy is on paper and, in our department at least, in practice completely equitable." Some respondents noted that partners took leave only if they were tenured or observed that partners who took leave had to give up their salary to do so.

Others referred specifically to gender-based constraints and expectations: "I do know women who have taken maternity leave while pregnant, but not partners who have taken leave"; "They have tried to take as much time as they can, but dads rarely take much leave." Another respondent highlighted the informality of parental leave: "Nothing formal. People generally take a few days but no more." One respondent observed the "fatherhood bonus" of using parental leave time to get ahead: "One colleague did take a parental leave when his spouse gave birth. He was quite open (at least with some colleagues) about the fact he wanted to use the parental leave to add to his productivity—he was not planning on changing nappies!"

In examining awareness of whether and how colleagues negotiate and use parental leave, we can start to understand how campus and department norms shape a parent's willingness and ability to take leave. As many of our respondents indicated, the norms and logistics surrounding leave for parents who did not give birth seem slow to change. The partner who uses their leave time to advance research or go on the job market both epitomizes and entrenches the system that continues to view parenthood as a liability, and one that is specific to women.

Best Practices for Extending Support to *All* Parents

What university administrators can do:

- Establish and communicate clear and universal parental leave protections for all faculty and staff, regardless of gender and marital status.
- Ensure compliance with existing policies, such as Title IX protections.
- Communicate with departments and units about the importance of compliance with university or college policies.
- Foster family-friendly norms through formal and informal on-campus programs and resources.
- Explicitly recognize and support the diversity of family structures.

What department chairs and unit heads can do:

- Support colleagues by assisting with coverage for special programs, courses, and service roles as needed.
- Check gendered biases against extending the tenure clock.
- Apply departmental and campus policies equitably across individuals, including non-tenure-track faculty.
- Work together as a department or unit to create a set of policies and norms that comply with university or college parental leave policies, but go beyond these policies to close any gaps in leave and support resources (e.g., peer coverage for courses and service roles when the university provides for eight weeks of leave when the semester is fifteen weeks long).
- Encourage and support colleagues of all genders who take parental leave (e.g., if a junior colleague is about to become a new parent and is uncertain about utilizing parental leave resources, encourage the colleague to do so and support them when they do).

What faculty can do:

- Learn about your department's or campus's parental leave policies as soon as possible and speak with your department chair or unit head and administrators as soon as it is appropriate to access those resources.
- Know your department's and campus's tenure clock extension policy.
- Put everything in writing, and get everything in writing.
- For tenure track faculty: stop the tenure clock.
- For non-tenure-track faculty: maintain and foster your connections in the broader discipline.
- Work with other faculty to negotiate systemic changes like healthcare, leave policies, lactation rooms, and childcare on campus.

On a domestic note, many survey respondents mentioned the unfair allocation of household labor between them and their partners. Women do tend to provide more of the cognitive and emotional labor for the household—things like scheduling doctors' appointments, remembering birthdays, and meal planning. This unpaid third shift adds to women's uncompensated workload beyond formal professional and parental roles (Ciciolla and Luthar 2019). One survey respondent suggested that parents "not keep score" about who does what and that "over time, the workload often balances out." But sometimes it doesn't. Another respondent said, "If both people aim to do 80 percent, it might end up fair." Becoming parents means renegotiating responsibilities and relationships. Sleep deprivation and injustice (perceived or real) can make tempers flare. Many survey respondents implored that partners be generous and gentle with each other and themselves. One wrote succinctly, "Always assume best intent."

As the vignettes in this chapter all suggest, the need for support extends beyond formal parental leave (although adequate leave is essential for academic parents' success). We urge departments, colleges, and universities to truly embrace academic parenthood and families in all of their forms and begin to view children not as private goods—for whom parents alone pay all the costs and from whom parents alone gather all the rewards—but as full-fledged members of the community whose lives enrich that community in the long term. Once that view of parents and children is our norm, policies and support structures will be more inclusive of the many paths to parenthood. Some soon-to-be parents will need support and accommodations for medical care and adoption logistics long before their child arrives as well as after their arrival. Others will need to drop everything very suddenly in the middle of the semester to fly somewhere in the world to meet their baby. Some families will finally conceive that long-anticipated baby and require flexibility for frequent monitoring appointments. Some parents will have medically unremarkable pregnancies but give birth early and need extended leave to care for an infant in the neonatal intensive care unit for months. The paths to parenthood are diverse; some are short and easy, while others are winding and overwhelming at times. The need for support is a constant across all families, but the exact needs will look different, and that is where we see the importance of empathy for our colleagues, students, and selves.

Notes

1. "Where Americans Find Meaning in Life," Pew Research Center, http://www
   .pewforum.org/2018/11/20/where-americans-find-meaning-in-life/.
2. We note here that we asked survey respondents about their professional responsibilities during and after gestation or adoption in a separate section, so adoptive parents likely responded to those questions instead of the question posed to the partner of a parent who gave birth.

6 Sick and Tired

The Physical Toll of Parenthood

The physical consequences of family formation are significant contributors in the lower-level processes that lead women to drop out of academia. The only recognized, legally protected time for new parents is during the weeks immediately following the birth or adoption of a child. Most Family and Medical Leave Act leave is unpaid for academics in US institutions. Survey respondents from other countries almost universally remarked at the inhumanity of family leave accommodations within the United States and the dire implications for women's health and parent-child bonding. While the federally mandated FMLA employment protection is twelve weeks, the process of expanding a family often encompasses a much broader timeline that starts well before a child's birth or arrival and for at least a year after. Pregnancy and the postpartum phase can be hard; the subsequent years can be even harder. A colleague's partner, when asked how his often-sick wife was doing, would wryly reply, "Never. Better."

Women may spend months or years undergoing fertility treatments involving hormones that affect their physical, mental, and emotional well-being. Interventions for addressing infertility are also financially costly, which can increase prospective parents' stress levels. Miscarriages are common and also taboo; academic women in male-dominated fields likely do not share this information with colleagues, supervisors, or administrators. (We address this issue comprehensively in chapter 7, "Love, Loss, and Longing.") Women experience a wide range of pregnancy symptoms, from few or none to quite severe. The first trimester is known for morning sickness, which many pregnant women will acknowledge as a complete misnomer as the nausea and vomiting can occur at any point in the day. As one survey respondent said, "It was a harder than average pregnancy, but healthy. I was nauseated (just nausea, no vomiting) for about twenty-two weeks. Then I had about eight good weeks. Then I developed symphysis pubis dysfunction and could barely walk for the last two months. I was exhausted and anemic the whole time but had a normal teaching schedule, which meant that I got almost no work done on research."

There is such variation in women's experiences with pregnancy. In extreme cases, women with hyperemesis gravidarum—a condition in pregnancy with severe nausea, vomiting, and dehydration that often requires medication or hospitalization—are persistently sick for the duration of their pregnancy. Other survey respondents had similarly difficult times: "Pregnancy was extremely debilitating and difficult. I had extreme nausea and extreme fatigue as well as body aches and other issues. It was hard to breathe and I always felt faint. I had to lay on the floor once while teaching. I couldn't have my laptop or sit at a desk so I had to construct this whole contraption to be able to type. I wrote a whole book while pregnant, so despite the difficulties I overcame them." Another said,

My pregnancy was especially difficult. I had hyperemesis gravidarum from five weeks until basically the minute my child was delivered which, even with medication, was challenging to manage while working. When people ate stinky food in common areas I could not avoid, I would become violently ill and need to get an infusion at the hospital. For this reason, I asked for accommodation but was denied. I was not allowed remote work abilities. I was forced to also work and do a significant commute up until five days before delivery with pelvic girdle pain, which basically immobilized me. It was the worst experience of my life and definitely made me a more stressed and less productive person because I wasn't eating at all and wasn't sleeping.

Some women require weeks or months of bed rest to maintain the pregnancy, while others continue a regimen of running and exercise until the day they give birth. For some women, labor and delivery are quick and unremarkable, and they rebound quickly, as was this woman's experience: "It was pretty quick, maybe a few days until I was on my feet and another week or two until I was healed up. But again, I did not have to work at the time." For others, labor and delivery can last for days and complications can require surgery. One mother expressed the depth of complications with her delivery recovery experience, "It was long. It took about six months and several minor surgeries before the injuries fully healed." Some deliveries require medical intervention, such as unplanned C-sections. C-sections are major medical procedures, and physical activity is restricted during the healing phase. Other women have traumatic birth experiences: One had "some post-traumatic stress disorder related to emergency premature delivery. High levels of anxiety associated with preterm birth, low birth weight infant. Child did not sleep well for three years. Impacted everything. I dealt with it by transitioning to more administrative (work) to better control workload. Research not recovered."

And all of this comes *before* the onset of routine childhood illnesses that an entire family cycles through during the first several years of daycare or pre-school. (The academic dad's vignette in chapter 5, "Doctor, Parent," speaks to the persistent illnesses that even overall healthy children and their parents face in the first years in childcare.) Birth and non-birth parents of all genders fall prey to missed workdays and sleepless nights due to teething infants, sleep regressions, ear infections, and the myriad viruses and communicable germs that characterize the years spent in the trenches. These missed daycare or school and workdays contribute to the daily stress parents have to manage, but FMLA protections cover only the first several weeks of a child's birth or arrival. Society and the academic profession rarely take notice of the sick and tired parents struggling to balance work and parenthood during the demanding early years.

"Will I Ever Feel like Myself Again?"

Parenthood is physically demanding. In this chapter's first vignette, Susan Allen talks about getting a years-long headache while on the tenure track—and wanting to start a family—that redefined her self-identity. People may expect that their self-identity will change when they become parents. However, people underestimate how prolonged illness can also change their self-identity from being a regular, productive faculty member to being an excited new parent—to becoming exhausted, congested zombies. Parents underestimate how they may become traumatized by the onslaught of waves and waves of seemingly never-ending illness that boomerangs from child to child to parent to parent. During the early years, parents often wonder, "Will I ever feel like myself again? Will I ever feel well again?"

New parents, especially those who are recovering from the physical processes of pregnancy and childbirth, need support. The after-effects of childbirth in particular are often shrouded in mystery and seen as too taboo for polite—and certainly for professional—conversation. Take, for example, the Frida Mom ad that US television network ABC refused to air during the Academy Awards in early 2020. In the ad, a new mother wakes to the sound of a crying baby, stumbles awkwardly to the bathroom in her hospital-issued

The Headache

Susan Hannah Allen
The University of Mississippi

The sun was shining and the bluebirds were singing, I was a year into a job that I loved, and things were going great. I'd come in on a shortened clock and I was starting to feel more confident about getting tenure. My husband and I had started talking seriously about starting a family.

And then, one afternoon I came home from the office with a headache—a headache that didn't go away (or even abate much) for the next four years.

I saw every type of doctor under the sun—internists, rheumatologists, allergists, dentists, endocrinologists, oral surgeons, and more. I had appointments with neurologists in four different states. I went to the Mayo Clinic and saw the "headache guru." I had acupuncture, I tried Botox, and I had a disastrous visit to a chiropractor that left me unable to get out of bed for several days. I meditated and did lots of yoga. Nothing seemed to help. I tried countless drugs—some hopped me up, some dulled me down, some made me anxious, some made me manic. Throughout this meandering journey through the healthcare system, I had to find ways to keep doing my job. I also had to adjust my ideas about starting a family because all of these drugs were Class C drugs, which doctors strongly recommend against getting pregnant while taking.

Teaching a full load while taking drugs that alter your brain chemistry poses an interesting challenge. Recognizing that I was unable to concentrate well enough to lecture or guide a class discussion for seventy-five minutes at a stretch set me down a path of some of the most innovative teaching of my career. I still had to convey the same material to fifty to seventy students, but I had to find new ways to do it. We did a range of small-group activities, writing activities, simulations, and role playing—honestly, anything I could think of that might help the students teach themselves.

Looking back on these experiences, I think they have made me a better and more creative teacher, but it was a strategy born of desperation. I was desperate to keep the balls in the air when all I really wanted to do was take a nap.

On the research side, things were even more difficult. Since I started graduate school (and probably before that), I'd been defined by how well my brain works. What did I think about today, how well did that mesh with what I'd thought of yesterday, how could I connect that with things I read a week ago, a month ago. Suddenly I couldn't concentrate and I couldn't remember. I couldn't remember what I'd read a paragraph ago, much less a week ago.

My frustration and sense of helplessness was tremendous. I had conference papers and article drafts that I needed to complete, I had coauthors I didn't want to let down. My doctors were telling me that the drugs they were giving me were my best option to manage the pain, but they left me in a clouded state that didn't work with my job or my definition of self.

Finally, one day in the office of my primary care physician, I dissolved in tears and told her that I couldn't keep taking the drugs that my neurologist said were the best bet for me. I couldn't keep living in a haze, feeling like my brain was wrapped in cotton. She looked at me and said simply, "Then stop." Her response was such a relief, but I knew it also might mean the start of a new trip on the medical and pharmaceutical merry-go-round that I had felt trapped on previously.

Because my general practitioner is married to an academic, she understood how important mental clarity was, especially with the specter of a tenure review hanging over me. While many of the neurologists were unable or unwilling to listen to why a particular drug did help with the pain but wouldn't work for my career, this doctor saved me by saying that we'd just have to figure something else out.

In the end, the solution came out of the blue. Not in a doctor's office or a drug trial but by way of a new year's resolution. Unrelated to the headache issues, my husband and I decided to give up gluten for the month of January. Every year, we try a little experiment to kickstart healthier living in the new year, and this particular year, his boss had given up gluten and found that he had more energy. We decided to try it. Eliminating gluten made a huge difference for me and made my headache much more bearable.

This headache is still there—on the fringes. When I don't get enough rest or when the barometer drops quickly, it makes its presence known. On the other hand, the sun is shining again, I got tenure, my husband and I adopted an amazing little boy who holds both of our hearts in the palm of his hand, and the bluebirds are singing again.

mesh underwear and struggles with common post-birth physical necessities like hemorrhoids and vaginal tears. While the ad is not particularly graphic, decision-makers for the Academy Awards and ABC considered it unsuitable for general audiences. This is a fitting metaphor for postpartum health and recovery in the United States: in addition to the lack of paid parental leave, there is a distinct lack of social support and general awareness of what exactly happens to a woman's body during and after childbirth. Support for new parents varies across cultures (Baker 2017; Wisler 2016), and the notion of the postpartum body as taboo is not a given. Both within the academy and generally as a society we need to do more to recognize the physical and emotional changes that occur in the family formation process.

In the postpartum phase, birth parents may experience postpartum depression or anxiety—both of which tend to be underdiagnosed. Women's pain is often discounted (Hoffmann and Tarzian 2001). Women often tell their loved ones and their doctors about their symptoms, but if the problem is not gravely acute—if the mother is not a danger to herself or the child—they are often left to suffer. Well-meaning friends and physicians may say things like "Can you get some more sleep? Maybe go get a massage? You need a housekeeper. Who cares if the beds aren't made? Order your groceries online!" All these are great suggestions, but they will not treat the underlying condition of postpartum depression or anxiety. Worse, mothers may feel even more guilty for not being able to keep it all together. The solution for postpartum depression and anxiety is not more naps or outsourcing housework. Recall that hysteria—derived from *husterikos* (Greek) and *hustera* (Latin) meaning "womb"—was long believed to be a women's disease originating in the female sexual organs. Women experiencing pain are still considered hysterical, irrational, labile, and unstable, and their underlying medical conditions continue to be regarded with skepticism and dismissal. While women's emotional and physical experiences are minimized, men who are new parents are, as one survey respondent described, "fawned over" as new dads.

One mother wrote,

> I was always unsure if my physical experiences were normal and when I would call my doctor's office and speak to the nurse, they generally would pass everything off as typical without examining me or checking on my mental health or other supports. More help is truly needed. After one of my pregnancy losses, I was really depressed and no physician was seeing me at that time. No postpartum care, per se, from the infertility specialist who performs surgery following these losses. I spoke to them about not feeling right, but they chalked it up to typical sadness. I knew something was really not right, and finally saw a primary care physician who diagnosed me with postpartum depression and treated it.

Physicians tend to focus on the most extreme symptoms and indicators, such as the danger of hurting oneself or child. "Milder" symptoms such as irritability, anger, and rage can be damagingly disruptive to the household and to the mother's short- and long-term well-being.

The words of one survey respondent sum up how parents fall through the cracks during the postpartum phase:

> I had postpartum anxiety, and probably depression too. Although it never looks like what people tell you it's going to look like. If you're not crying and despondent, there's really no help for you. I was showering every day (almost), being incredibly productive, putting on a good face for the world, so nobody saw what was going on. I was living multiple double lives—putting on a show for the world that I was balancing everything and excelling, and putting on a show that my former department didn't suck. It takes incredible emotional effort to convince yourself to show up to work and be peppy and positive and productive when your department is unsupportive, telling you your work is inferior (even when you're succeeding in measurable ways that are being noticed in the discipline), that your PhD program is substandard, and that you're not good enough for a tenure-track job. I have subsisted on chocolate and sugar for years. Neither of my kids is a good sleeper, so it's only been in the past few weeks that I have started sleeping through the night. In short, the past five years have been the most brilliant and hellish of my life.

New Parents Need Better Support Systems

Lack of sleep, irregular sleep, and the physical demands of the early days and months of parenthood are exacerbated by unsupportive family leave policies that create additional stress. In many of the work-life balance discussions, colleagues and experts suggest that taking time for oneself is critical to having a happy, well-adjusted life. In reality, the early years of parenting are moment-to-moment crisis management with little time for extras, like exercise and socializing. In our survey, we asked respondents to prioritize three of the following: work, sleep, family, friends, or self-care. The results confirmed our own experiences. More than half of the respondents chose work, family, and sleep (in varying orders).

The mind-numbing fatigue might be the worst: "For the past five years, every single day I have been exhausted. From the day I got pregnant I have been sick—morning sickness plus all the germs from kids being in school, and a weakened immune system from lack of sleep and toxic stress." Furthermore, academics often live far from family and support networks and must weather the stressors of being new parents in intimate isolation. Because there is often no family nearby to serve as informal childcare, the children of academics often enter daycare early. As disease vectors, children in daycares introduce a host of new illnesses, such as hand, foot, and mouth disease; impetigo; colds; respiratory viruses like RSV; ear infections; and the flu. Sleep deprivation and stress can depress adults' immune systems, and parents regularly catch the same bugs as their kids. Sick kids can't be sent to school, and sick parents have to suffer through their most important work obligations with little external support. It is worth noting that parents of children with chronic health conditions and devastating diagnoses face even bigger hurdles as they struggle to care for their children and meet their work obligations.

In our survey, most parents reported missing at least one day per month due to illness; many reported missing two to three days of work per month, while some missed four or more. As we discuss in chapter 5, "Doctor, Parent," academia does afford some flexible time (i.e., time spent away from the office while not teaching, advising, or otherwise on campus), and this can give academic parents some leeway to rearrange their work schedule to accommodate sick children and emergency calls from school or daycare. Academic jobs do not require faculty to punch a clock, but faculty do have time-constrained responsibilities to be present in the classroom; teach high-quality courses; grade and return homework, papers, and exams in a timely fashion; and hold office hours. A missed workday for an academic might not look the same for someone in the corporate world, but tolerance for illness in academia is often lower than you might expect. Most survey respondents who identify as birth parents reported that they carried out their regular responsibilities throughout pregnancy, and often soon afterward as well. As one respondent wrote,

> I taught a 3-3 during my pregnancies and preschool years. In order to achieve excellent ratings in my annual reviews, I also had service obligations and a minimum of one publication annually and one conference presentation annually. I met all these obligations but coauthored the publications and sent my coauthor to the conferences. This was accepted by my department, and I was still ranked excellent (anyone without children would have gotten the same ratings, so this was NOT an accommodation).

Parental partners are often each other's confidante and sole support system. These relationships also suffer during the early years of parenthood. One respondent recounts,

I did gain thirty pounds after each delivery, rather than lose weight as most women do. I was never able to sleep for more than two hours at a crack. I often had to work late into the night, as that was the only time I was not holding a baby. I stress ate, never had a second to exercise. My husband and I didn't see each other much. We have no family in the area and had not lived here long enough to have friends. We were never relieved of our parenting responsibilities, even for a few hours. We just muscled through it, knowing it was temporary, but it was hard on us, on our marriage and on my job.

Family formation accommodation is imperfect for tenure-track faculty. It is downright bleak for those filling in the gaps who comprise the academic "underclass"—the graduate students, the visiting assistant professors, the instructors and lecturers, and the adjuncts. Graduate students and adjunct professors may not have health insurance at all. Non-tenure-track faculty are often underpaid and overworked, and as this chapter's second vignette contributor notes, there is no tenure clock to pause. Thus the expectations and demands compound, with fewer resources and safety nets.

Empathy, Gender Norms, and Family-Friendliness

It's hard for colleagues without kids to understand the physical demands of family formation. The responses to our survey about the family-friendliness of departments varied widely. Departments where many faculty—both men and women—were parents of young children were rated as more hospitable, charitable, and flexible. On the other hand, respondents whose departments have few parents of young children reported a more anti-family, hostile climate. As one mother wrote,

> I am the only tenure-track woman and the only junior faculty member in my department. We are five tenured men (four of five are full), one tenure-track woman (me, second-year assistant professor), and two part-time spouses who lecture in the department (one is my partner). All faculty have children, but due to the gap in age/seniority, my colleagues' children are all older, ages ten to twenty-seven, while my daughter is two and a half, and I am due next week. I am the only member of my department with childcare expenses. My departmental colleagues do bring children to the department on occasion, and some of them are vocal about their parenting responsibilities.

The Constant Sickness Cycle

Anonymous non-tenure-track professor

I became pregnant with my first child six months after earning my PhD, and I was at the cusp of qualifying as a high-risk pregnancy because of my age. I got a late start in academia and was the oldest person in my cohort by far, even older than some of my professors. Due to geographic and my partner's employment constraints, I took the first and only available academic position, a non-tenure-track job with a heavy teaching and service load. My department head, an Ivy League graduate, told me early on that I would face an uphill battle getting a tenure-track job due to the "subpar" doctoral program where I had received my degree. At that point, I was undaunted and unreasonably optimistic about transitioning to a tenure-track job, but in retrospect, I should have recognized this statement as a strong signal about my future prospects in the department. In retrospect, I wish I had known that I could never be seen as a serious scholar in that department or improve either my salary or my job title. This is an important point: whatever level you enter an organization determines how you will be treated and limits the potential for upward mobility. My starting salary was well below the poverty line, and I would have qualified for public assistance were it not for my partner's income.

The chasm between doctoral degree and gainful employment is already enormous. As the *Chronicle of Higher Education* (June 2012) notes, graduates of the top eleven PhD-granting departments in political science get 50 percent of the tenure-track jobs. With an oversupply of qualified PhDs, the teaching and service gaps are often filled by underpaid and overworked adjunct, temporary, and non-tenure-track scholars. I had no idea how much I had stacked against me or what kind of an uphill battle I would face over the next few years. Junior scholars are often advised to get clear guidelines from their department and institution for tenure standards; this is sound advice also in moving up from temporary to permanent positions. Because departments appreciate the cheap labor that non-tenure-track faculty provide, such as carrying high teaching and service loads, and because of the difficulty in obtaining new faculty lines from the university administration, it is generally against the department's best interest to have underemployed faculty succeed in their careers (read: transition from non–tenure track to tenure track). In other words, why buy the cow when the milk is an inexpensive, known quantity? I mistakenly allowed the department to throw me a baby shower, which further solidified the perception that I was on the "mommy track" rather than the tenure track. The job market process is fraught enough without the added stress of starting a family at the same time.

I had two medically uncomplicated pregnancies in the next several years after I was hired, but I suffered severe morning sickness until roughly halfway through with both. When I was not queasy and vomiting, I was exhausted. My first labor and delivery was arduous and I labored, without medication, for three days. During this time, I was working on my computer in my hospital bed through Pitocin-induced contractions that felt like getting hit in the face with a cast iron skillet every few minutes. After my child was finally born, I took six weeks of sick leave, since the university had no family leave policy at the time. Since I was not tenure track, I had no tenure clock to pause, and the demands of producing publications compounded with each pregnancy and postpartum period. I had none of the protections of a tenure-track position and even more of the penalties. I nursed both children for more than a year, and since we live far from family, we had very little built-in childcare support. We have pictures of my child sleeping on my chest, with the computer on my lap, and sleeping in the baby carrier while I stood at the kitchen counter to work. I didn't have an uninterrupted night of sleep for six years.

When my first child was less than a year old, I had a career-changing success that ironically served to alienate me from my department in the short term but helped me subsequently land a better position. I thought that my department head was looking out for my best interests and bargaining on my behalf, but after being passed over for several tenure-track positions in my subfield in the department, I sought mentorship and advocacy from outside sources within the university and the discipline. The lesson from this is that you have to work to be competitive in the discipline, not the department. As Theodore Parker said, "the arc of the moral universe is long but it bends toward justice"; good work will generally be rewarded.

During this time, I also had two early miscarriages, one of which occurred while I was out of town giving a presentation. I quickly got pregnant with my second child, and the childbirth this time was fast and easy. However, the next few years were a blur of sickness after sickness, alongside postpartum anxiety and depression, and some of the medications had drowsy side effects that made me even more tired. My immune system was devastated from the pregnancies, the lack of postpartum support, the constant inundation of germs from daycare, and the stress of the long hours of working to improve my academic position and my salary. I had several surgeries to address underlying illnesses during this time as well.

I went on the job market both while pregnant and with a newborn. My second child would not take a bottle, so when the baby was a month old I hired a nanny to provide childcare in my office while I taught an evening class so I could nurse halfway through, until someone complained about children in the department. My partner then had to bring the baby to campus so I could nurse in the parking lot. I nursed and pumped milk on interviews and at conferences, in deans' offices, public bathrooms, and supply closets. I explained the mechanics of pumping milk (while hooked up to the flanges, milk spraying) to the provost who had leaned in for a close-up look during a break in the annual general faculty meeting. I missed conferences that did not have childcare or accommodations for nursing mothers.

All along, I was the epitome of a research productive overachiever. Other than constant illness, there was no visible trace that I was suffering inside so profoundly. And yet I was deep in the throes of postpartum depression and anxiety (PPD/A), compounded by depression from prolonged illness. I was constantly filled with rage at everyone, including my supportive partner. Because I was outwardly thriving, none of my family, friends, or medical providers identified or diagnosed PPD/A. As I later learned, extreme anger is a manifestation of depression and anxiety. Laurie Penny (2017) wrote in *Teen Vogue* that "most of the women you know are angry"; while it might be a sign of righteous indignation, it's also possible that chronic, endemic depression and anxiety are the root cause of a woman's anger. Women in academia and in the workplace more broadly are suffering, because we are outwardly high functioning and successful, with undiagnosed PPD/A.

This takes a toll on a relationship as well. When two people enter into a committed, loving partnership and they utter the words "for better or for worse," they probably don't consider just how bad it can get and how underprepared partners are for dealing with the nuances of new parenthood, early-career demands, and maintaining a partnership. Supporting the career ambitions of female partners is very different in theory than in practice: the reality is much messier and difficult than anyone will admit. I was resented for my exhaustion and constant illness, for my short and furious temper, for my inability to be the person I had been before. Had I been in my partner's position, I would have felt the same way. We practiced attachment parenting and outsourced very little in the way of help. In retrospect we could have made different choices to alleviate some of the stress, but we did the best we could. For years, my partner and I considered it a success if we felt neutrally about each other most days. But we endured the profound isolation that academia enforces, and the bright spot is that we always delighted in parenting and in our children.

Sheryl Sandberg (2013) tells women to "lean in" but fails to provide any counsel for what happens when you lean in and fall on your face. Lean in works when you can afford to outsource childcare and spend time on self-care and relationship care. Lean in works when you have a village or a stay-at-home partner, but not when you are isolated from family and friends and have a working partner. Lean in is a trust game, where you surrender yourself to the fall because you know that people will be there to catch you. It felt too selfish to ask for me time, given all the demands on our family, but in retrospect it probably would have improved my health and overall well-being. Anne-Marie Slaughter (2015) is more realistic, saying that women "can't have it all," at least not all at once. Randi Zuckerberg tweeted that women have to make the choice between "work, sleep, family, fitness, or friends" and that we can have only three of these at once. I chose work and family, and in a distant third place, sleep. Hoekzema and colleagues (2017) found measurable differences in maternal brain structure and gray matter that persist up to two years after childbirth; researchers have yet to quantify what effect this has on work productivity in academia.

Early-career academia and starting a family is a series of constant crises that a male-dominated field with androcentric milestones is scant prepared to understand, much less accommodate. The dizzying, disorienting, incoherent, zombie years of sleep deprivation feel impossibly long and unsurvivable. Men, and our women colleagues without children, have no idea what we endure.

After years of being sick, tired, underappreciated, and underpaid, I ultimately got a job offer that placed me in a supportive and appreciative department and in a tenure-track job. The kids got older, and as many people foretold, things got better. I am not the person I was before, but over time I did get back to feeling like a version of myself that I recognize—and that my partner still chooses to love. I don't think things would have been so difficult if my department had been more accommodating and if we had better family support. At no point did I ever entertain giving up, but I can understand why women do. This is how the leaky pipeline happens. This is why women leave the profession.

Exposure to faculty starting families, and with young children, seems to soften academic departments and increase empathy: "I have a relatively young department. We've had some recent turnover in staffing, but three of the four current faculty have or are expecting children. We are sensitive to childcare issues (especially in our small, rural community) and are welcoming of children at department meetings and events. We also have an annual department dinner for families, and the institution has an all-campus picnic each fall semester open to students, staff, faculty, and families. It is a relatively family-friendly climate." Other departments are less kid-friendly: "Kids do not exist. Kids are a disruption to work/life/productivity. Kids were never seen. Even so, my infant was brought to my office every afternoon after daycare and was there with me for an hour or so before I went home. No one was hostile to me about it, but I was clearly the *only* person who did this."

In many ways, antiquated gender norms still persist: "Most female faculty are recently tenured and unmarried without children; most males have children the age of my children and a spouse that primarily stays home. Some recent hires at the assistant level are women and men with young children." This sentiment seems to indicate that the scenario of a (man) professor with a stay-at-home wife continues to be an unchanged cultural standard. Another survey respondent wrote, "Not much of a family climate. One colleague compared my leave to being in an extended vacation and said he should get himself a baby to take a break too. I bring my children to my office on occasion and turn down some requests due to conflicts with my kids' schedules. I do not believe this has harmed me, but I do not feel particularly supported." In other cases, department and unit heads may be accommodating and family-friendly, but colleagues may not: "My department is very gracious about letting my kids hang out in the department, and four of seven of us are parents. One of the nonparents is constantly complaining about the 'extra' support that parents receive that she does not receive, but she can't articulate what this 'extra' support actually is. (Because other than allowing the kids to sit quietly in the office, there is none.)"

We want to believe that things are better now than they were thirty years ago, and in some ways they are. Tenure clocks are stopped. Mentorship keeps women in the game. But the underlying cultural expectations have yet to fully evolve to embrace a world where working women can become parents without being penalized in both overt and subversive ways. Universities rely on sick leave to accommodate family formation rather than implementing actual family leave policies. This means that when parents—especially mothers—need to take sick leave to care for themselves or their sick children, they have fewer days to draw from.

The physical consequences of parenthood—the crippling fatigue and revolving door of communicable diseases—imperil academics' health and well-being for several years. Sick and tired faculty may suffer from lower student evaluations and ratings during these years. One survey respondent wrote, "I got terrible evaluations the semester I was pregnant. I missed the last class and the final because I was in the hospital, and I had not yet revealed that I was pregnant to my department, colleagues, or students so I did not justify my absence to them other than that I was ill. One student wrote that I had abandoned them at the end of the semester, and how could I?" This is not necessarily an indicator of the individual scholar's long-term potential but rather a symptom of the physical, emotional, and cognitive challenges that new parenthood poses. The academic system is fundamentally not set up to support parents in these situations. Far from support systems, academic parents muddle through the first few years as best they can. As many of the survey respondents and vignette contributors noted, illness and fatigue can take an immeasurable and unseen toll on academic parents.

Best Practices for Accommodating the Sick and Tired

What university administrators can do:

- Separate FMLA from sick leave so that parents can use sick leave for its intended purpose.
- Adopt a family leave policy for birth and adoptive parents.
- Provide affordable, accessible, on-campus childcare.

What department chairs and unit heads can do:

- Engender compassion among faculty for colleagues with young children.
- Support, rather than punish, faculty who take sick leave.
- Weight student evaluations less in overall faculty evaluations, as they are already gender biased.
- Encourage faculty to take care of their physical and emotional health and well-being.

What faculty can do:

- Take sick leave when you need it.
- Document everything.
- Ask for collegial help. Helpful colleagues and solutions may or may not be found in your own department or university. Keep going and keep pushing until you find someone who will help you.
- Ask for medical help if you are sick and especially if you have post-partum depression or anxiety.
- Offer help to your colleagues.

7 Love, Loss, and Longing

Fertility Struggles, Adoption, Miscarriage, and Infant and Child Loss

Nothing speaks more to the invisible, lower-order processes that affect productivity, work-life balance and happiness, and progression through the rigors of graduate school, the job market, and the grueling pre-tenure years than the process of becoming—and staying—pregnant or hoping for a successful adoption process. While family formation affects both parents, the physical demands of childbearing fall uniquely on women. But it's more than just the physical act of becoming pregnant that takes a toll: it's the uncertainty, the cost associated with infertility treatments, the emotional and very real hormonal changes that affect a woman's health and well-being. It's the unobserved biological changes during the precarious first trimester, before most people announce pregnancies. It's walking the line between maintaining "normality" and business as usual while cultivating the seeds of a growing family, along with the aspirations, hopes, and disappointments that are statistically probable along the way.

While some women get pregnant right away, others spend years or even decades, counting tens or hundreds of months on the fertility roller coaster. Between 10 and 20 percent of known pregnancies end in miscarriage (American College of Obstetricians and Gynecologists 2018). The proportion is much higher for some groups of women, and the overall statistic may suffer from under-reporting bias, as many miscarriages happen before women even know they are pregnant. In the same way that many women try to time their pregnancies to coincide with university breaks—so as to not inconvenience their colleagues—women also minimize the experience of pregnancy loss. This is society-wide and not a unique feature of academia. According to one survey respondent, "I miscarried during class . . . in the bathroom. It didn't affect my work." Another wrote, "When we started our second round of IVF, I was TA-ing with my chair and thought I was going to pass out in the class, so I told her we were doing it and to not worry if I passed out in class and that I might have to miss class unexpectedly. So she was aware, but not my department." In short: women tend to put others' social comfort before their own health.

One Size Doesn't Fit All

The biggest and most important truth about family formation in academia is that the process varies substantially from person to person. Some pregnancies and adoptions are easy and straightforward. Others—many others—are more complex and nonlinear and require more nuanced accommodations. Academic institutions and departments—actually the entire system of health care and legal parameters in the United States—address the bare minimum requirements for accommodating faculty welcoming new children. FMLA policies kick in only once the child has arrived, despite the challenges parents and families face in the weeks, months, or even years before the child is born or adopted.

Imagine what it might be like to endure years of infertility and fertility treatments. Imagine what it might be like to require bed rest—to be confined to your house or a hospital room—in order to sustain your pregnancy. Imagine what it might be like to have a much-desired adoption fall through mid-semester. Again. Or imagine what it might be like to get the long-awaited news that your adoptive child can come home with you—in the middle of the semester. Imagine how it would feel to have another month of not getting pregnant, or another chemical pregnancy, or another miscarriage. Imagine the grief of parents suffering a late-term miscarriage. Imagine the challenge of keeping it together at work while experiencing some of the most profound grief and loss that human beings can feel.

Under the best of circumstances, miscarriages happen in the privacy of home. Family formation is nothing if not inconvenient, however. As one survey respondent confided, "I had a miscarriage in my first semester as a tenure-track faculty member—actually it happened during a department meeting—and this was also a significant event in the conjunction of my reproductive/parenting life and my professional life. I missed one class as a result of the miscarriage (nine weeks along), and because it happened during a department meeting, it created a very awkward situation with my (all-male) colleagues . . . and I did not feel comfortable announcing to all of them what had happened." Another respondent wrote about having a miscarriage during a prestigious invited talk.

Unspeakable Losses

Jana von Stein (2013) published her reflections on losing her firstborn child, Sophie, in the *Chronicle of Higher Education*. In a piece titled "When Bad Things Happen to Untenured People," she wrote about the effect that her child's prolonged illness and the subsequent grieving period following her child's death had on her identity as an academic and her professional record. She and her then-husband, also an academic at the time, were granted tenure extensions by their home department, but as she wrote, "for some people, legitimate challenges to productivity can be long-lived. Calculating the 'appropriate' extension in cases like those is next to impossible, but it is worth trying." Some departments and institutions try, and that is met with much appreciation and gratitude from parents.

Our point in addressing the hopes, desires, effort, and persistence it can take to become parents is that the road to parenthood is not always easy. And the struggles of the journey are often invisible. At present, family formation policies in institutions in the United States are woefully inadequate for accommodating the myriad paths to parenthood. The tension we identify is between the letter of the law and the spirit of the law. The letter of the law—the FMLA policies on the books—should serve as a ground floor and a bare minimum. Departments and institutions should foster a culture of embracing the process of family formation, if for no other reason than new faculty are expensive, faculty searches are also costly, and failed tenure cases damage the reputation of departments. Talented scholars can also be parents. If departments are concerned about faculty misusing family formation policies, they should direct their suspicions toward men, who are the more likely candidates to abuse parental leave in order to better their careers (Wolfers 2017).

We make two critical distinctions in our pleas for embracing family formation in academia. First, institutional and departmental policies should be more equitably and clearly articulated; second, institutions, not individuals, should be responsible for determining and implementing policies. Through our online survey, vignettes from our named and anonymous contributors, and many conversations with peers and colleagues, it is evident that many scholars receive accommodations for family formation not because of fairly communicated or applied policies but because they had an individual in their corner willing to advocate for them.

To be clear: these accommodations were not above and beyond the letter of the law; on the contrary, these accommodations have been, writ large, individual scholars fighting for the bare minimum—the letter of the law—to be applied. In far too many cases, department chairs or deans have capricious and unilateral power to deny accommodations, even in violation of the law. And, for the most part, parents and families must accept what is given them.

And yet the amount of time a person spends pregnant, lactating, and raising young children is relatively short compared to the larger population morbidity statistics for problems like heart disease. Nearly half of people in the United States have some form of cardiovascular disease, yet people with heart problems, cancer, or other diseases do not face the same discrimination as pregnant women—or women trying to get pregnant or start families. Family formation engenders a particular form of disdain and resentment from individuals and institutions, different from other types of medical conditions. In many institutions, parents must use sick leave—intended for medical illness —in lieu of a family leave policy. Institutions want it both ways: they want women to use their sick leave for pregnancy but they also lack the compassion, generosity, and accommodations afforded to other colleagues with chronic illnesses. Perhaps it is a question of agency: parents make a deliberate choice to be parents and as such *deserve* their misery, whereas disease *happens* to other people, and their conditions warrant more understanding.

In some sense, comparing who is suffering more is pointless. Pain is real, and compassionate policies should apply equitably to all people experiencing medical conditions—from bypass surgery to dilation and curettage following a miscarriage. Yet as Jessica Winegar (2016) writes, similar to the deliberateness of getting pregnant, miscarriage carries blame: "Unlike Japan and other societies, Americans have no cultural script for this encounter. We have the word—miscarriage—which seems to blame women for the loss. After my first miscarriage, a caring friend who surely didn't mean to blame me asked, 'What did you do?'"

A Hundred Tears of Solitude

Suffering in silence, however, incurs a particularly personal type of pain. It is noteworthy that both of our vignette writers for this chapter made their contributions anonymously. Pregnancy loss and infertility are social taboos, unlike heart disease. Broadly speaking, women's health is a taboo topic, and many studies have validated that women's pain is taken less seriously than men's. Women are more likely than men to be prescribed sedatives than painkillers (Chen et al. 2008), and pain related to internal sex organs (such as endometriosis and menstrual pain) is frequently dismissed. Society tells women to suffer in silence through infertility and miscarriage and also discounts their pain when they do speak up. Dear reader, most women you know have probably had a miscarriage.

The majority of our survey respondents who indicated they suffered a chemical pregnancy or early miscarriage said they did not tell their supervisors, chairs, or colleagues. Those who did share the news mention a variety of outcomes. One respondent said, "I have experienced two second-trimester losses, and my department was aware of both, mostly because they occurred so late in pregnancy. For both, I took about two weeks off and my courses were covered by colleagues. I did not file any official leave paperwork for either." Another respondent said their miscarriage "didn't really affect work but was stressful and distressing for the pregnancy because I knew there were issues to worry about all pregnancy. Also people were really not wanting to talk to me afterward and basically shunned me."

As Winegar (2016) notes, some cultures lack language or widespread culturally accepted rituals for dealing with miscarriage. Because women's health issues are so taboo, many people avoid reaching out to colleagues. If a story about infertility, miscarriage, or a failed adoption is shared in confidence, it is important to honor the privacy of that information. However, colleagues and supervisors can do several things, including asking what, if anything, the person needs, and if this information may be shared among colleagues for the purposes of support. Chairs, supervisors, and deans can ensure that in the moment of grief, their colleague is aware of departmental and university policies available—such as bereavement leave—to help them get through the loss.

Work and Productivity

Some women report severe interruptions in their ability to work and concentrate while dealing with infertility and pregnancy loss. Some indicate that pregnancy hormones complicate their ability to cope emotionally and psychologically, and most mention how profoundly they have been affected by grief and the grieving process. One woman's experience reveals the complexity of challenges in conceiving:

> My fertility process involved flying to a different state every time I ovulated for nine months, then six months of more traditional (in the doctor's office in my city) fertility treatments. I also had one early miscarriage. One of my colleagues knows the extent of the time we spent trying to have a kid, but nobody else does. And the one colleague who knows about our fifteen tries before getting pregnant doesn't know about the miscarriage or the extraordinary amount of emotional energy and money it took. I have been repeatedly, if politely, dissed by others in my department for publishing less during that period.

For pre-tenure academics, the physical and emotional stress related to having children may mean that they need special accommodations on the tenure track. One option is implementing a policy for stopping the tenure clock for pregnancy loss and bereavement. As one woman wrote, "It was nearly impossible to do intellectually demanding work during the months in which I was waiting to get confirmation that the baby was very sick, as well as in the months following the loss. I went to work and sat in front of my computer like I always do but was able to produce very little tangible research." Another said, "I experienced pregnancy loss at seventeen weeks. Several people in my department were aware, since it was impossible to hide, but there was no kind of support."

Other women used work as a distraction from the experience of miscarriage. Per one survey respondent, "I still worked my normal hours. It was a good distraction once I was cleared to return to work." Another echoed this sentiment: "I experienced miscarriage. I used work to avoid thinking about it. This was not the healthiest way of dealing with it." Women who miscarry are not the only parents who suffer: another respondent mentioned missing days of work and going to therapy to help deal with grief arising from their spouse's miscarriage.

The Waiting Game

Families going through the adoption process have similarly invisible struggles, marked by hopes and disappointments. Adoption timelines are rarely linear, and adoptive parents also endure months if not years of preparation and uncertainty. Some adoptive parents also experience the psychological and physical demands of trying to conceive. As one survey respondent lamented, prospective adoptive parents have no growing belly to show and to mark the forthcoming arrival of a new child. Their ride on the roller coaster of highs and lows, with its promises and plummets, is unobservable from the outside. They are in a state of perpetual anticipation, hopeful that a family will choose them to adopt their baby and hopeful that the process goes smoothly. Most—if not all—of this process is done in profound isolation. Colleagues don't necessarily know when an adoption falls through. Adoptive parents may not celebrate any of the social and cultural rituals and milestones associated with gestation and birth. Many of the official policies and options available for birth parents are not accessible to adoptive parents. Adoptive parents may also be simultaneously dealing with complicated emotions and physical effects related to infertility while awaiting a positive adoption

Silencing Ourselves

Anonymous Associate Professor

The loss of a child is too much to bear alone. When I suffered a pregnancy loss, God, my family, and my friends helped me to move forward one step at a time. I walked into my classroom, my office, and meetings holding back tears. I told only my chair and three colleagues about the pregnancy. When the baby died, I told only these same people. They comforted me, but I tried to keep the conversations short. As the days went on, I felt increasingly weak. Our department assistant convinced me to call my doctor. Unable to walk to my car alone, she took me to her car and drove me home. My doctor told me that everything was proceeding normally and that I would likely recover my strength soon. So I kept working, convinced I would be overdramatic if I asked for some time off.

Beginning my second year in a tenure-track position, I feared looking weak. As a woman still in her childbearing years, I feared being seen as a liability. I was convinced that I had to keep publishing, teaching, and serving and never let them see me sweat. When I felt faint, I closed my office door, sat down, and prayed for strength. I am the sole provider for my family of small children and a stay-at-home homeschooling dad. We moved from family and friends to take this job. I could not fail. I did not totally neglect myself. During the month after the initial loss, I continued to see my doctor, telling her that something felt wrong. She assured me that all was fine and that it was a difficult process that would end soon. To be sure, she took some blood tests, but she felt I had nothing to worry about.

Following her advice, I went to the airport, ready to board a plane and attend a scholarly conference. I knew I had to present my research and make connections. I said nothing to my chair. I feared wasting the department's money spent on financing the trip. As I was about to board the plane, my doctor's office called. The nurse said that my hemoglobin was dangerously low and I needed a blood transfusion. I asked if this could wait until after my trip. She told me that if I did not get a blood transfusion immediately, I might die. I called my department and told them I could not go to the conference. I spent two days in the hospital, fearing I would lose my job. I received an email from my department chair. He told me I had nothing to fear. He arranged for me to take two weeks of sick leave, and colleagues agreed to cover my classes. He told me I must spend the next few weeks at home recovering. In addition, he spoke to the dean of my college and obtained assurances that this would not impact my evaluations in any way. I never spoke about what happened to the colleagues who covered my classes; I only thanked them. I do not know if my chair told them anything. My evaluations have not been affected, and no one has mentioned these events to me since.

Reflecting on this time, I am grateful for the support of my chair and my colleagues. I realize now that I silenced myself, and I still do not know if that was necessary. I will never know if I could have shared this loss with my department. I wanted desperately to tell people about the child I lost, to honor his life. But I could not know how it would affect my career. I was blessed with a compassionate and understanding man who had suffered a similar loss years ago as my chair. I could not have predicted that. I think for many women suffering pregnancy loss in academia, it is the fear of the unknown that burdens them, perhaps silencing them too.

outcome. While the adoption stories shared in this book ultimately worked out, they were filled with uncertainty, disappointment, and dashed and then fulfilled hopes. Not all stories end well, however.

In "Silencing Ourselves," this chapter's first vignette contributor describes the psychological and physical health consequences of having a miscarriage. She feared professional repercussions for failing to meet conference-related expectations. She credits a supportive chair and helpful colleagues for helping her get through the near-fatal consequences of her miscarriage. It bears contemplating what this scenario would have been like had she suffered a heart attack, something also requiring acute and immediate medical attention. It's acceptable to talk about a heart attack; it's not acceptable to talk about a miscarriage. Women self-censor, for sure. But we do it because of societal expectations that miscarriages are not appropriate topics of conversation.

The second vignette, also anonymous, addresses the precariousness of being in a non-tenure-track position while starting a family. The writer experienced multiple miscarriages and had high-risk pregnancies resulting in the birth of two healthy children. This scholar's story is important because it demonstrates how she continued to work at full capacity while enduring miscarriages, fertility treatments, and medically complicated pregnancies. She describes trivial but not insignificant barriers like access to her own small office refrigerator and a toxic work environment with hostile colleagues who scheduled non-optional meetings while she was on mandated bedrest, which was required to sustain the pregnancy. During maternity leave, her years-long efforts and work were erased from a nationally prominent grant in the year

A Complicated Path and Hostile Work Environment

Anonymous Non-Tenure-Track Professor

I am a research assistant professor—a non-tenure-track position—in education research and policy. Unlike most academics who have a more flexible schedule, this position is a year-round faculty appointment with a typically corporate schedule, every day with a full day's time in the office or in the field, held accountable to a director or supervisor. While there are benefits to the more predictable, routine schedule in many ways, when it comes to childbearing and childcare, it would be helpful to have a more flexible schedule to work around medical and family needs.

The restrictiveness of my position made it difficult to balance the desires of growing our family. Infertility appointments, countless treatments, and miscarriages were all part of our journey. While my bosses verbally expressed support and concern, their expectations for our unit were applied equally and "fairly" for all. This meant they could not allow a team (faculty) member to have a flexible or compressed schedule to meet work obligations while balancing other treatments or surgeries or doctor appointments. Precious paid time off or unpaid leave were the primary options to "support" this journey. Given that my role is not dissimilar to other academics, my bosses could have accommodated a more flexible situation under these circumstances. In these circumstances, equal treatment was not fair for all.

It was no small feat to conceive and successfully carry two high-risk pregnancies. I became pregnant with my first son three years after a miscarriage that resulted in continuous fertility treatments, progressing in intensity. During those years, I continued to work my typical schedule, rarely missing a day of work due to illness or treatments that had their own set of challenges—keeping medications refrigerated while administering multiple times per day, and so on. This was an exhausting process to begin trying to grow our family. A small but poignant barrier was that I had to ask permission to bring in my own personal refrigerator in my office, which needed a sufficient explanation for approval by my supervisor. It was approved without issue, but I had to ask and share that personal information in order for that to happen. I did not want to disclose this pregnancy to my work colleagues or supervisors until I knew it was certain—and I was lucky that the early weeks of morning sickness were kind to me. With projects that took me into the field more than into my office, I was able to wait until almost twenty weeks to announce my pregnancy to my supervisors.

They were personally delighted and supportive that we were finally successful and would have our first child the following February. However, the conversation quickly turned to intense planning for the exchange of work tasks during my absence. I held numerous meetings and made many spreadsheets and lists of tasks and who would cover them while I was out on leave. My non-tenure-track position had recently formed some potential guidelines for promotion, so I also had those in the back of my mind. I also was desperately trying to maintain the productivity that was expected and needed, as heaven forbid something happen while I was out on leave and my job be dissolved, and then I would need to find a new position.

The university allowed for twelve weeks unpaid leave (FMLA) and the state allowed for four more weeks (up to sixteen). Given the time of year I was having my son and the childcare options around, my maternity leave needed to be at least fourteen of those sixteen weeks. That leave successfully took place to fourteen weeks, albeit some of it unpaid. Being on unpaid leave also created an additional financial burden, as I was responsible for insurance premiums we did not typically pay. Because of miscommunication with the human resources office, I almost lost the option to add our medically fragile child to my insurance the first year. My son was a slow-growing child, and doctors were keeping a close eye on him. It was truly a blessing to be unplugged and focused on my son for the first several weeks of that leave. It would not be until he was almost two years old that we would learn he has a genetic abnormality that systemically challenges his development. During this time, the stress and exhaustion only grew.

After returning to work, I experienced passive-aggressive retaliation for having a child and being out on leave. On the surface, I found my projects had been led in whatever ways those temporarily in charge had decided. Few of my detailed plans had been followed or supported, and my name and contributions were written out of the final report of a major project. I still hold no authorship on the public final reports of a high-level, nationally visible project for which I served as co-principal investigator for five years.

When I came back to work, it was also critical to my son's health to nurse him exclusively. He was not able to drink from a bottle effectively, and his daycare was far from campus. Each nursing session took about an hour round trip, and he needed that three times in a typical workday—meaning I had three more hours in each day that I had to find time for work before or after the typical schedule of 8:00–4:30. Initially I worked at night to meet those demands, but they took their toll. After a few months, I had to start pumping milk and sending it to his daycare, and thankfully he had grown enough to be sufficiently able to take a bottle. This routine lasted until he was eighteen months old.

Our second journey to conceive another child came with multiple pregnancy losses and infertility treatments, which were again half-heartedly understood and supported by my supervisors. During one pregnancy loss, I did not have enough sick leave remaining, so I had to be at work while miscarrying and took only one day off for the surgery. I let my supervisors know the day before the surgery that I would be out, and they seemed to comprehend what was happening. After the surgery, I was emotionally drained, and I needed a few more days to recover. So I asked my more supportive supervisor about the bereavement policy for the loss of a child. He did not feel it would apply but encouraged me to ask human resources. Through this, I did find out that the bereavement policy could apply to the loss of a pregnancy, but I felt comfortable taking only one of the three days for recuperation. Yet again, I was both physically and mentally exhausted more than I ever thought possible.

After two years of trying again to grow our family, we were blessed with a second son. This second pregnancy was much harder physically on my body, but I luckily avoided a lot of morning sickness in the first trimester. Things were going well until middle of the second trimester. At twenty-seven weeks, I began having contractions that put me into preterm labor, which luckily was stopped by interventions at the hospital. However, I was released on full bedrest and had to navigate how to continue working full-time because, again, I did not have the leave time accrued to go out three months prior to delivery. At this point, my remaining supervisor was the one who was typically more supportive, and he worked with me to work full-time from home. Still, meetings where I was needed would be scheduled with an unspoken expectation that I would come into campus because I was "working full-time." On most occasions, I had to ask to be conferenced in by phone rather than them offering for me to join remotely. This placed a burden on me to decide if I needed face time to show my full commitment to my roles and responsibilities, because if I did not, I was risking making progress in my career.

In the end, my second pregnancy went full term, and he was born completely healthy—two things I am eternally grateful for. During this pregnancy, it so happened that the university had adopted a paid parental leave policy for six weeks postpartum. I was truly thankful to then be able to utilize my small amounts of accrued vacation and sick leave, as well as the paid parental leave to take twelve weeks off with my second son. After about six weeks, though, I was getting calls and emails from work to handle "critical" issues, and they were ready for me to be back in the office.

As my pregnancy was harder on my body this time around, I needed physical therapy to recuperate, and my doctor requested I return to work on a part-time schedule, gradually working up to full-time. Going from four hours to six hours a day to full-time has been a three-month process. I am grateful that the university and my supervisor again supported the gradual return to work. But he or other colleagues then would schedule certain meetings where I was needed in the afternoon after my part-time hours would technically be over. I could shift my hours to afternoon only, but other morning commitments would often mean I would just have to stay longer than scheduled. Again, this placed the burden on me to have to step away and miss critical conversations, which could have jeopardized my progress in my career. Therefore, I stayed for as many of these situations as I could.

Overall, I would say that my academic research position, the supervisors I have had, and the policies in place at the university have been more supportive than not. The university's paid parental leave policy has been the best game changer and trendsetter in this arena. I am so thankful for that. But it is the subtle issues in being in a twelve-month academic position with less-than-flexible scheduling that make it so exhausting and so difficult to balance full-time work and the infertility, pregnancy loss, pregnancy, newborn schedules, lactation, and working with two children under the age of five that I have now experienced in my family life.

before she went up for promotion. And as a non-tenure-track faculty member, she faced different expectations regarding work-life flexibility; whereas tenure-track faculty may have more flex time, she was expected to be present in the office. Her story underscores the precariousness of scholar parents who are in non-tenure-track positions and who are reliant on the good nature and personal accommodations of supervisors when an institution lacks a family leave policy. And, most importantly, her experience demonstrates that a one-size-fits-all policy, applied dispassionately across all individuals, was not equitable, fair, or entirely legal.

Much like individuals and families often mark anniversaries of the deaths of loved ones, so do some academic parents recall the anniversaries of their failed pregnancies. One respondent wrote, "I *always* take off the day that my son died. My coworkers also know that my empathy reserves around that day are not for work. I have a difficult time concentrating around that time and my teaching isn't the greatest." Grief is complicated and persistent.

There are many important lessons to learn from this chapter, not the least of which is that miscarriage, complicated adoptions, and infant loss are all lower-order processes that contribute to higher-order outcomes. Miscarriages happen at work, in faculty and department meetings, while teaching, en route to conferences, and at invited talks. Adoptions fall through in private and heartbreaking ways, known only to the prospective parents. One respondent recalled, "My miscarriage was devastating to me. I couldn't concentrate, missed deadlines, acted like a jerk to people at work. It was awful. My boss was extremely supportive and without his help, I would have been even worse off." Support for parents and prospective parents experiencing loss is essential to their ability to recover, both personally and professionally. There is no one-size-fits-all approach to handling these situations, and a rigid set of policies applied uniformly to all cases would likely not meet the needs of all individuals. However, departments can craft general guidelines for accommodating a range of unforeseen circumstances, helping to offset some of the work-related concerns and helping parents grieve their loss. Increasingly, universities have a bereavement policy for pregnancy and infant loss, which, anecdotally, some women have begun to take. Having a set of guidelines helps the academic community to establish a set of expectations and contingencies for how the department will handle practical issues of covering classes and service obligations during personal emergencies and times of crisis.

The Long Game

Family formation is complicated and can contribute temporarily to a decrease in productivity. Broadly speaking, grief and loss of any kind, whether of a pregnancy, child, sibling, spouse or partner, parent, or other significant person—or pet—could contribute to a loss in productivity. Women are unique, however, in their ability to carry a child and experience the real biochemical, hormonal, physical, and emotional toll of fertility treatments, pregnancy, and the denouement and resolution of an unsuccessful pregnancy. Sometimes, grief and joy are intertwined, as another survey respondent revealed: "I had some miscarriages they didn't know about, but I also lost a baby at twenty-five weeks while his twin was born and was in the NICU. I had no leave because I didn't want it and just was convinced to give away one of my classes but wasn't happy about it."

We want to make it abundantly clear that while academic parents may experience temporary setbacks in their research productivity and teaching evaluations, women in academia with children outpace their peers in research productivity in the long run. Further, a recent study finds that it is gender—not children—that account for rank disparity between men and women. Being a woman, not being a mother, is the culprit in the differences between achieving tenure and promotion on par with men.

Best Practices for Supporting Colleagues on Difficult Journeys to Parenthood

What university administrators can do:

- Offer tenure extensions for documented infertility and miscarriages (Winegar 2016).
- Provide resources for support groups for faculty, administrators, staff, and students through campus counseling centers (Winegar 2016).
- Ensure that policies related to family formation, including adoption, miscarriage, and infant and child loss—including sick and bereavement leave—are communicated clearly and equitably to faculty and departments.

What department chairs and unit heads can do:

- Set up diversity training for department chairs, appointed mentors, deans, and tenure and promotion committees (Winegar 2016).
- Enact departmental policies for accommodating the teaching and service responsibilities during health emergencies.
- Communicate these policies equitably and clearly to all faculty.

What faculty can do:

- Expand mentorship foci to include issues along the family formation spectrum, including adoption, infertility, and miscarriage.
- Make use of university resources related to sick and bereavement leave.
- Be knowledgeable about your department's and institution's policies related to FMLA, bereavement, and sick leave.
- Be kind. If you know a colleague is experiencing a tough time with family formation, do not ignore this person.

8 Express Yourself

Breastfeeding and Lactation in the Ivory Tower

Breastfeeding is one activity that highlights the challenges that mothers *in particular* in the academy face. Pregnancy and lactation single out women for "unprofessional" behavior. Breastfeeding is time-consuming and often represents an opportunity cost for women scholars who must attend to feeding their babies. Milk expression, whether by pumping milk or by breastfeeding, averages thirty minutes per session, with an average of two to four sessions during the day. Not all parents choose to or are able to breastfeed, yet this does not stop others from commenting on their parenting decisions and passing judgment. Those who do breastfeed contend with medically supported reasons for regular milk expression, including the threat of dwindling milk supply and health complications such as mastitis. While breastfeeding has well-documented benefits, we strongly believe that fed is best and that parents should be supported in whatever feeding choices they make on behalf of their children and themselves. What many people don't recognize is that there are a lot of things that breastfeeding parents have to consider and weigh. We hope that this chapter will provide some insight into the tremendous amount of cognitive and emotional labor that is both unappreciated and uncompensated in breastfeeding and nourishing babies.

Our goal in this chapter is to meet you where you are: to acquaint you with the physical, emotional, and cognitive labor that accompanies breastfeeding—or not—one's child or to validate your experience in doing these things.

Professionalism and the Profession

Breastfeeding underscores how men's experiences and career trajectories are the norm or standard reference point in academia and in the broader workplace. When they breastfeed or express milk to feed a child, women are viewed as subversive, controversial, and unprofessional. Because the female body is hypersexualized in contemporary Western society, it is considered inappropriate to expose breasts or reveal nipples in public. While breast-feeding is exempt from public indecency laws, many public establishments routinely shame, ostracize, and even boldly confront breastfeeding moth-ers. Breastfeeding is not a sexual activity. While breastmilk is a bodily fluid like saliva, urine, and semen, the act of breastfeeding or pumping milk is not equivocal to using the restroom or self-stimulating. It is not a display of anything except for child nourishment. Yet men and other women alike feel embarrassed by witnessing the act of breastfeeding, and some of breastfeed-ing's harshest critics are women.

Breastfeeding is not unprofessional. Parents can and do work while breastfeeding or pumping milk. Brain function is not fundamentally compro-mised during lactation. In her *Forbes* article "What's the Etiquette for Breast-feeding at a Work Conference?" Jo Piazza (2017) says the following: "It is true that women should be able to breastfeed without harassment or shame. What is also true is that it still makes some people uncomfortable and in a work environment many women have no choice but to consider other people's feel-ings, no matter how outdated or misogynistic or crude." Note that the article is not directed at how men should accommodate or support women who are breastfeeding at conferences or help lobby on their behalf to change not only work culture but also conference and institutional policies. The entire focus of the article is how women can do better to pay attention to their work climate to see if it's appropriate or not and make accommodations for the benefit of other people.

Many Types of Breastfeeding Difficulties

Breastfeeding, especially with a first child, can be difficult. We asked our survey respondents about the challenges they faced in breastfeeding, many of which are related. Many breastfeeding parents reported problems with producing too little or too much milk. Many said that their babies had trou-ble latching properly. Some reported having issues with high lipase, which makes stored milk smell and taste differently, leading babies to reject it ("My Expressed Breastmilk Doesn't Smell Fresh" 2011). Many said they got mastitis and thrush. And many said that they experienced a lot of physical pain, includ-ing bleeding and cracked nipples. The physiology of breastfeeding means that in order for the parent to produce more milk, milk must be removed either by nursing, pumping, or hand expressing. When breastfeeding parents are unable to express milk, the short-term implications are painful engorgement, painful clogged ducts, and mastitis that feels like a combination of the flu and death. In the early months and through growth spurts, milk removal trains the mammary glands to produce more milk—a literal process of supply and demand. It is not feasible for breastfeeding parents to wait an entire day to express milk.

Supply

One of the primary concerns that parents report while breastfeeding is whether or not they are making enough milk for their child, if they have a low supply. The academic literature highlights that most breastfeeding parents are capable of making enough milk for their babies, but the perception is that the babies are getting insufficient nourishment (Amir 2006). In some cases, babies who are not getting enough milk may be diagnosed with failure to thrive, an infrequently diagnosed condition where a child is underweight due to insufficient caloric intake. The name of the condition—"failure"—rings in the mother's ear as she alone bears the guilt of not being able to provide breastmilk for her child. (We discuss a similar pattern regarding miscarriages in chapter 7.) A new mother reported the following on our survey: "Low supply due to stress, plus my asshole lactation consultant and mother-in-law scared me into using formula. I didn't need to but I had no support. The lactation consultant at my hospital was terrible, and I was hormonal and scared my baby was starving. I know now she was just cluster feeding." As another survey respondent wrote, "I had difficulty getting much volume of milk using the pump and so I would typically need to pump multiple times during the workday for twenty to thirty minutes to store enough milk. Supply was not a problem when I was feeding my daughter directly so this was frustrating." Some parents find that the breast pump does not remove as much milk as does nursing their child directly, so time away from the baby can be frustrating and the source of much stress.

Feeding the baby is an all-consuming activity, especially in the early weeks and months, and can be a very stressful time for breastfeeding parents. Some parents overproduce milk, and this can create problems with engorgement, leaking, and a predisposition to mastitis, or it can be the source of tummy troubles for the baby (Trimeloni and Spencer 2016). One mother reported the following problems: "Oversupply, which meant I had to pump to relieve engorgement after every feeding for the first four months. It was brutal. General anxiety around nursing enough, too much, etc."

Difficulty Latching and Other Problems

One of the first things baby and mother must learn is establishing a good latch to get the milk to flow. As many parents have experienced, nursing is one of the most unnatural natural activities. Breastfeeding takes practice and persistence, and within many cultures the process is supported by an extended community of mothers, aunts, friends, and grandmothers who help the new parent and baby learn this skill. In the United States, however, breastfeeding rates of children ever breastfed, or breastfed for several months, are shockingly low. This is in part due to the social stigma around breastfeeding as well as the work demands of parents who have highly variable access to professional protections for expressing milk. If lactating parents are unsupported at the start, they are much less likely to attempt or continue breastfeeding.

Poor latching is one of the most common problems. Some parents reported they needed to use a nipple shield for many weeks. This mother's experience summarizes those of so many others: "My child had a poor latch which led to milk blisters and ultimately mastitis. After I got mastitis I had a decreased supply and had to start supplementing with formula. This was around the time my child was eight months old. This also affected my pumping output." Another mother had a similarly hard time:

> You name it—I have had it. Plenty of mastitis and swelling and lumps and clogs. So painful. Lots of low supply. I had to pump around the clock for three months for my son while he was in the NICU. I had to spend one hour a day trying to teach my son how to nurse while he was in the hospital, but it took a while for him to learn how to breathe, swallow, suck, and do other things regular-term babies can do automatically. Both kids had severe tongue ties, and the guy who had done ten thousand of them said my son's was the worst he'd ever seen. The first three months of my daughter were pure hell, pain, severe pain, while nursing because of the tongue tie until it was fixed. I fed her over two years and my son is still nursing.

If the parent and baby are having problems related to latching, the parent may decide to exclusively pump. Pumping milk is much more time-consuming than breastfeeding, including the preparation, sterilization, and clean-up of pumping supplies. Some babies who have trouble latching will refuse pumped milk in a bottle if it is high in lipase. Lipase is an enzyme that breaks down the fat in milk, and an excess of it causes the milk to smell and taste sour or spoiled. While it is safe to drink, some babies refuse milk with high lipase. Other babies have food allergies or sensitivities, and mothers often have to adjust their diets. For example, some babies are sensitive to when the breastfeeding parent consumes dairy products or caffeine, which can present as colicky symptoms.

In other cases, the baby refuses a bottle and will only nurse directly from the parent. One mother wrote, "Baby would not take a bottle of breast milk (ever) so it was just me!" Another mother said, "I nursed my daughter in the car parking lots all around campus—my husband would bring her to me—there was not scheduling accommodation for her nursing. She spent a lot of time in my office nursing." Similar to advice given women in pain, many people suggest that women just "leave their babies at home" and that the "babies will figure it out"—meaning that they will get hungry enough to take a bottle. This may be true, but it is also patently unsupportive of the type of motherhood experience that a particular woman chooses to have.

Just leaving the baby at home does not solve the problem of breastmilk removal either, since the parent will still have to pump to retain their milk supply and avoid problems such as mastitis and clogged ducts. As one survey respondent said, "I often found I had to skip pumpings throughout the day due to meetings, classes, or advising which was often frustrating." Exclusive pumping carries a whole different set of challenges. Some offices are shared spaces, and some workplaces do not have dedicated lactation rooms. Electric pumps can be onerous to carry, and sometimes a critical pump part gets left at home. Many survey respondents noted they had bought last-minute manual pumps to get them through the day. Pump parts must be washed and sterilized, and milk must be stored in a refrigerator. And parents must remember to bring that milk home at the end of the day.

Moreover, time spent expressing breastmilk is time spent not working. If lactation facilities are not readily available, the process of expressing takes longer if the parent must relocate to find an appropriate space to express milk (Peters 2016). Sustaining and nourishing children can eat into the amount of work time available for women. Further, all of this adds to the mental load of attempting to balance work and parenthood.

Mastitis and Thrush

Mastitis is a serious illness resulting from incomplete milk removal, introduction of bacteria, or clogged milk ducts. Upward of 10 percent of breastfeeding people get mastitis, and many experience repeated bouts with it. Mastitis often requires antibiotics and can lead to stopping breastfeeding. Many mothers in our survey reported problems with mastitis, the symptoms for which include high fever, malaise, and breast pain and swelling. In extreme cases, breast abscesses from mastitis require lancing and draining.

Sometimes babies do not remove enough milk because they have thrush, or oral candidiasis, and nursing is painful or difficult for them. Sometimes, parents who take antibiotics for mastitis can get thrush, since they can cause an overgrowth of the body's natural yeast. The thrush-mastitis cycle can be difficult to break and is a continual source of frustration and pain for both mother and baby. As one mother wrote, "Pain! So much pain at the beginning. We saw a lactation consultant, then another one, and then went to a breastfeeding clinic in the hospital (which is a great resource that we're lucky to have). It was excruciating pain every time I nursed (which was about every two to three hours every day) for the first eight weeks. I didn't know if I was going to make it. But I did!" It is well documented that medical professionals discount women's pain, and as a result we know comparatively little about how to manage pain-related problems because they are routinely ignored, underdiagnosed, and poorly treated (Calderone 1990; Chen et al. 2008; Robinson and Wise 2003). For some women, pain associated with breastfeeding is met with a call to "just quit," which does little more than gaslight their experience.

Fed Is Best

Some parents are unable to breastfeed, or they choose to give their children formula. All parents should be supported in their decisions, free from judgment. Yet those who supplement breastmilk or rely on formula to feed their babies report obstacles related to social stigma, pressure, and guilt, all of which complicate the early days of parenthood. One woman wrote, "I have felt shamed by friends, caregivers, and coworkers for not breastfeeding in ways my coworkers who chose to breastfeed didn't face. Women who nurse are very encouraged to do so where I work." In the first vignette, Christina Fattore describes the troubles she faced breastfeeding, and the relief she felt in choosing to give her second child formula from the start. As one survey respondent said, "The mythology around breastfeeding creates a ton of pressure for professional women. As with all decisions around pregnancy, childbirth and childrearing, it's basically another opportunity for people to judge women. You're damned if you do and damned if you don't." Academics are prone to perfectionism, and this extends to parenting decisions. We are each our own toughest critics. In emphasizing that parents should be free from judgment with respect to how they feed their infants, we call on parents—especially mothers—to avoid self-judgment.

Healthy Moms, Healthy Babies, and Formula-Feeding

Christina Fattore
West Virginia University

Like most academics, we're taught that input equals output. If you study hard, you'll get an A. If you work hard at your writing, it will improve. If you write a lot, you'll publish a lot. We are socialized to think that we have control over our situations. If you don't get a job your first time out, there was clearly something wrong with your job packet. If you didn't get tenure, it's because you didn't publish enough. Success weighs heavily on your input. If you do the right things, you will enjoy the fruits of your success. It shouldn't surprise anyone that this is how I approached motherhood.

When I was pregnant with my son, I was convinced that I would breastfeed. I read all the books, went to all the classes, and talked with my friends who had done it with success. I did my research. It seemed as though my body was just supposed to know what it was doing. That sounds easy, I thought. My mom told me about how much she'd loved breastfeeding me, how she didn't have any issues, and she made it eleven months. I expected to do it for a year, which was my comfort level. I also was going to have a vaginal birth because, again, I read all the books and went to all the classes. Easy, right? I did the work, I studied hard, I was going to ace being a first-time mom.

I never expected what happened next. After being put on bedrest with pregnancy-induced hypertension, I was induced two days after my due date. The induction didn't take. I didn't feel one contraction. Almost forty-eight hours after I checked into the hospital, I was taken down for a C-section because the baby was just not coming on his own. During my C-section, my blood pressure dropped, and so they took me off the hypertension meds I had been on. I knew that I needed to get the baby to latch on as soon as I got back from the recovery room, and so we kept trying and he latched pretty quickly. I had it in my head from all the classes I took and the books I read that he didn't need that much because his stomach was the size of a walnut. Well, he cried. He cried and cried and cried. I kept trying to feed him. You have no idea how much is actually coming out of your breasts in those first few days. Three days after his birth, I spoke with the hospital's lactation consultant who agreed that he was getting enough and that he was satisfied, even though he would cry almost constantly. We went home that evening, and for twenty-four hours, I kept waiting for my milk to come in, for my baby not to cry, for him to be satisfied. Instead, what happened was at 2 a.m. four days after his birth, we went to the ER because he wouldn't stop crying and was running a low fever.

At the ER, he was crying and I was crying. He had also gotten down to seven pounds from his birth weight of eight pounds and thirteen ounces. The ER doctor checked him out and said he looked just fine. She asked me to feed him in front of her so she could make sure he was latching. As I was bawling, I tried to get him to latch. An angel in the form of a nurse came in and asked if I would be OK if she got me a bottle of formula. Formula had been vilified by all the books and classes I had consumed. It was a setup for failure. If you gave a baby a bottle, that's all it will want, and it won't want the food that was made expressly for them. But, in those five days, I realized how little control I had over the situation. I wanted my baby to stop crying. If this was the solution, do it. And guess what? He guzzled those two ounces of formula and finally settled in. The nurse sent us home with a bunch of samples to tide us over until we were able to buy some formula the next morning.

I kept trying to breastfeed him in the next few days and supplemented heavily with formula because my milk never came. I tried pumping after every feeding to attempt to trick my body into the first letdown. And it never happened. It wasn't until later that I realized that my milk never came because, after my son's birth and that initial drop in blood pressure, my hypertension returned with a vengeance. I had headaches, and my hands and feet swelled. I was borderline preeclampsia and so they put me on Lasix, which is a heavy diuretic. Put it together: diuretic plus a breastfeeding mother . . . not a recipe for success. But in my postpartum mind, I blamed myself. Why wasn't it as easy as other people said? Women in my online mom's group were complaining about an oversupply, and I was as dry as a bone. After that night in the ER, I cried every day, every time I tried to feed him and he was still hungry, every time I hooked myself up to my breast pump at 2 a.m. to keep the cycle going. After about a month of this torture, I had enough. I knew I wasn't ever going to be able to breastfeed my son. I also recognized that I had postpartum depression, which was something I attribute to my difficulties with breastfeeding. I wish someone had shared their struggles with me so I had a more realistic idea of breastfeeding and knowing I wasn't alone.

I spent four years with a bit of shame, as friends and family were able to successfully breastfeed. I couldn't be a part of their conversations because I fed my son formula. He was also sick a lot during that first year in daycare, so it was hard not to say, "Oh, breastfeeding has all those natural immunities built into it and he's not getting any."

Blaming yourself is easy. A friend of mine who also formula fed and was comfortable in her decision said something to me that stuck: If you line up a bunch of two-year-olds, can you tell which were breastfed and which were formula fed? How about a bunch of six-year-olds? High school seniors? Thirty-year-olds? The answer is no, you can't.

Unlike the good social scientist I am, I completely disregarded the variables that might come into play as I transitioned into motherhood. I did the research, I studied hard, it should have come easy. But like we learn in academia, success doesn't have constant returns to scale. There are roadblocks. Sometimes, reviewer 2 hates our paper when everyone else recommends publication. We might butt heads with someone in our department who holds a grudge come tenure time. There are greater systemic issues in academia that are beyond our control. It shouldn't be so surprising that there are certain things in motherhood that are beyond our control as well. Once you rid yourself of the expectation that motherhood is filled with situations you can anticipate or control, the easier it becomes. I learned this lesson in time to enjoy my second child.

Four years after the hardest month of my life, I gave birth to a beautiful baby girl who I decided to exclusively formula feed. Actually, my husband and I both discussed this decision, and he fully supported me. After watching my disappointment and my stress with our son, he thought it would be an opportunity for me to experience motherhood and that newborn stage without the extra stress of worrying if my milk would come in or not. I agreed with him because I would do anything to avoid postpartum depression again. The second time around, it was all different. My C-section was scheduled and went very smoothly. I was able to hold my daughter while still on the operating table, while I wasn't able to with my son. When I got back to my room, it was just my husband and my daughter. I was able to do skin to skin with her without the expectation of trying to get her to latch, and it was amazing. I felt that I was able to be a good mom to her and also to my then-four-year-old son.

I never realized what a fog I was in when my son was born because of my depression. In those first few weeks with my daughter, I was able to soak in all her loveliness and enjoy snuggles with her while she napped. I was able to read to my son and enjoy his first days in preschool. It makes me sad that I wasn't more aware of my son's newborn days because I was just going through the motions. I will also admit that I had a hard time bonding with him because my focus was on my milk production. I was able to bond much more quickly and easily with my daughter without that stress. More importantly, to me, I felt in control with my daughter. There are so many variables when it comes to childbirth and that whole first year. Who knew if she would have reflux like my son? Or if she would be a good sleeper or a bad one? What if she got sick? I could handle all those things because I recognized my emotional limits.

I do feel like I get judged by people sometimes when I say that I exclusively formula fed my daughter. People have asked "you didn't even try?" Nope, no I didn't. I also feel awkward when other moms are talking about their breastfeeding experiences at the bus stop or someplace like that and I have nothing to contribute. I feel offended when I read things online that formula feeders can't bond with their babies. I snuggled my babies through every bottle. Of course I bonded with them! I am also hurt by people who say that fed is *not* best, that you're giving your baby chemicals, you don't love them enough if you don't even try. I can honestly say that my son could have dehydrated badly or even worse if I hadn't started supplementing after that visit to the ER. However, I tell my story because I want other people to know that it is OK to formula feed, that fed *is* best, and that your mental health trumps the expectation that you should bend over backward to provide milk for your baby. I'm happy that I was able to do it all over again differently with my daughter, and I am confident that I made the right choice. And, for the record, if you line my son up with a bunch of other first graders or my daughter with a bunch of other toddlers, you can't tell if they were breastfed or formula fed.

Conferencing while Breastfeeding

One of the biggest challenges facing academic parents of young children is traveling while breastfeeding. To start, some women avoid conferences or other travel, which poses a career cost to them. Missing conferences means time spent not working, networking, researching, and engaging with peers and colleagues. Women considered many aspects of staying home from conferences in their survey responses; here, we list a sample of their reflections:

- I have brought grandparents with me to conferences to keep the babies—taking taxis to and from meetings to feed, hauling breast pumps and breastmilk through security, getting harassed by gate agents over whether the breast pump is a medical device and if I've exceeded my carry-on limit. It's a total hassle. I have had to cancel more conference appearances than I've actually attended in the past four years.

- I do it. I have brought my whole family to many conferences. I have breastfed at sessions or right after. I have held my baby while at conferences on other campuses and students passed by whispering about that "poor student with a baby" (they were talking about me). I was thirty-six and a professor. I skip lots of conferences that I would have to be at overnight.
- I sent my coauthor to conferences and have not attended them much since becoming a parent. I didn't like them before becoming a parent, and really didn't want to go afterward.
- Just pumped—I traveled only for short times so I wouldn't have an enormous amount of milk to travel with.
- None. I didn't attend any when I was breastfeeding.

Accommodating breastfeeding often means added expenses, such as paying for grandparents, partners, or other caregivers to accompany a nursing mom to conferences. In addition to greater travel expenditures, many breastfeeding parents elect to stay at the conference hotel, which may be more expensive than other surrounding options. As another mother wrote, "I had to pay extra money to stay at the conference hotel and pay for my mom to stay for the conference to provide childcare. In between sessions I would go back to the hotel room to nurse. I also ended up letting other mothers use my conference room to pump because there were no nursing or pumping facilities set up for conference-goers."

Everything Is More Difficult

The logistics of transporting children and their accoutrements, or leaving children at home and bringing breast pumps and associated parts, is complicated. At the very least, the parent will be flying with more baggage than usual or preferable. Gate agents have been known to give mothers a hard time with bringing their breast pumps—which is a medical device—as carry-ons. When flying with milk, the Transportation Security Administration may want to scan it. Flying with pumped milk entails its own challenges, including keeping it cold during transport. As one mother said, "The hardest part of breastfeeding as an academic was the travel. Not the conferences themselves, but the lack of a space to pump in airports and difficulty in transporting milk." While most airports now have lactation rooms or pods, this has not always been the case.

Both in transit to conferences and at the conferences themselves, women have been asked to pump milk in public bathrooms. One conference-goer made headlines in 2016 by pumping milk in the hotel lobby, when she had been directed to a public bathroom. Pumping milk in bathrooms is not only unsanitary but also demoralizing and dehumanizing.

Most survey respondents reported that conferencing while breastfeeding was at the very least difficult. Their words and experiences say more than we could describe, so we list several illustrative responses here:

- Not good. Even conferences that had seminars on work-life balance and family issues did a terrible job with that.
- Complicated, messy, embarrassing.
- Difficult and uncomfortable.
- I don't find conferences very compatible with bringing babies. Even if childcare is offered, it means sitting in a hotel room every evening. I avoid bringing my children.
- I was unable to take my infant. Stored breastmilk in advance. Pumped and dumped at conferences to continue production.
- I took my son to one conference when he was nine months old. I breastfed him in my hotel room and in the back of some sessions. There were no breastfeeding facilities.
- If the baby was at home, very inconvenient (lack of facilities/cold storage).
- I returned to my room repeatedly to breastfeed my daughter; I did not carry her around with me at the conference—she was sick, I didn't have breastfeeding-friendly professional clothes, I was interviewing and didn't want search committee members to see me in the hallway nursing an infant.
- Rushing back and forth to my hotel room frantically not to miss feedings, finding hotel staff walking my crying baby up and down the hotel halls, giving my spouse a moment of relief.
- The only conference I attended as a breastfeeding mom was the International Studies Association's 2016 annual meeting in Atlanta. My mom and daughter (twelve weeks old at the time) came with me. The main conference was in the Hilton with the Sheraton a couple blocks away. We stayed in the Sheraton which is also where the Kiddie Corp was housed. The only space for pumping was in the Sheraton. There was *no space* for pumping in the Hilton. Since I would have to return to the Sheraton for privacy, I just opted to go back to my mom and nurse. This meant, though, that my time at panels was limited. I couldn't easily pump between panels and go to more.

Some parents—albeit far fewer—reported different, and easier, experiences:

- Conference breastfeeding has been easy. My experience at the American Political Science Association's annual meeting in 2017 was great.
- I attended a conference during my parental leave and took the baby with me. It was not an issue although there were no specific facilities for this.
- I breastfed each of my kids at conferences and had no problems.
- I just brought my three-month-old to a small National Institutes of Health conference. It was great, but there were no changing tables in the bathrooms! Otherwise, people were very supportive or just neutral about the fact that I was nursing during sessions.

Our survey respondents offered a range of do-it-yourself solutions they have employed to manage the difficulty of traveling while breastfeeding or pumping. They recalled arranging private spaces to pump or breastfeed in the absence of a dedicated lactation space or mother's room at the conference; one respondent made use of a conference organizer's hotel room, another used a presenter's hotel room, and several others emphasized the importance of staying at the conference hotel to make it easier to go back to your own room for pumping or nursing breaks. Given the added expense and limited availability of conference hotel rooms, we recommend that conference organizers take care to ensure there is a dedicated space for breastfeeding or pumping parents in attendance.

On the Job Market

This chapter's second vignette contributor writes about going on the job market while breastfeeding. Women get competing perspectives about whether or not to reveal their "humanity" while on the job market. One survey respondent's account highlights the potential for campuses to embrace academic parents: "I set up a nursing lounge (pump, food, water, etc.) in a private office for nursing candidates. The department loved it, I had a crib in my office the first year, took the baby to research and faculty meetings. The parents all support each other." This family-friendly atmosphere is not universal. As related in chapter 2, women are sometimes advised to remove wedding bands and not reveal they are pregnant while interviewing. However, breastfeeding poses a different set of constraints: ignoring bodily cues to nurse or pump can quickly lead to serious health problems such as mastitis. Women are torn between needing to ask for breastfeeding accommodations and not wanting to seem un-serious about the position. Women may wonder, *If I ask for accommodations now, will my future colleagues perceive me as being on the "mommy track" and not a serious scholar?* Because some questions are illegal to ask during job interviews—such as pregnancy status and plans for future children— prospective employers may dodge important conversations to comply with official employment equity regulations. Cautionary tales abound: some scholars have had employment offers withdrawn after revealing they would need FMLA accommodation in their first semester. It is clearly illegal to negatively discriminate against someone based on their family status, but are there benefits to actively embracing a candidate's family status?

For a few short years when children are very young, everything is very hard. It's hard to manage work and family obligations when the stakes in both environments are very high and where the tenure-track and breastfeeding parent is often singularly and simultaneously responsible for success in both. For example, one parent mentioned her child cluster feeding; this developmentally appropriate phenomenon occurs during growth spurts and means that (1) the baby wants to nurse nearly constantly and (2) the breastfeeding parent has little time to sleep, work, or do much else (Krapf, Ursprung, and Zimmermann 2014; Mui 2014). The evolutionary point of cluster feeding is to increase the parent's milk supply to meet the nutritional demands of their growing baby. During these times, the effects of sleep deprivation are profound. Outsiders are nearly universally obsessed with whether or not the baby is sleeping through the night, a myth that is out of step with physiological developments. Mothers often feel the urge to throat-punch people who inquire about their child's sleep, as they too are feeling the negative consequences of interrupted sleep. It is important to remember that these precious and difficult times are fleeting and that an academic parent's scholarly output and teaching evaluations may suffer during the early years of parenting but are likely to rebound. We again reiterate that mothers in academia outpace their colleagues in publications in the long run (Krapf, Ursprung, and Zimmermann 2014; Mui 2014).

The next vignette captures how breastfeeding coincides with other significant life and academic milestones. This mother-child experience represents more than infant nourishment: it is emblematic of much larger struggles women academics face. Women have had to fight to prove they have been sexually harassed in both home and scholarly environments; the #MeTooPoliSci hashtag was born of egregious, decades-long, and institutionally protected cases of harassment and discrimination. Individual academics

Breastfeeding in the Academy: A User's Guide

Kelly Baker
Assistant Professor, Small Liberal Arts School in the Midwest

Before I start my story of being a nursing mother in academia, a few confessions: First, I had this vignette about 90 percent written in October and on my calendar to send out by the first of the year. I'm now five days late and counting. Sometimes it's hard to get to the finish line with two little ones, even when you're almost there. Confession part 2: as I finish writing this, I am sitting in a recliner at my parents' house, where I'm visiting for winter break, wearing yoga pants and a tie-dye shirt my students made for me last semester, nursing my daughter and awkwardly typing over her sleeping, suckling little body. This is how I've written throughout my "break," nursing a toddler and typing one-handed. I've finished a revise and resubmit and gotten a new article out the door, all the while singing the Itsy Bitsy Spider and playing Play-Doh and wrapping presents and hiding antibiotics inside yogurt to help clear up a pesky ear infection. Breastfeeding in the academy has become a self-reinforcing mechanism of keeping my career and my parenting somewhat in balance, where my body physically reminds me to take a break, stay grounded, and check in with my kiddos. The first draft of this vignette was also written while nursing, late at night on my iPhone notes app, twilight nursing and thinking about the peculiar condition of breastfeeding and the ivory tower.[1]

I had my son when I was in graduate school, and my daughter was born my third year on the tenure track, so I've breastfed my way through plenty of academia. I've been pregnant or nursing for the past six years and had to balance the needs of my very young children with my career for virtually the entire time I've been part of the academy. In many ways, my family is very lucky. My husband and I have been able to trade off and arrange schedules so neither child had to go to daycare before they were about a year old. I was able to use a dissertation writing fellowship to stay home full-time and write once my son was born, and then I took half a semester of (fully paid) maternity leave with my daughter. My husband had a month of paid paternity leave with our son, which he used to help me find pockets of time to write my dissertation. After our daughter was born and I was back to work full-time, my husband was finishing his master's thesis, so he wrote and stayed home with our daughter. This made it easier to keep her exclusively breastfed during the early months. My husband was able to pick up expressed milk from work when the supply ran low or bring her to my school so I could nurse her between meetings. For us, there is a constant blending of work and life in order to keep both of them more or less functioning.

Interviewing. My son was fourteen months when I started applying for academic jobs, and at that point I'd never been away from him overnight. The whispered advice floating around my graduate program was not to wear a wedding ring or mention anything about your family during the interview process. Families and tenure track, we were warned, did not mix—it brought up questions of divided loyalties, trailing spouses, and dual hires. Better to appear safely unattached. I kept my ring on, but no one had advice for me about breastfeeding—or the inability to do so when I was at interviews. None of the interviews I had that year asked about accommodations, nor did I feel confident enough in myself as a candidate and mother to ask for them.

The first on-campus interview is a nerve-wracking process for anyone. For a nursing mom, there's an added layer of anxiety. How do you pack a pump? Is there enough freezer stash for while you're gone? Pump and dump or try to freeze and bring back? Will you be able to store it? I had no idea, but these logistical questions paradoxically kept me preoccupied from really worrying about the substance of the interview (Will they like me? Will they think I'm smart? How will I teach a room of strangers for seventy minutes? How can I eat Thai food for dinner without spilling soy sauce down my shirt?). My sole point of contact for that first interview was the male chair of the department who was (I figured) at least forty years my senior. When he sent me the schedule for the visit, with no down time from 8 a.m. to 8 p.m. (not even a bathroom break), I figured I would just have to bear it. So, for the first time in more than a year, I went twelve hours without pumping or nursing. My body revolted. As I talked research and teaching strategies, my breasts screamed. "Where is your baby? Did you leave the baby in the forest? *Your baby is hungry! We have milk!*" It hurt. I leaked. I put back on my suit jacket and hoped it didn't soak through my new suit. I was filled to bursting when at last I got back to the room and was able to pump. I looked at pictures of my baby giggling and pumped fifteen ounces in one go.

Two weeks later, I had my second on-campus interview. En route, I lost the little plastic attachment that allows the pump to express milk and learned that the small town I was in did not sell one for my model of pump (let alone the social logistics of asking the male chair of the department, a mere two decades my senior, to drive me to a Target or Walmart). I was stuck. I tried to hand express, to little avail, and went an excruciating thirty hours without pumping or nursing. The interview was terrible. I didn't belong there. Again, my body pleaded with me, this time for a day and a half, to nurse my missing baby. I tried to pretend I was interested in the position. The only woman on the search committee told me it was a horrible place for women to work. By the time I got home, I was engorged, had developed mastitis in one breast, and was a hormonal, tearful mess.

The day-to-day. Luckily, I was offered, and accepted, a job at the first school I interviewed with, a small liberal arts university in the Midwest. My daughter was born at the beginning of my third year on the tenure track, which meant half of a semester off, and then back to teaching. I had to adjust to leaving my three-month-old at home and to the different rhythms around pumping. I could never build up a freezer stash, so I was constantly calculating—what if she's going through a growth spurt? What if I get home late? Will missing that pumping session to talk to a student about their paper mean my daughter doesn't get enough milk? It was always fine, but it was always a calculation—a blending. Even at work, I was responsible for my child's well-being. There is a lactation room on campus, but no one ever told me where it was. (It was created after an assistant dean was pumping in the bathroom because her office had glass walls). Luckily, I have an office with no internal windows and a door that locks.

I had requested a Monday/Wednesday/Friday teaching schedule so I could work from home on Tuesdays and Thursdays. Despite obvious advantages, this schedule gave me forty minutes between classes, which seems like a lot until you race against the clock, knowing you need to pump before you teach again. After class chatter: 5–7 minutes. *33 minutes remaining.* Rushing to the bathroom after students leave (pumping makes you thirsty, and having babies means you have to pee all the time). *30 minutes remaining.* Finding way to office, locking door (crucial!), assembling pump, reattaching weird plastic thing for fifth time, taking shirt off or pulling dress above hips and hoping no one can see through the blindless windows of your third-floor office. *24 minutes remaining.* Pumping, while scrolling through Facebook or Twitter or videos of your giggling or sobbing child to convince your milk to come down (8 minutes per boob, unless you're a superwoman who can pump two-breasted). *8 minutes remaining.* Storing milk, wiping suspicious milk drippings from clothes, floor, phone, anywhere else.

4 minutes remaining. Figuring out what you're teaching, grabbing supplies, filling water bottle, peeing again, and walking into class ready to go, right on time, with 0 minutes remaining. Piece of cake.

But of course, meetings get scheduled. Students need you. Colleagues think you're standoffish. Friends who want to go to lunch don't understand why pumping isn't optional. The grumpy chair who hired me once told a student, "I know she's in there—just pound on her door 'til she answers." I looked down, saw my topless self, hooked up to a cone and bottle, milk pouring from my breasts, and decided I could wait the student out.

Although my institution really didn't adapt to my needs as a nursing professor, it's important for me to note that I experienced no real backlash or recrimination. My administration was very visibly, vocally supportive of my leave (my dean and associate provost covered my classes themselves), but there aren't any faculty my age who have kids, so there was no real model. When I got pregnant and I asked some of the faculty with older children for advice navigating parental leave, I was told one of two things: "No one has ever done this before so you'll be the guinea pig" or "We just had babies in grad school or in May, so we didn't inconvenience our department." One woman told me that she rented out the apartment next door so her best friend could come take care of her baby so that she didn't have to take parental leave. When I pointed out that I didn't want to return to work so early—I wanted to have as much time as possible to bond with my new baby and to recover from pregnancy and birth—people were supportive but seemed puzzled as to *why* I would want that. Overly conscious of my status returning from parental leave, I overcompensated by doing more new course preps and taking on more committee work. I wanted to live my politics and be very public about being a parent, but the perfectionist voice inside my head insisted that I had to be doubly productive so no one could accuse me of putting my family over my job.

Travel. My five-year-old has been on two international research trips with me, and my one-year-old has been on one. They'll both come with me abroad this summer, grant funding permitting. I won't lie—in many ways international research is easier to conduct solo, but the on-campus interviews made me realize that, so long as I was nursing, I didn't want to be away from my family for my job anymore. I didn't want to be absent on weekends at conferences and weeks at a time on research trips. I also wanted my kids to experience the world. So my husband and I just started figuring out how we could make academic travel overlap as family travel. Last summer, we traveled to Greece. I'm currently writing a paper about the protests I studied while I was there, and my son's memories of Greek playgrounds, kind Greek grandmothers, and delicious Greek pastries weave together with my memories as I write. He wakes up, remembering a beach we played on. We look at pictures of that beach trip, which conjures memories of the LGBT rally we attended the next day. If my daughter wasn't nursing, perhaps I would have made different decisions and left them at home, choosing not to travel with a car seat and a stroller and the extra gear. But. People let their guards down around children. They strike up conversations, overcome language barriers. They explain to you what they want for their own children, how they see their future. Children take you to playgrounds, which is where I discovered the staging ground for the United Nations High Commissioner for Refugees humanitarian intervention for refugees in Thessaloniki. My children help me overcome impostor syndrome from being in a new place, they help me experience life as a local, seeking out sweets and a bathroom every thirty seconds. As a social scientist seeking to explain the social world, what could be more beneficial to a researcher?

For some people, this may sound like their nightmare. The constant blurring of worlds might provoke a permeant identity crisis, living partially in two worlds so never being fully present in one. And that's OK. If pumping works best, then do that. If formula works best, then do that. For me, I have moments of not being able to finish a thought and of wanting my body back. But it's also made me a fighter and an advocate for rights for parents in general and nursing mothers in particular. This year I was part of a subcommittee on diversity in hiring, and I was able to advocate for a universal design approach to faculty interview schedules, where breaks were built in to hopefully increase the success of a variety of candidates, including mamas who pump. I've started to advocate for dependent child travel scholarships to pay for airfare and childcare out of our professional development money.

Even as I write about breastfeeding and the academy, the act literally inserts itself—for parents in general (and breastfeeding moms in particular), the two are both constantly present, comingling and competing for attention. My daughter, now fifteen months old, nurses for comfort and to reclaim my attention. She toddles over, squares off her tiny shoulders, pushes my laptop closed, and clambers up onto my lap, nestling in to nurse. My son sees his opportunity and comes over with a book. Climbs up too. Nursing on the right, reading on the left. Time to put work aside, make a note of the last sentence, frantically push Command + S (who has time to redo work for deleted documents?), and slide back into mom mode. Later, my son goes to play basketball with his dad, and my daughter's eyes get heavy and close as she suckles in her sleep. I inch open my computer screen, begin awkwardly typing with my left hand, hoping to finish another few sentences before I get pulled back into mom world.

The truth is, there isn't a level playing field in academia. Nursing academics accomplish the same thing as our peers, but dripping milk and with a constant suckling companion. We have to logistically calculate how our bodies can produce food for a tiny human on a day-to-day basis, and for the days, weeks, and months we're sometimes expected to travel. And it's totally doable. It's possible to nurse, be a fabulous mom, publish, write, do research, and teach—but it helps to have resources. Talking about those resources doesn't make you weak—it makes these things possible. So ask for them. Time. Flexibility. Money. Understanding. Perspective taking. Understanding partners and colleagues. A few changes of clothes and extra accessories for the pump. We've got this.

Postscript. I think this is the first paper I've ever written where I continue to live what I'm writing about. It's a funny thing. When I finished the first draft of this piece, I was visiting my parents over break and enjoying the madness that comes with trying to get work done while the kids aren't in school. Now, I'm finishing revisions for this piece at a professional development conference with members of my administration. It's the first conference I've ever gone to without my kids, and I'm gone for four nights. Traveling here felt like I was missing a limb—I packed only a small rolling bag and a backpack. No stroller, car seat, LEGOs, diapers, wipes, or small people. It's amazing how easy it is to move through the world that way. My daughter still nurses in the morning and at night, more on weekends, so I brought along a little manual breast pump. More than being worried about my supply diminishing if I don't pump for this long, I'm worried she won't want to nurse when I get back, that this trip will wean her. So although I was feeling optimistic about balancing nursing and the academy when I wrote this initially, I'm feeling pretty emotional as I finish the revisions, wondering if our nursing relationship is actually over and I don't know it yet. Even if she's done, of course it's not the end of our bond. Both of my kids will still need me; I'll still bring them with me to see the world everywhere I can. But the necessity, the urgency, will be diminished. We'll be able to exist in the world apart from each other for a little longer at a time. But because it's so fleeting, because nursing lasts such a short period of a baby's life, it's all the more important for academia to make room for nursing relationships and not to force parents to make a choice between nursing and success in the academy.

and whole departments may support feminism and other efforts to de-bias the academy *in theory* in that they believe in democratic liberalism and are supportive of women's rights broadly defined, but when making hiring decisions and voting on tenure cases, feminism in theory yields to entrenched gendered stereotypes in practice, and those decisions and votes do not go in women's favor. Thus the nuances of breastfeeding are symptomatic of bigger issues in the academy, as the anonymous contributor illustrates.

The point of this chapter is to illuminate and validate the challenges that scholar parents face around the choice to breastfeed or not. If breastfeeding coincides with infrequent but important career events, such as conferences or job interviews, parents may feel they have to choose between their child, their health, and their career. The discipline broadly and departments and institutions in particular can help resolve some of these problems for scholars by proactively making accommodations for lactating colleagues, conference-goers, and prospective employees.

Best Practices for Supporting Parents as They Feed Their Infants

What conference organizers and program chairs can do:

- Ensure that there are adequate accommodations for nursing parents. This includes refrigeration and private non-bathroom spaces to pump milk or nurse a baby.
- Provide official networking opportunities as a part of the conference itself so women, especially nursing mothers, are not excluded from unofficial after-hours networking events.

What university administrators can do:

- Ensure that lactation facilities are available across campus.
- Encourage departments and units to proactively offer breastfeeding accommodations to job candidates.
- Promote university culture change to embrace.

Between Feminist Transformation and Maternalist Bias: A Personal Testimony from within the Chilean Academy

Jael Goldsmith Weil, PhD
Associate Professor, Centro de Estudios del Desarrollo
Regional y Políticas Públicas, Universidad de los Lagos
Funded by Agencia Nacional de Investigación y Desarrollo
(ANID), FONDECYT/INICIACION/ N° 1180717

Note: The author has changed positions and institutions since the time of writing; her narrative reflects her previous experiences and not those at her current institution.

It's June 6, 2018. I'm standing in the middle lane of downtown Santiago's main boulevard: on my left, the so-called *históricas*—those feminists who bravely battled Chile's military dictatorship in the 1980s. Occupying the lanes to my right, thousands of young feminists approach us—mostly college students fed up with sexual harassment and gender-based violence from their teachers, classmates, on streets, in universities and homes. They have been on strike since April of this year, managing to take over most educational establishments, including all of Chile's major universities. The first public signs of this began in 2016, when two students from the prestigious Universidad de Chile publicly outed a professor for sexual harassment. This triggered a #MeToo moment with a wave of testimonies from students with similar experiences of abuse from their professors ("Anuario de las mujeres 2017" n.d.; Carlsen and Miller 2018; "Sexo, mentiras y denuncias" 2016).

The first university to be closed down by the feminist movement was the Valdivia campus of the Universidad Austral de Chile after the university failed to address cases of sexual harassment and abuse denounced by students and university workers and students (Bartlett 2018). It was followed by other universities hitting a peak with thirty-two of the country's major universities paralyzed by late June ("Más de 30 universidades ya están movilizadas por demandas feministas" n.d.; "Recalendarización del año académico" 2018). During these takeovers, students occupied whole campuses (day and night), barricading the entrances off with desks and chairs. They held feminist consciousness raising and masculinity deconstruction workshops, organized cleaning and cooking crews while negotiating with university authorities on the necessary conditions under which they would return the buildings to the university. The longest of these takeovers lasted seventy-four days and was in protest to the decision to maintain the tenure of a law professor found guilty of sexual and work harassment ("Estudiantes ponen fin a toma feminista en Facultad de Derecho en la U. de Chile" 2018).

Today's protest will become known as the apex of the 2018 feminist mobilizations. It has brought together somewhere between one hundred thousand (according to organizers) and fifteen thousand (according to police accounts) protestors, was extensively covered by international press, and downplayed in the local news. I'm excited to be at the march, thrilled to see the joy and force of this feminist outbreak, a little jealous it didn't happen when I was in my twenties, and feeling old. I'm forty-two, an assistant professor in the political science department, and the mother of two young children. The sun feels good, but at the same time I am strung out, intellectually half alive. Last night my four-year-old daughter couldn't sleep, and the night before my baby son nursed six hours straight. While I affectionately observe the older women and get super excited to see the younger women march, my partner and baby-daddy is at home in the role of unwilling househusband.

Chile has maternal benefits that make my US colleagues green with envy: six months paid leave, two years on-site or fully financed daycare, one hour a day designated for breastfeeding, and a charter that pro-hibits firing women during this two-year period. However, these gen-erous maternal benefits—classified as "maternalist beyond the floor" (referring to the fact they go beyond International Labour Organiza-tion recommendations)—also bring long-term gendered legacies that work against women's advancement in the workforce (Blofield and Martínez Franzoni 2015). The idea of a "special" set of rights reserved for mothers has been inscribed in the Chilean state since the early twen-tieth century, conditioning female citizenship and crossing political frontiers and regime changes (Goldsmith Weil 2017; Goldsmith Weil 2020). Outcomes of this highly maternalistic organization of state ser-vices include extremely low infant and maternal death rates. They also include low levels of female incorporation in the workplace and one of the highest gender salary gaps in the region. While penalizing women in the workplace for having children is illegal, de facto discrimination is inscribed into the law. For example, employers with more than twenty female employees are obligated to fund daycare, providing incentives to hire men over women; fathers are allowed to take paternal leave only if mothers cede it to them; and men public employees have replacement salary caps lower than their women counterparts, which discourages their use of postnatal leave.

As the students march by with their multitude of performance arts, costumes, chants, and messages, my focus of concern shifts between whether the topless protestors remembered to put sunscreen on their nipples and my progressive discomfort as time for my next pumping session creeps up. I was born in 1975, international year of the women, grew up in the progressive United States of intellectual Jews, and have been a feminist for longer than most of these protestors have been alive. However, the struggles I am involved in at the moment seem premodern at best. This week I got the results of my tenure process. In spite of the fact that my numbers put me in the associate camp, the classification seems to hedge on whether I met my teaching obligations during the semesters I was on pre- and postnatal leave—an issue that had already come up in a productivity ranking in 2017. After formally protesting the verdict, I received a brief note with a few vague sentences and a phone call from the provost clarifying that the decision could not possibly be gender biased given that the committee included women.

Next to me on this sunny winter day is a colleague who has spearheaded and led the department's feminist initiatives and is sent to every single meeting where anything gender related is discussed. She is worried about repercussions if seen by the department authorities at the march. I don't really understand why but try to convince her being here is fieldwork, part of her job, and ultimately remind her it is lunchtime and there are no legal restrictions on where she takes her break. Lately, my academic world has become extremely uncomfortable and split into gendered spheres. While our students march under the banner of being the granddaughters of the witches, my male colleagues complain of what they call a witch hunt, where accusations of harassment, sexual misconduct, and rape could "happen to anybody."

At the same time, my closest group of female colleagues and friends are being delayed or denied tenure for reasons that just don't add up. Most recently, a colleague from another university just won two very prestigious and large grants. She also pre-applied for tenure, had two kids, made Mickey Mouse cookies for her son's birthday, took care of her father in his last days, and regularly publishes papers in peer-reviewed journals. The longtime dean in charge of elevating and presenting her case to the university-wide committee—without a comparable academic, publication, or breastfeeding record—advised her to wait until further accomplishments to submit her papers. Another colleague, whose teaching and mentoring practices have earned her important recognitions, has acted as an advisor in senate hearings, publishes in peer-reviewed journals and books, personally monitors her two kids' play dates, was ranked by the Chilean national science foundation as "highly productive," and has a pivotal role in professional organizations, was poorly evaluated for her "interpersonal relations" and "low productivity." These perhaps can be decoded as not aligning herself with the decisions to support anticipated tenure to young male colleagues who show promise, to delay tenure to a colleague with significant achievements (single mother, recently signed book contract), or to support the hiring of faculty members whose past conduct has been misogynistic.

As the march continues, my phone buzzes. I get a text message from a colleague—a single mother of two children—who is putting together an edited volume on maternalism. The pause in the semester caused by feminist takeovers has finally allowed her the time and space to finish the book, another unexpected connection between our students' revolutionary feminist fervor and professors' everyday struggles to simultaneously teach, breastfeed, research, mentor, advocate within our disciplines, write, engage in public outreach activities, organize birthday parties, advance ourselves professionally, and engage in feminist activism. Having gotten enough of the march, my colleague and I walk back to the office: she brings back a flag as a souvenir. I bring an empanada to eat at my desk while I pump and prepare classes and feel squished between the optimism of this feminist revolution and the persistent experiences of bias against mothers in academia.

What department chairs and unit heads can do:

- Ask job candidates what breastfeeding accommodations they need—and provide them!

What faculty can do:

- If you are traveling while breastfeeding, your pump counts as a medical device and does not count against your carry-on quota.
- Print out and keep handy your airline's breastfeeding policy, including pumping supplies.
- If possible, pack your milk in smaller quantities (five ounces or less) to meet Transportation Security Administration standards.
- Support breastfeeding colleagues.

Note

1. Twilight nursing is where a baby (and hopefully the mother) doesn't fully awaken but nurses in a semi-asleep state. Think of an all-night milk buffet.

9 Looking Back, Moving Forward

Conversation Starters for a More Inclusive Academic Environment

To normalize academic parenthood and foster more inclusive campuses, we must recognize and engage with the difficult realities that individuals and families struggle with as they try to balance their personal and professional lives. Some of these truths are ugly. They expose double standards for women and men, shifting benchmarks for tenure processes, stacked decks against non-tenure-track faculty, and unrealistic expectations for graduate student parents. But many of these truths highlight the very best of our nature: administrators who uphold the values of transparency and diversity, supervisors who advocate for their colleagues and who treat their faculty and students with empathy, coparents who work together as a team, and colleagues who pick up the slack when they are needed most.

The previous chapters have explored some of the most challenging times in an academic parent's life and career, highlighting shortcomings in university support systems and suggesting potential improvements. As we noted in the book's introduction, we speak most directly to the experiences of academic parents in the trenches of early childhood and early career. Many scholars with older children have repeated with encouragement, "It gets better." In this chapter, we look beyond the strategies for just getting by to encourage some measure of optimism: work and life are imperfectly balanced and full of challenges, but there is joy and meaning in the struggle.

Society often treats children as private goods that consume their parents' time, attention, and resources, and parents, alone, reap the pride and joy benefits of their offspring. This view misses the big picture for why our work as scholars and parents matters: we are raising the next generation of scientists, teachers, artists, medical professionals, civil servants, and contributing members of society. We are also raising the standards for how women are treated in the workplace and in the home.

How can academic parents not only survive but *thrive*? If we can answer this question, we can begin to have the conversations that make our campuses, departments, professional associations, and informal networks more inclusive, supportive, productive, and representative. To start, we must remember that the onus to make academia more supportive of women, parents, and families should not be on women alone. Men must be active advocates for institutional change alongside their women colleagues, students, friends, and partners.

Academia is a profession that rewards innovation. Colleges and universities strive to be on the cutting edge, to embody innovation, and to make the most of human potential. To live up to these standards, colleges and universities should be on the forefront of efforts to reduce gender gaps and level the professional playing field (or board game, as we envision it). As we have discussed throughout the book, universal, transparent and clearly communicated, and equitably applied parental leave policies and other accommodations go a long way toward embracing parents in the academy. In the United States, this means that colleges and universities should be exemplars of sound policies that go beyond the bare minimum protections provided at the state and federal levels.

At the outset of this chapter we discuss our survey respondents' answers to the following question: "What is the best advice you have received or given about work-life balance?" We have grouped responses into five broad categories to offer insights into best practices for navigating common obstacles or concerns that arise in both professional and personal life. The two vignettes in this chapter feature the voices of senior scholars whom we asked to reflect on what the profession meant to them as they started raising families and what it means to them now. After the first vignette, we outline suggestion for policies and initiatives colleges and universities can implement to support faculty, staff, and students who are navigating academia with children on the way or in tow. This discussion is also rooted in our survey responses and offers faculty, department leaders, and campus administrators a list of practical suggestions to consider. The chapter's second vignette follows the discussion of best practices and offers reassuring commentary from an academic mama and her grown and successful children. It is our hope that this chapter will underscore to readers that the work done as graduate students, researchers, faculty, administrators, and other academics, and the work done as parents and caregivers, matters.

Best Practices for Daily Survival and Success

One of the most enlightening sections of our survey of academic parents involved advice for academic parents in the proverbial trenches, especially those who are in the early stages of their careers while starting or growing their families. We asked our survey respondents to share the most helpful advice they have either given or received on the subject of managing work and family life. In studying their responses, we have identified five categories of best practices for the individual academic parent's daily survival and over-all success. (Later in this chapter we turn to the university- or department-level practices that can help foster a more inclusive campus and profession.) These categories include self-care, partnership, multitasking, the profession, and parenting.

Self-Care

Survey participants emphasized the importance of self-care for navigating the tenuous early years of academic life and parenthood. Self-care is among the easiest aspects to neglect, and women are often praised for their selflessness and ability to prioritize others' needs before their own. Yet self-care is the cornerstone of keeping the delicate balance between home and work in check. One survey respondent said, "I can't be 100 percent in all my roles all the time," and another said, "You can't do everything well—learn to accept doing some things mediocre." Self-care can mean different things; importantly, it means *not* excluding things that matter to your individual well-being. Put differently, you can give your 100 percent effort to the activity you are doing at that moment: If you are in parenting mode, be fully in parenting mode. If you are working, be fully present at work. If you are engaging in self-care, whether that be having a shower, a walk, a workout, a quiet lunch, an hour with a coffee and a magazine, a kickball game, or a commute, give that activity your full attention. Give yourself permission as well to delineate firmly between work and home activities.

Self-care can be difficult to prioritize because of pervasive guilt about working too much or too little, or not spending enough quality time with kids and family. One senior scholar advised not working on evenings or weekends. This may seem like a radical and impractical suggestion, but it is possible with a few exceptions, such as time-sensitive deadlines. People who work late into the evenings and on the weekends—and especially those who humble-brag about it via social media—may not be as productive or happy as they think or portray (Primack et al. 2017). As Cal Newport (2016) suggests, doing the deep work involved with writing may be made inefficient and less produc-tive with social media intrusions, and this can be compounded by a keeping-up-with-the-Joneses strategy of staying at work later than your colleague across the hall.

Efficiency, not time logged, is a better determinant of success (Pozen 2012a, 2012b). One respondent also noted that children may make academics *more* efficient, simply because there is no time to waste. Susan Sell's vignette in this chapter echoes this sentiment. At the heart of the suggestion to avoid working during evenings and weekends is the notion that an important element of self-care is the practice of setting limits or boundaries. Several respondents offered advice urging parents to simply "say no!" to tasks that take time away from children and partners, from the research and writing that are essential to tenure and promotion, or that sap the energy and creativity that are already in short supply. If you have a hard time saying no to things, consider flipping the script and focusing on what you are saying yes to when you affirm and uphold your boundaries. In our culture of FOMO (fear of missing out), it can be hard to turn down requests for fear that you may forgo a great opportunity. Opportunity costs are like that! If you have a clear roadmap and vision for your scholarship and work priorities, it may be easier to turn down requests that do not serve your long-term goals. One respondent suggested to "focus on what you will think is important to have achieved when you're ninety." If that means only attending the required department or university events and service obligations and saying no to the rest in the early years of parenting, then so be it.

In a similar vein, one respondent advises that when the kids are young, you should do what you can just to survive. With near universality, our survey participants mentioned that the most difficult time is during the early years of parenthood, which are characterized by sleep deprivation and sickness. Another respondent observes that it isn't just the early years that present challenges for parents and that every stage of child development and family life has its own advantages and disadvantages, but also that each difficult period is only temporary. Several other respondents recited the line "This, too, shall pass."

In the spirit of doing what is possible to get by, a common piece of advice from our survey respondents was that parents should be gentle with themselves. Both academia and parenthood can be exhausting, with far more opportunities for (self-)criticism than praise, so showing oneself grace is essential for overall well-being and even professional success. Several survey respondents offer absolution for personal and professional shortcomings: *Be kind to yourself, and forgiving.*

A little stress can be a great motivator, while a great amount of stress can inhibit action. Letting stress accumulate is counterproductive, and in order to survive simultaneous parenthood and academia, you have to figure out a way to hit the reset button. Forgive yourself for a crappy lecture, giving your kids too much screen time, or eating that whole box of Girl Scout cookies. Forgive other people, too, like your partner.

In *The Four Agreements* Don Miguel Ruiz (1997) offers sage advice alongside forgiveness: "Don't take anything personally; always do your best; be impeccable with your word; don't make assumptions." We add an important caveat to Ruiz's advice: women are socialized to care what others think, and we would be remiss to overlook the powerful social and institutional forces that shape gendered responses to criticism, failures, and setbacks. An important element of self-care involves seeking out colleagues, mentors, and coauthors whose advice is constructive and empowering rather than destructive and belittling. Furthermore, recognizing the institutional factors leading to inequities problems will help create positive change. In our call for self-care and forgiveness, we are not advocating for accepting or ignoring inequities. Academia and society in general need more people working for structural change, so an important element of self-care may involve—for those who are able—challenging injustices as they arise.

Partnership

Partners, spouses, and coparents are key players in the strategies for managing work and family life. Several of our survey respondents gave advice specifically on the subject of partners and best practices for surviving and thriving *together*. Many of these responses emphasize the importance of choosing a partner wisely, finding someone who supports and understands the work that goes into a successful academic career. One respondent observed that it may be best for academics to find non-academic partners, which may alleviate the two-body problem, reduce the potential for competition, and broaden the focus within the household beyond the peculiarities of academic life. But, of course, these decisions are highly personal and outside the scope of this book. What many of our respondents did emphasize was the importance of balancing responsibilities within the household and working together.

Given the tendency for faculty members to have some degree of influence over their schedules and, if they have a manageable teaching load, flexibility during typical business hours, it can be easy for the academic parent to become the default person to handle doctor's appointments, school events, and household tasks like meeting the plumber for emergency repairs. Once again, this flexibility does not readily apply to adjunct or contingent faculty or other faculty with heavy teaching loads. For those academics who do have a more flexible schedule, it is easy to fall into a pattern wherein the partner with the more forgiving schedule handles the inflexible tasks and events.

Sharing the load is essential. Whatever this looks like in each individual household, a system of divided responsibilities helps to ensure that one parent is not taking on the majority of the household management and parenting load. As one respondent wrote, "If both people aim to do 80 percent it might end up fair." Finally, communication is paramount. As one respondent cautioned, "Babysitters are cheaper than divorce." Prioritize your partnership, and check in to make sure both your needs are being met.

We acknowledge that the survey respondents who offered advice on work-life balance related to partners and burden sharing in the home write from the perspective of academic parents who do have partners living under the same roof. For academic parents without partners or dual-academic couples separated by long distances, the strategies for balancing professional and family responsibilities will look different. For these parents especially, informal and institutional support systems are key to success. The next category of advice—on multitasking—has broad appeal for parents with and without partners.

Multitasking

Work-life balance is a myth. Several survey respondents suggested that perfect balance between the personal and professional is unattainable, and that instead parents are better off focusing on management of competing demands. Identify systemic solutions to help make fraught times easier. For example, one academic parent puts her children to bed in the next day's school clothes instead of pajamas to avoid morning tantrums; another family plans meals for the week to avoid last-minute "what's for dinner?" panics; screen time can help parents balance working from home to meet research deadlines and teaching obligations with children at home. These solutions are feasible for harried parents, given a little creativity and preparation.

Many of the responses that fall under this category recommend delegating or outsourcing the time-intensive but mundane household tasks and paying for quality, reliable childcare. Respondents noted that if the household budget permits, hiring someone to clean the house, having the groceries delivered, and buying pre-prepared foods will save time that can be better spent actively involved with one's family or engaged in teaching and research. In one respondent's words, "pay for your time back." Of course, this advice assumes that families have the financial means to pay for time-saving services, which is not the case for many families and may be especially out of reach for graduate students, contingent or adjunct faculty, and families with one income earner. Not everyone can pay for their time back. Yet the underlying message, one that is universally applicable within academic parenthood, is to focus on the most important things that will foster personal and family well-being and professional success and to find shortcuts for the tasks and demands that will not.

There is too much advice about parenting, parenthood, and work-life balance to reasonably digest, much less implement. Similar to the advice from chapter 8 on breastfeeding, do what works for your family. One of the advantages of the internet is the prevalence of support groups for new parents who have questions about everything. For many survey respondents, finding a local online group led to a cascade of benefits. New parents do not need to reinvent the wheel; they need to get connected to the information that will help them make the best decisions for themselves and their families. And the great thing about online parenting groups is that someone is almost always guaranteed to be awake at 2 a.m. to respond when you have a question.

Proximity to support networks helps to alleviate some of the pressure on multitasking parents. Two respondents specifically lamented their distance from their children's grandparents and other family members, advising those who can to live and work near family to have a support network to rely on. Another respondent observed that friends and neighbors can provide much-needed social support. Given the realities of the academic job market, many academic families build their informal support networks with friends, neighbors, or colleagues to compensate for their geographic distance from relatives. Whatever the composition of this network, it can be essential for the times when there are more tasks than time to complete them or money to outsource them.

At the heart of this discussion of multitasking is the observation that everyone is just trying to make it through each day with health, children, and job intact while parenting in the trenches of academia and child development. As one respondent remarked, everyone will be able to do different things at different times in life. There will be periods in which the demands of family formation and parenting are all-consuming and work takes a back seat. There will be times when professional demands require parents to lean on support networks, family, babysitters, or longer days in daycare to meet book manuscript deadlines, assemble a tenure portfolio, or grade exams. There may also be times when your support networks can't come through for you, and you will learn the depth of your own strength. Our goal here is to move the conversation from getting by to thriving. A significant part of that transition involves finding solutions to daily challenges, but much of it must come through better institutional policies and support systems, which we discuss later in this chapter.

The Profession

The formula for academic success varies by department and institution, and each person should have a clear understanding of the guidelines and expectations for a successful tenure and promotion case. *Ask what is required for tenure and promotion, and adhere to those parameters.* These parameters are not often clear or clearly communicated, and no one enters academia knowing how to put together a dossier, so seek them out, write everything down, and prioritize the tasks that will lead to tenure and promotion. Best practices, such as maintaining a strong, explicit focus on short-, medium-, and long-term goals, can help formalize your workflow and minimize distractions. Many successful scholars believe that accountability is an important aspect of getting projects through to publication. Find your academic support system—the scholars who will read your early drafts and give you feedback, who will nominate you for awards, and who will help publicize your successes. And then pay it forward and do the same for them and for your students and junior colleagues.

Women often spend time on activities that do not bolster their chances for successfully earning tenure and promotion, including taking departmental or university service opportunities that are low profile and yield modest accolades. *Do things that will foster your portfolio and earn the esteem of your immediate colleagues and broader peers.* Students often seek attention and advice from women scholars for non-academic problems, especially mental health issues, which are on the rise. *Connect students with university resources that can best help them and protect your work time.* Successful academic parents—especially those at research-intensive universities—protect their writing time.

Many scholars offered the advice to do a "good enough" job. Yet it's difficult to know whether being good enough is actually good enough, especially in preparation for critical times like mid-tenure review or job market interviews. Being good enough means taking the sage advice of senior scholars who advise early-career scholars not to perseverate on manuscript drafts: get your papers out the door and under review. Being good enough means choosing service assignments wisely and making excellent use of your time at work so you can be fully present with your family at home. One senior scholar practices the art of "chipping," meaning that every time she has a few free minutes—like waiting for students during office hours—she chips away at tasks that can be accomplished in short bursts of time. She codes a few lines in Stata, grades a few assignments, preps the next day's lecture, or responds to a few emails. The end result is that she captures an hour of time in small segments to accomplish tasks that don't require the focus, stillness, and concentration dedicated to writing time. Similarly, another scholar protects her writing time by charting her online activity, introducing automated accountability (via RescueTime), and not letting small intrusive tasks interrupt the time she has devoted to working on manuscripts (Collins et al. 2014).

Academia is beginning to understand the special challenges that women and their partners face during the early childhood years. In our profession, groups funded by the National Science Foundation, such as Journeys in World Politics and Visions in Methodology, offer mentoring opportunities aimed at plugging the leaky pipeline and keeping women in the profession. Conferences have started offering informal cafés and early-career scholar networking opportunities, such as the Pay It Forward program in the International Studies Association, which has now diffused to regional conferences, and the mentorship program in the American Political Science Association.

Parenting

With near universality, scholars report that the early years are the hardest and that things get better as kids get older. However, academic parents of very young children may find this reassurance cold comfort. Either the experiences with newborns, toddlers, and young children or the upheaval of starting a brand-new academic job far from family and social support systems would be difficult. Combined, these two life events together can feel isolating and overwhelming. On top of this, the injustices new academic parents face—such as unequal policies where mothers must use their sick leave after childbirth while men continue to accrue theirs, or where fathers treat family leave as a sabbatical to improve their CV or go on the job market—compound feelings of frustration. New academic parents scarcely have time for their work and families, much less for challenging systemic inequalities.

Time is often of the essence for academic couples, especially women who may be entering later years of childbearing age and undertaking the risks associated with this. There is never a good time, or a perfect time, to start a family. The right time is when it is right for the prospective parents, and that is a decision concerning only those people. If you are on the job market, you are allowed to bring your baby on job interviews. If you are pregnant, you may also request assistance. You do not need to remove your wedding band. You are allowed to be a person with a life. An on-campus interview is physically and mentally exhausting enough without adding pregnancy or an infant to the equation. Ask for the accommodations you need, including time to nurse or express milk. This is especially true if your baby is exclusively breast-fed. This will give you the opportunity to decide whether a department will be a good fit for you as well.

Our hope for this book is that readers will understand that the individual-level stories are representative of a cohort of scholar parents and are not idiosyncratic or unique. The struggles the vignette contributors describe speak to systemic issues like the two-body problem, unobservable problems like infertility, and the extended months and years of sleepless-ness and sickness that early-career new parents contend with. Still, many of these stories have happy endings and point to successful careers *and* close relationships with children and partners. Professor Susan Sell's vignette is one of those stories.

Susan Sell, professor at the Menzies Centre for Health Policy at Austra-lian National University's School of Regulation and Governance, recalls the lack of women mentors during her graduate student days and discusses the practicalities and joys of parenting in the academy. She recounts the day she watched a senior woman graduate student give a confident presentation of her research and how the inspiration and encouragement she drew from that (unwitting) role model shaped her early career. Sell also details the influence of motherhood on her academic productivity, benefits of an academic career for parents, and the joy she derives from mentoring younger women in the profession.

Best Practices for Navigating and Setting University Policies for Family-Friendly Campuses

Each chapter contains a list of best practices related to the chapter's theme, and here we present several overarching recommendations for improving parent-scholars' success in academia. We derive these recommendations for individual scholars, department or unit heads, and administrators from sur-vey responses and the vignettes, best practices from evidence-based litera-ture, and our own experiences in mentoring workshops in the profession. We have broken this section down into three categories to highlight the practices that are most directly relevant to individual scholars, department heads, and administrators, but we recommend that readers who are not short on time read each set of recommendations to take in the bigger picture of the work that lies ahead.

The Lack of Women Mentors

Susan Sell
Professor, Australian National University

I grew up in a lively family of seven. Once I decided to give up my original dream of becoming a nun when I was six, I knew that no matter
what I wanted to be a mom. Always interested in history, writing, and
geography, I grew up thinking that I would become a lawyer like my
dad. He loved what he did and shared that enthusiasm with me. Our
family dinner table conversations were often about history, politics,
Vietnam, Watergate, and the civil rights movement. Two of my broth-
ers were of draft age during the late stage of the Vietnam War, and my
mother was active in civil rights. I found these animated discussions to
be fascinating and the issues important and urgent. I had a wonderful
woman high school US history teacher who devoted a lot of class discussion to Watergate and who taught me how to write papers. In college I majored in political science with a focus on political theory. One
summer during college I had the opportunity to work in a law firm and
realized that it was not the right path for me. A political theory tutorial
at London School of Economics in my senior year of college helped me
realize that I really wanted to be a scholar.

Pursuing a PhD in political science as a woman in those days was
not so easy. My college advisor discouraged me from pursuing an academic career. He told me that I "talked like a sixteen-year-old" and that
the scholar's journey was a lonely one. He said that I found the world
to be "a big and interesting place," and he recommended that I pursue a career in library science instead. I ignored his advice, as I usually
have when someone tells me that I cannot do something. I entered the
University of California–Santa Barbara's doctoral program in political
science as one of about three to five women in a program of about one
hundred in total. I had no women professors and not many women
role models. While I had some fine professors there, there was a lot
of sexism and harassment then and no formal channels or procedures
for reporting it. I ultimately transferred to UC Berkeley to complete my
PhD. UC Berkeley had a higher proportion of women students than did
Santa Barbara, but we were still a distinct minority. There were very few
women in international relations, my concentration, but the UC Berkeley experience was excellent and I had a wonderful mentor.

I had no women professors for my coursework. At UC Santa Barbara I observed how my women colleagues presented themselves in
academic settings. Some prefaced their remarks in seminars with "this

probably isn't important but . . ." or some self-effacing comment. My high school history teacher constantly reminded me not to preface my in-class remarks with "this is probably going to sound stupid but . . ."; it was a habit hard to shake. One fellow student flirted with her professors, complimenting them on their wardrobe or giggling at their not very funny remarks. A few others tried to act more like men. None of these offered very appealing role models for me. At UC Berkeley I took a research seminar that combined students just starting to develop their dissertation projects (me) and students finishing up. One woman fellow student, who was presenting her findings in her last semester, gave an impressive and confident report. I thought to myself, "That is the way that I want to come across as a female academic!" She was calm, fully in command of her material, articulate, and serious. She also was comfortable expressing gaps in her knowledge without apologizing for that. This was a revelation for me, as I had not witnessed that before; I found it to be very inspiring, and the memory has stuck with me all of these years.

Before I started my family I suffered from some measure of perfectionism. I never thought my work was quite good enough and wasted too much time worrying over paragraphs. I was slow to send things out for review and had a fraught time getting my dissertation published. However, once I had my son, I let go of the perfectionism and learned to use my time more wisely and efficiently. We had less than full-time childcare but knowing that I had only x hours of childcare each week really got me to focus. I had to let go of perfectionism and spend more time producing and less time fretting about it.

In the early days of motherhood, pre-tenure, I would find myself trying to get work done when the baby was napping. More than once I found myself feeling irritated when the baby woke up and interrupted my work. I felt terrible about feeling irritated by my newborn. So I made up my mind that from then on, when I was with my baby I would be 100 percent with my baby. When I was at work or my baby was in childcare I would be 100 percent with my work. That was a really constructive and helpful mind-set for me. I started doing mainly busywork during my babies' naps, answering emails, and so on, so interruptions would not be a big deal.

My university had a six-week parental leave policy, but since my son was born in July it made little difference. I had two months of bedrest before he was born and some medical complications afterward. I was barely healed when the semester started up in late August. When my second son was born in late September, I had to teach the first four weeks of class. A substitute took over for the middle six weeks, and

I returned to finish up the last few sessions. It was not good for the students or for me. My fellow women colleagues and I fought to get a better parental leave policy in place for our junior colleagues. We did not want others to go through what we had gone through. Ultimately academia caught up with our lives and adopted more generous parental leave policies.

Academia offered many benefits for motherhood. The flexible schedule was a godsend. My husband had a nine-to-five job, but when I was not in the classroom I could be available to take our children to the doctor or dentist or whatever. One of my sons received special assistance from the county, and I was grateful to be able to be home with him when the therapists came to the house. I could learn from them and better help my son. On days that we had no childcare I could stay home if I was not teaching or in important meetings. If my child was sick I could stay home. More than once I brought my kids into the big lecture hall with coloring books and other distractions. If I got an urgent call from the daycare I could usually pick up my children if I needed to take them for stitches or other medical issues. I might have to wait a few hours to finish teaching my class, but I could get there.

I felt very fortunate to be in academia for this flexibility that helped me to balance my professional responsibilities with my most important job as a parent. I had good friends in other professions that were not so accommodating. One friend and mother was in a high-powered law firm. Once she had children she could see no path to the partner track. When you are a litigator your client needs you to be available twenty-four-seven. A number of women lawyers I know left private practice and took government or public interest jobs that had more predictable hours.

My first post-PhD position was as a visiting assistant professor. At a fall semester department barbeque a handful of women students approached me, gushing with enthusiasm that they would finally have a woman professor. I found it unsettling. I told them, "You don't know anything about me. I may be horrible." It bothered me to be seen as a category rather than as a person.

One of the great joys of my career has been mentoring younger women in the profession. I joined the faculty at George Washington when it was in a rebuilding phase. We were doing a lot of hiring and hired a number of terrific women faculty members. For a time, there were three senior women in international relations, and we hired four more junior women. I knew of no other department in which women were so well represented in international relations. It was wonderful to see how the profession was opening up to women in what had traditionally been considered the men's subfield.

I have loved supporting my PhD students and following their journeys as academics and parents. The work-life balance is always a challenge and the stresses of academia are real. I never feel like I have quite gotten that balance right; it's a continuing process. One bit of advice for new parents—make the time to go on dates. We never did enough of that, but it is time well spent. I cannot imagine a more rewarding career—a lifetime of always learning, always being challenged, and being inspired by students, colleagues, and peers. But for me the best job of all is mom.

Individual Scholars

We offer the following recommendations to individuals who are or hope to become academic parents:

Be knowledgeable of your department's and campus's policies for tenure and promotion as well as family formation. For tenure and promotion, find out how, when, and in what form mid-tenure review occurs and begin compiling the materials you will need for your dossier, starting in your first year. Keep notes on your courses, ongoing research projects, service work within and outside of the university, relevant community service or civic engagement, and contacts within the discipline who may be in a good position to serve as external reviewers for your tenure file or peer-reviewed research. For family leave, find out how much leave time the department or university allows for pregnancy, childbirth, adoption, and bonding; this is most relevant for scholars in the United States and other countries that lack parental leave policies. Learn about job protection provided through local and national government policies like the Family and Medical Leave Act or universal parental leave policies in the countries that require employers to grant leave for new parents. Do not be afraid to ask for help clarifying the department or university's policies surrounding tenure and promotion or family leave; as our survey respondents observed, many institutions have policies that are vague, difficult to access without intimate knowledge of the recesses of the human resources department, or inconsistently applied or that have recently changed.

Be organized, be prepared, and ask for what you need (within reason). When it is time to negotiate family leave, if you must negotiate it, first draft a plan proposal with what you realistically need given the guidelines of your department and university, and do not show up to the meeting unprepared. Determine who will cover your classes and responsibilities in your absence. In many cases, the individual—not the department chair or unit head—will be responsible for finding a teaching replacement. Put everything in writing, and get everything in writing. Write an email to your department chair, unit head, dean, or human resources representative (as appropriate) summarizing your in-person conversation with the negotiations and concessions. Once your family leave begins, set an out-of-office response and protect your family time. When it comes to family leave, the dissertation or tenure clock, and campus job interviews, ask for accommodation; you most certainly will not get what you do not ask for.

Foster relationships in the profession. These connections are valuable for all scholars, but especially for scholars who do not have tenure yet or are not in tenure-track positions. Colleagues can write letters of recommendation for jobs or tenure applications, collaborate on research projects or course development, be an advocate on job search or tenure and promotion committees, advise on research or professional development, or simply lend moral support and friendship.

Make excellent use of your time. When you are at work, be present. Reduce distractions as much as possible and focus on the work that will help you finish the dissertation, compile a stellar job application, secure tenure and promotion, teach engaging courses, and foster professional relationships. Do not procrastinate; children have a way of running fevers just before a conference paper, journal review, or manuscript submission deadline. When you are at home, be fully present with your family. Time spent away from research and teaching is vital for creativity *and* for familial relationships.

This advice will not eliminate the structural obstacles confronting academic parents, especially mothers, but should empower individuals to make the best use of their limited time and ask for the help and resources they need to stay in the pipeline. The advice that follows speaks to department and unit heads in their capacity as gatekeepers, mentors, and advocates.

Department and Unit Heads

We offer the following recommendations to department or unit heads, so that they may foster a more equitable environment for their students and colleagues:

Departments should provide and maintain an accessible list of departmental and campus policies related to family formation, childcare, and lactation. These include policies about family leave, teaching and service responsibilities, stopping the tenure clock, on-campus childcare or support for childcare emergencies, and breastfeeding and lactation support. Many survey respondents noted they were unaware of their department's, college's, or university's official policies. Many others reported that such policies do not yet exist or are unequally applied. With near universality, survey respondents pleaded for more transparency with regards to the availability of this information and the equitable application of family leave policies, especially among individuals in the same department. The caveat for this is, of course, that family formation processes vary widely, including easy and difficult pregnancies and adoptions, and some individuals may need special accommodations given the complexity of their cases. If the university maintains an on-campus childcare center, ensure that information on this service is available to all eligible students, faculty, and staff. Similarly, if there are policies related to children in campus buildings or contingency planning for childcare emergencies like illness or weather-related school closures, make those transparent. Ensure that the department complies with local and national policies that support breastfeeding and lactating parents, including provisions for non-restroom space and time to express breastmilk or feed an infant. To the best of your ability, apply departmental and university policies equitably across individuals, including non-tenure-track faculty.

Negotiate with your faculty. Put differently, do not fail to negotiate with your faculty. We have been appalled and shocked by the number of survey respondents who mentioned that their chair or dean refused to negotiate with them or denied their requests for accommodation in flagrant violation of university regulations or even state or federal law. You can contact your union representative, university ombudsperson, human resources, or the Title IX office to begin a formal complaint if you so choose.

Do not discourage your women students or assistant professors from starting families. Many respondents shared stories of colleagues or supervisors admonishing them about getting or being pregnant at perceived inopportune times, such as during graduate school or before earning tenure and promotion. Our point here applies to students and faculty of all genders, but the advice to delay parenthood is almost exclusively given to women students, not to their peers who are men, and as such is inherently sexist and biased.

When your employees are on parental leave, respect their time away. Refrain from unnecessary intrusions, such as emails or phone calls, about details that can be resolved in their absence.

Connect job candidates with a local real estate agent during on-campus interviews. This person can serve as an impartial third party who can answer questions that candidates may not want to disclose to the hiring

committee. These could include questions about housing prices and neigh-
borhoods, school districts, childcare availability and costs, and other personal considerations.

Department chairs and unit heads possess sufficient leverage to shape
norms within the department, if not more broadly within the university. We
encourage these individuals to use the resources at their disposal to ensure
that their faculty, staff, and students are able to survive and thrive in the academy even as their responsibilities at home and off campus increase. Department leaders, like individual scholars, are not fully able to eliminate the
factors that lead to the leaky pipeline phenomenon, but with commitment to
the cause they can help create a more family-friendly atmosphere.

Administrators

We offer the longest list of best practices here, as policy change within academia is often most successful when the commitment starts at the top. At the
most basic level, support looks like enforcing and communicating existing
policies.

**Communicate family leave policies to department or unit heads, who
should themselves communicate the policies to faculty and staff.** In our
survey, we found significant knowledge gaps and disparities between men
and women regarding knowledge of official policies. This should not be a
"women's issue." Women should not be burdened with carrying the institutional knowledge of family formation policies, or even norms within departments. Men should be as knowledgeable as women in this domain.

**Provide a list of university policies related to family formation, child-
care, and breastfeeding and lactation support on campus—unprompted—
to all job candidates.** The campus visit for a job interview might involve
oblique discussions about school districts and daycare availability that send
signals to the candidate about family-friendliness. These features about the
local community should be standardized and provided to everyone. This will
help protect the department and university from entering the dangerous
realm of asking illegal questions of a candidate, such as "Are you married, do
you have (or want) children, or would you like to know about family leave
policies?"

**Grade yourself. Run university-wide annual surveys about parent-
hood and family formation to understand the needs of faculty, staff, and
students on campus.** Ask faculty in anonymous annual reviews or an annual
survey of the department or university about family formation policies, and
publish the results of the survey. This promotes a culture of transparency and

demonstrates a commitment to fostering an equitable work environment with accountability.

If administrators and department heads work together to foster transparency and consistent application of family leave policies, model and respect work-life separation, and communicate the relevance of family leave policies to faculty, staff, and students of all genders, campuses can begin to be more supportive of parents. Support for existing policies is, however, the ground floor. We urge academics and administrators with the capacity to do so to push for systemic change that moves our profession past the ground floor of basic human decency and creates a more humane, supportive, and diverse academy. To that end, we propose the following best practices for moving beyond common existing policies:

Use the cluster hiring model. This approach to hiring helps to increase the number of new faculty and staff from underrepresented populations and provides better support for those newly hired faculty and staff through cohorts. Be mindful, however, that giving faculty two tenure homes can set them up for failure. Joint appointments in different departments can mean that a new faculty member will potentially have to satisfy different disciplinary and departmental requirements that may be at odds with one another.

Institutionalize mentorship programs for junior and senior faculty across departments. Mentorship is a vital component for success. In some departments no senior women colleagues are available or willing to mentor junior women scholars, so these programs are especially important for academic women. The Pay It Forward model established by the International Studies Association, which pairs junior and senior women scholars in a research workshop setting, has been very successful. Mentorship is also important for ensuring the success of involved academic dads, LGBTQ+ faculty, and faculty of color, so implementing mentorship programs that support the range of intersecting identities among faculty will help foster a more inclusive campus.

Establish a policy of mandatory paid parental leave and apply it universally. Consider how other countries get it right with respect to parental leave and family support initiatives and model these approaches. This advice applies to campuses within the United States. If the US government will not institutionalize paid parental leave, colleges and universities can at least do their part to provide this benefit for their faculty, staff, and students. Parental leave is not sick leave, nor is it vacation. Parents should not be required to use these policies for family formation purposes. Under the broad umbrella of universal parental leave, the following policies and practices will protect vulnerable students and faculty in the family formation process:

Ensure job and course protections for adjunct faculty who take parental leave. Accessing parental leave benefits should not cost contingent faculty their jobs.

Ensure protection for graduate students who take parental leave. Provide parental leave accommodations to graduate students and give them the option to pause the degree completion clock. Encourage faculty and departments to accommodate student parents who need to make up coursework missed due to childbirth, adoption, or miscarriage.

Offer course reductions for women with tough pregnancies/ infertility and parents working through difficult adoption processes. While willingness to disclose these situations will vary, a policy permitting course reductions for faculty experiencing these medically and emotionally difficult processes will improve accommodation options available to faculty and departments.

Ease the process of extending the tenure clock. Offer a universal and automatic tenure clock extension option for new parents. This will help to reduce the likelihood and impact of departmental repercussions, since arrangements will not be ad hoc. Establish an automatic tenure clock extension for each birth, adoption, or guardianship. Offer the possibility of extensions for miscarriages and infertility. Consider making the tenure clock more flexible, with half-year or semester extensions instead of full-year extensions as appropriate. Include the option to forgo the tenure clock extension at the individual's request. Institute a similar and equitable policy for non-tenure-track faculty to ensure they get the privileges and protections their tenure-track colleagues receive.

Establish or improve mechanisms for reporting harassment and discrimination. Establish a system of anonymous reporting for people facing discrimination in an effort to reduce toxicity, discrimination, and harassment within departments. Create positions for or expand the availability of Title IX office help or liaisons for academic parents. This is especially important for women experiencing bias or harassment related to pregnancy or parental leave. Further, adopt an official stance (similar to anti-bullying policies) in support of faculty parents facing departmental backlash, and reiterate this position as cases arise.

Facilitate campus discussions and initiatives to support parents. The university ombudsperson or equivalent advocate is a central figure well positioned to facilitate discussions on ways to improve support for academic parents (both students and faculty), but individual faculty and department heads can spearhead dialogue and workshops as well.

Some of these suggestions go well beyond the policies and practices in place at most colleges and universities today, and that is the point. Each of these recommendations contributes to a more hospitable climate that provides scholars with an intellectual home in which they can thrive. This supportive climate will inevitably lead to improved recruitment and retention of diverse faculty and students and ensure that talented scholars are not forced out by institutional obstacles.

The chapter's second vignette contributor considered quitting but stayed in the game and has devoted much of her time to ensuring that junior scholars have the support they need to do the same. Kelly Kadera, associate professor of political science at the University of Iowa, writes about the daily struggles of early family life—including the attempts to balance her graduate work and her partner's job constraints, and later to balance work and parenthood in an effort to lean in—and the joy of witnessing her children's academic successes and activism. Professor Kadera's children—Lily, Madeleine, and Maxwell Moloney—coauthored the vignette with their mom, offering the perspectives of adults who not only survived but thrived as the children of an academic mom.

The View from the Ground Up: Work-Life Happiness and Why Lower-Order Processes Matter

In documenting large-scale gender discrimination within the academy through observations of Chutes and Ladders, discrimination in faculty hiring processes, unequal benefits of family leave, unequal service burdens, discrimination in student evaluations of teaching, and the gender gap in citations and syllabi, existing studies point to a need to understand better the sources of bias and inequality within the academic profession. Studies of widespread gender-based discrimination necessarily focus on macro-level processes and outcomes. We see a need for better understanding of the lower-order processes, the often unseen daily realities that shape the observable phenomena.

The lower-order processes we have described in this book point toward toxic work environments for women and parents. Research demonstrates that academic institutions that fail to support work-life balance risk losing women faculty to stress-induced burnout, via departure to another institution

Journeys of and with an Academic Mama

Kelly Kadera and Lily, Madeleine, and Maxwell Moloney

At several early points in my academic career, I considered quitting. The multiple demands of conducting research, teaching, and raising children seemed like too much. But when I contemplated alternative lifestyles, I concluded that being an academic mom was the best one for me and for my kids. My three children have grown into young adults, making this a good time to reflect on that decision. Was it the right choice? Did I make mistakes, or do I wish I had done things differently? What were the trade-offs and challenges? What advice would I give young academic parents today?

Decision Making in the Early Years

While in graduate school at the University of Illinois, I got engaged. Shortly before the wedding, my fiancé was offered a job in a mid-sized southern city without a university. He asked me to move with him. Moving would have advanced his career, and would have greatly slowed, if not halted, my progress to a PhD. I thought of other graduate students who lived away from their home programs and how hard it was for them to finish their degrees. I thought of the years of living on food stamps as my mother tried to survive on her server's wages and tips and sporadic child support from my capable but unwilling father. If I gave up on being a political scientist, how would I ever be financially independent? How would I care for my future children if I ever had to do so alone? How would I earn a living and also have time to help with homework? The choice was easy. I refused. He married me anyway, and we had three children. Consequences, mostly good, and some difficult, arose.

Maddy was two years old and Lily just two weeks old when we packed up our two-bedroom apartment in Champaign, Illinois, and moved to Iowa City, where I had taken a job at the University of Iowa. Until this time, Maddy enjoyed a charmed life: learning to fish with her Snoopy pole in the little fountain pond in the middle of the apartment complex, playing with Robbie Diehl when his mom, Martha, and I traded childcare, visiting with Tío Gary (Segura) or Uncle Ron (Maggi), attending Illini basketball games as a lap child, and only occasionally going to a sitter's while Mama worked on her dissertation. Now there was a new baby in the family, strange men took away the boxes containing all her toys, we moved to a new house, we didn't see Robbie anymore, Papa didn't go to work, Mama was gone a lot, and when Mama was home, she was preoccupied with nursing and caring for Lily. Maddy, who had been a very easy baby and toddler, suddenly began sucking her thumb and acting out. What had I done?

But just as I began to wonder whether I was capable of "leaning in" or whether that was even the right approach to life, Maddy did something ordinary yet extraordinary. She played dress up, swapping out her red Snow White cape for a pair of my shoes and my briefcase. As she clumsily paraded through the house, I asked her what she was doing, and she proudly proclaimed, "I'm going to work, Mama!" In that moment, I knew. I could not give up, even with the extra stress and challenges. Maddy and Lily deserved a world where strong women thrive and where they could expect rich life options.

Two years later, after assuring my mother that her desire for more grandchildren would not be satisfied by me, I got pregnant with Max. That baby boy became my strongest feminist. Maybe it was predestined, but I couldn't be prouder.

The Upside

All three of my kids grew up in ways that challenged traditions and gender roles, perhaps in part because their own mother challenged them. My young women, Maddy and Lily, are both pursuing careers in science. Maddy is completing her BS in environmental science, with the goal of teaching science at the elementary level. Lily is a PhD candidate in chemistry, working with a female PI on nanoparticle synthesis for solar materials. She, as part of an all-women team, has just published her first article (Lee et al. 2018). Max, my young man, loves languages and is pursuing an MA in Spanish, with research interests in masculinities, gender performance, and violent memory in twentieth- and twenty-first-century theater. Attending the 2017 Women's March in Washington, DC—advocating for women's equality, LGBTQ rights, and science—with them remains one of the most rewarding and meaningful experiences of my life.

Raising a family also influenced my own research and teaching. One fundamental social process of early childhood, the spread of disease, which I watched unfold as Max and Maddy got chicken pox and I decided to immunize Lily, influenced my conceptualization of transmission rates in conflict contagion (Kadera 1998, 374). And much of the hazard analysis of my article on democratic survival was written in a hospital (Kadera et al. 2003) while I simultaneously read medical studies on risk factors affecting recovery after bypass surgery and cared for my mother who was recuperating from that surgery. My sense of my students' life experiences and circumstances has evolved as my children became college and graduate students themselves, filling out

Professor Kelly Kadera (*left*) with her children Lily, Madeleine, and Maxwell Moloney. *Kelly Kadera*

frustrating FAFSA forms, finding part-time jobs, searching for meaningful fields of study, and finding amazing mentors.

The flexibility of professorship, more than any other feature, provided these benefits. Many professions allow women to succeed, be good leaders and mentors, and make important contributions. But few provide the same ease in scheduling parenting duties like attending conferences with teachers, sports competitions, and performances. That flexibility came with trade-offs because it became hard to tell my kids, extended family members, or volunteer coordinators that I was unavailable. People believe professors have almost unlimited free time and comment on how nice it must be to teach only two days per week, ignoring all the other work faculty must squeeze into their schedules.

The Challenges
Raising kids while getting tenure, and even afterward, challenged my physical, emotional, and intellectual strengths in ways I can only appreciate now. I remember, for example, moving through some of the kids' youngest years, sleep-deprived, like an automaton. My husband found a job in Iowa City a few months after we arrived, and we traded the kids off, with occasional daycare until they went to school. They pursued hockey, gymnastics, ballet, volleyball, orchestra, and show choir, with all the attendant chauffeuring and volunteering that went with those activities. And my own extracurricular life was nonexistent until I realized, in my early forties, how much of a toll that was taking on my own physical and mental health.

Professional challenges of motherhood and academia started right in my home department. They included tense exchanges with senior colleagues about gendered norms in a department that often began or extended meetings past 5 p.m. and where the wives of male colleagues regularly attended dinners with women job candidates. I remember teaching in a computer lab so small that my pregnant belly could not squeeze between rows to help students analyzing data and students who commented that women professors should keep their personal lives at home but lauded male professors as kind and modern when their young kids came to the office or class on odd occasions.

Conferences in the days before childcare services meant attending fewer conferences and leaving the kids at home when I did. A few months after Max was born, I drove to the ISA Midwest meeting in Saint Louis with a man colleague. When we arrived at the evening reception, a senior man scholar greeted my colleague by name, and then turned and asked me, "and what do you do in Iowa City?" He clearly assumed that women accompanying men must be wives. Stunned, I simply replied, "I do international relations research, like everyone else at this conference." After the reception, I went with a group to dinner, but the restaurant was only a bar, with cocktail waitresses dressed in short black skirts and leather bustiers. As a nursing mom, I needed real food, and I walked back to the hotel to try to find something there while the others (all men) stayed to drink and network.

Once the kids reached preadolescence, they took turns accompanying me to conferences, where they watched me present my research and explored the world's museums, historical monuments, wildlife, and cultures. As a real treat, I coauthored a paper with Max (and Cameron Thies and Laura Sjoberg), and we presented it at the Global South ISA conference in Havana, Cuba, in 2017.

Happily, I can also report that we've collectively made real progress. My department has (mostly) shifted to normal hours for official events, and child production and care has become more evenly normalized for men and women faculty. I've helped provide childcare for guest speakers, workshop attendees, and participants in Journeys (a mentoring workshop for junior female IR scholars run by myself and Sara Mitchell), by recruiting Maddy as a sitter. Maddy, as a fortunate consequence, has met some incredible young women academics and their kids and has attended several Journeys research and career and gender sessions.

In Their Words
I asked my kids to offer their own thoughts on what it was like to have an academic mom and told them their observations could include

difficulties too. They all chose to write short lists, which readers might appreciate. After presenting them, I briefly reflect on themes.

Lily J. Moloney
My mom being a professor means

- Knowing how to write good undergraduate, summer internship program, and graduate school applications
- Knowing what to look for or avoid in choosing a school or a mentor
- Understanding professors are people
- Respecting professors (you best believe you are calling your professors "Dr. X" unless told otherwise, and the grade you got was the grade *you* earned)
- Knowing work sometimes needs to come before play
- Observing a woman role model in a nontraditional gender role who also advocates for others (including me) to break away from these roles
- Getting advice when you call about an academic problem (such as grading or writing your first publication)

Madeleine M. Moloney

- Help with homework and school
- Advice with academic choices
- Incredible role model
- Permission to be intelligent
- Seeing the fun side of school
- Bragging rights about how smart my mom is
- Mom's absence from some dance competitions
- Chances for me to go to conferences in state and out
- Journeys (seeing strong, smart women leaning on and supporting each other)
- Financial freedom to do things like ballet
- Having a mom around for school breaks
- Having a mom around before school in the mornings

Maxwell T. Moloney
Pros:

- She taught me to challenge myself and others around me.
- She inspired me to develop and value relationships with people different than me. I think this has especially taken shape in my relationships with mentors and professors who are women.

- Because she is an academic and an educator, her work schedule has always been similar to my school schedule, so she was always around while school was in session, and our breaks lined up.
- She always helps me reason through homework and projects whenever I need it, even if it's something she isn't familiar with. In high school this meant she would help me work through chemistry problems. Now it means she helps me reason through Spanish linguistics articles and my own projects about Spanish literature.
- Her job takes her to interesting places all around the world, and sometimes she takes us with!
- Curiosity may have killed the cat, but it certainly didn't kill my mother. Among the infinite things my mom taught me, curiosity is undoubtedly the thing I value most. Not only is she curious and inquisitive, but she did a lot to make my sisters and me the same.

Cons:

- (This one's a little bit silly.) She's way smarter than me so I can never win an argument, which was pretty frustrating as an angsty teenager.
- I remember times where she seemed exhausted. I have a lot of memories of her grading, reading, and writing while everyone else in our family was getting ready for bed. My sisters and I used to sit in bed with her while she graded papers before going to sleep.
- Looking back, I don't think my mom was able to prioritize herself, especially while my sisters and I were young. She always had a lot on her plate, and self-care seemed to take a backseat for a long time.

Much of what Maddy, Lily, and Max shared surprised me. Maddy pointed to our family's financial stability as affording her opportunities. Max said that he remembers me working when he and his sisters went to bed. Lily offered a pithy maxim about work before play. These observations surprised me because I hadn't considered that they were aware of these truths of ours. We had never discussed them before. Lifestyles teach kids lessons that they may not articulate until they are adults.

All three also talked a lot about academics. They mentioned me helping them with various aspects of their academic lives, including homework, research, publications, and choosing universities and mentors. Notably, they also reflected on how that support translated into their current scholarly lives. My parenting philosophy has been to help my kids, much my like students, find what they're passionate about, equip them with the skills to pursue those interests, and encourage them to explore and develop their own, strong identities. Seeing the payoffs when my young adult children value intellectual playfulness and curiosity, when they express pride and confidence in their own minds, when they respect others' perspectives, and when they develop and practice good strategies and habits pleases this academic mama.

Max alone mentioned the toll parenting took on me, and he and I talked about this passage after he wrote it. He told me he remembers me asking if it was OK if I started to take a Pilates class. This part of my life was both sad and transformative. Every person in my household, save me, was deeply involved in two extracurricular activities: the kids each playing a sport (or two) or dancing plus playing an instrument, and my husband playing two sports. My time outside work involved making and packing lunches, coaching homework, chauffeuring the kids, volunteering, household chores, and so on. When I started to take Pilates, and then yoga on a regular basis, everyone revolted. I heard complaints about me not being home, demands that I miss Vinyasa to accommodate others' schedules, and frustrated queries about why I was being so selfish and no longer laundering everyone's workout clothes and equipment. Proudly, I stood firm. And one day, Max and his sisters told me that I was so much more fun to be around than I used to be. They were right, and so was I.

Advice
As a summary, let me offer a few words of advice for young academics of today, including my own children.

Ensure your own path. My mother left her server job to go to business school and worked her way up managing credit accounts for a Midwest business. I have reaped great intellectual rewards from coauthoring and much help from important mentors. But I always made sure I was also able, if need be, to make my own way and demonstrate my own contributions, whether in terms of family finances or scholarly ideas. Knowing you can go it alone if necessary gives you the confidence to build strong partnerships with others.

Find good allies. Despite what I said above, many people helped me by trading childcare, advocating for changing gendered norms in my department and in the profession, and by insisting, when I questioned it, that I had important contributions to make to the study of world politics.

Put self-care above everything and everyone else, and do not wait until your children are older to do this. Even if your goal is to provide for others or to do great research, you must first be well rested and a healthy, whole individual. If housework or yardwork slides, hire help. Make a family budget for self-improvement activities, in terms of both monetary and temporal costs, and allocate resources fairly across all family members. You will be teaching your children to put their own self-care first, giving them life skills too.

If you choose to have a partner, choose wisely. Ask what expectation they have about who does laundry, fixes broken cars, attends parent teacher conferences, stays home with sick kids, and so on. Ask what roles their own parents performed and if those were gendered. Ask what kind of family model they want to provide their children.

Involve your kids in your intellectual and professional life. Model this life and teach them how playful and fun it can be. Let them experience the joys of academic success and passion of scholarly dialogue. Whether they become academics or not, they will use these lessons as students, as homework coaches, and as responsible citizens of the world.

or from academia altogether (Gardner 2012). Political scientist Anne-Marie Slaughter (2015) suggested that women can't have it all. Yet this proposition itself is gendered: rarely do we pose the question, *Can men have it all?* A significant narrative has emerged over the past several years since Sheryl Sandberg (2013) urged women to "lean in" and not to "be gone before they're gone"—in other words, women should not surrender their career ambitions just because they are pregnant. This is easier said than done, and the notion of leaning in has received a well-deserved dose of criticism, including from former First Lady Michelle Obama (Goldstein 2018; Wamsley 2018). In our survey, many respondents noted that the work-life balance is a myth and that the metric for measuring which part of life is the frontrunner changes almost daily. In other words, work-life balance is not a fixed formula but an ever-shifting algorithm that adjusts to the needs of its inputs: children, partners, self-care, sleep, and deadlines.

The literature on bias and the leaky pipeline in academia highlights a number of shortcomings that are pervasive but fixable with recognition and the will to implement both formal and informal support initiatives. Each of the book's chapters demonstrates that the call for more consistent and transparent norms and practices that support academics during the family formation process and throughout the stages of parenting comes not from one lonely voice or even a small group of voices but from a persistent chorus of academics working in all stages and settings within the profession.

New scholarship on gender and citations in the *American Political Science Review* offers encouragement, noting that women's journal submissions have doubled in recent years and that women are as likely as men to have their work accepted for publication (Breuning et al. 2018). Efforts to improve parental leave policies and support families have increased over the years, as demonstrated by the fact that many of our survey respondents note that their universities have done more in recent years, but the need for transparent, consistently applied policies and institutional support structures remains. The academy has come a long way toward making the elusive work-life balance possible, but there is still a long way to go.

Many of the daily experiences and decisions that build up to create setbacks along the winding path through Academic Chutes and Ladders relate to issues that are uncomfortable—or even taboo—to discuss in the workplace. For example, women and their partners may feel that they cannot discuss a pregnancy loss that occurred before the couple publicly announced the pregnancy or the outwardly unobservable emotional toll of fertility struggles. It may be difficult enough to confide in close friends or family members, and the prospect of broaching the subject in a professional setting (with one's department chair, dean, or colleagues) is unthinkable for many individuals, yet the physical and emotional health effects of pregnancy loss and infertility are real and present challenges for day-to-day personal and professional activities. If there is little to no expectation of formal or informal institutional support for these common but traumatic experiences, academics and their partners who are in the midst of pregnancy loss or fertility struggles may neither ask for nor receive the help that they may need and desire.

Academic parents of preschool- and school-age children may find that the university calendar and local school calendar are out of sync, leading to days during the academic year when a parent must cobble together childcare arrangements. Many academic families do not have the luxury of choosing their locale and as a result live a great distance from family support structures (and the possibility of free backup childcare provided by family or friends). If the university or department norms create the expectation that bringing children to work is unacceptable or reflects poorly on a parent, the simple issue of scheduling care on teacher workdays, early dismissal days, or holidays that the school system recognizes but the university does not creates added stress. Add to this the ad-hoc and rarely well-timed occurrence of childhood illnesses or bad weather days resulting in absence from school or school closure, and parents of preschool- and school-age children often find themselves navigating logistical hurdles and a hearty dose of guilt or envy that their colleagues have bonus snow days to spend on research.

These are just a few examples out of many daily challenges facing academics with families—or academics who are contemplating starting families—but they are rarely accounted for in formal university discussions of institutional support for faculty or in studies of gender-based discrimination in academia. We aim to change that. In writing this book, we have explored many of the daily struggles and decisions that come together to form the difficult—but not always insurmountable—realities of academic parenthood.

Concluding Thoughts: It's on All of Us

We all have a role to play in making the academic profession a more welcoming one for parents and families. As we noted at the book's outset, the path from graduate student to full professor is rife with hurdles that threaten to force women to take an early exit. Representation of many types matters. It matters to have role models of similar demographics to nurture and mentor graduate students and early-career scholars. It matters to attract and retain talented scholars and increase the diversity of the academy, congruent with the stated missions of most universities.

There is tremendous competition to recruit talented scholars, and offering equitable, transparent, and generous parental leave policies and support initiatives will help achieve this goal. Survey respondents from outside the United States found many of our questions non-issues. Parental leave policies fall under the purview of national legislation, and many provide financial incentives and compensation for childcare. Many countries' family leave policies are measured in months or years, not weeks or days. All parents are encouraged to take the necessary time to welcome children into their families. Women are not hustled back to work, leaving newborns in someone else's care. It is unsurprising that maternal well-being indicators show universally lower rates of postpartum depression and anxiety and that mothers outside of the United States breastfeed at higher rates and for longer. This work matters because we are changing workplace norms, cultures, and policies so that our children learn a different—and better—set of standards.

In our society, parents of all genders face unrealistic expectations and competing demands for their time, energy, and attention. For individuals working in a profession that requires creativity, clarity of thought, and the ability to meet deadlines (at least most of the time) mental and physical exhaustion threatens to derail one's career. The academy is losing talented scholars, but it does not have to be this way. As our vignette contributors in this chapter illustrate, there is ample room for joy, passion, and success in the academy, and parenthood can even magnify all that is good in the profession. We do this work because it is worth the struggle.

This book matters because so many women and families suffer alone, in isolation. It is important to share our stories and reveal how common-place and gendered family formation bias and discrimination is. Many of the vignette contributors confided that the process of writing was cathartic and provided clarity, especially those who have written anonymously. We hope that readers will consider the research discussed herein, the real and raw stories of the best and worst of parenting in academia written by our vignette contributors and encapsulated in our survey excerpts, and the advice in this chapter, and start conversations about parenting in the academy. Significant work lies ahead, but the promise of a more equitable, humane, and supportive profession is far too great to ignore.

Survey Questions

Q2.1 Please select the age range that applies to you.
- 15–19 years
- 20–24 years
- 25–29 years
- 30–34 years
- 35–39 years
- 40–44 years
- 45–49 years
- 50–54 years
- 55–59 years
- 60–64 years
- 65–69 years
- 70–74 years
- 75–79 years
- 80–84 years
- 85–89 years
- 90+ years
- Click to write Choice 17

Q2.2 With which gender do you most identify?

Q2.3 With which race or ethnicity do you most identify?

Q2.4 What is your nationality?

Q2.5 Number of children currently living in household?
- 0
- 1
- 2

- 3
- 4
- 5+

Q2.6 At what age did you first become a parent?

Q2.7 At what age did you add another child (if ever) to your family?

Q2.8 What is your current partnership status?
- Single
- In a relationship
- Married
- Divorced
- Separated
- Widowed
- Prefer not to answer
- Other _____

Q2.9 What is your degree of highest attainment?
- Bachelor's degree
- Master's degree
- Juris doctorate
- Doctorate
- Other _____

Q2.10 What is your current professional employment?
- Unemployed
- Adjunct
- Instructor
- Visiting Assistant Professor
- Postdoctoral Fellow
- Research Assistant Professor
- Assistant Professor
- Associate Professor
- Professor

Q2.11 Do you currently have tenure?
- Yes
- No

Q2.12 Did you have tenure before you had your first child?
- Yes
- No

Q2.13 What salary range best reflects your current position?
- Less than $10,000
- $10,000–$19,999
- $20,000–$29,999
- $30,000–$39,999
- $40,000–$49,999
- $50,000–$59,999
- $60,000–$69,999
- $70,000–$79,999
- $80,000–$89,999
- $90,000–$99,999
- $100,000–$149,999
- More than $150,000

Q2.14 If your primary residence is the United States, which region best describes where you live:
- Northeast
- Southeast
- Deep South
- Midwest
- Plains
- Pacific Northwest
- Southwest
- West Coast
- Mountain States
- Outside the United States _____
- Other _____

Q2.15 What institution type best describes your place(s) of employment? (Select all that apply.)
- Community College
- Junior College
- Comprehensive University
- Liberal Arts College
- Research University

- Minority-Serving Institution
- For-Profit Institution
- Public Institution
- Private Institution

Q2.16 What is your academic discipline or field?

Q3.1 What is your institution's parental/maternity/family leave policy? (Feel free to paste a link to a webpage that explains the policy, if one exists.)

Q3.2 Did you negotiate with your department chair/head and/or university administration to take parental/maternity/family leave?
- Yes
- No
- Other (please specify) _____

Q3.3 If you did negotiate to take leave, how did you do so?

Q3.4 What is your department's parental/maternity/family leave policy? (Feel free to paste a link to a webpage that explains the policy, if one exists.)

Q3.5 Has your university and/or department's parental/maternity/family leave policy changed over time? If so, how?
- Yes (please describe) _____
- No
- Not sure

Q3.6 To the best of your knowledge, is your institution's policy consistent across all departments?

Q3.7 To the best of your knowledge, is your department's policy consistently applied? (Give specific details as appropriate.)

Q3.8 What were your professional responsibilities during gestation or adoption?

Q3.9 What were your professional responsibilities immediately after birth, adoption, or change in family status (e.g., foster parenting or otherwise acting as primary caregiver)?

Q3.10 How satisfied are/were you with your department's/university's parental leave policies?

- Very dissatisfied
- A little dissatisfied
- Dissatisfied
- Neutral
- Satisfied
- A little satisfied
- Very satisfied
- Other _____

Q3.11 What factors influenced the timing of your choice to become a parent?

Q3.12 What responsibilities did you have in preparing for your absence from your position (for extended parental/maternity/family leave)? (Examples might include preparing lectures and exams or finding course coverage.)

Q3.13 Describe the "family climate" of your department. (For example, I am the only one with kids; other faculty have kids; other faculty have older kids; faculty members bring children to the department on occasion; family events are held by the department, etc.)

Q3.14 Describe an important experience that stands out for you in your department or university you had prior to giving birth, adopting, or otherwise taking on a child caregiving role.

Q3.15 Describe an important experience that stands out for you in your department or university you had after giving birth, adopting, or otherwise taking on a child caregiving role.

Q3.16 What are your childcare arrangements?

Q3.17 Open ended: Please add anything else you want to tell us.

Q4.1 If you experienced infertility or pregnancy loss, was your institution/department aware? If so, what forms of leave or other support did the institution/department offer? Did you utilize leave or other forms of support (e.g., unofficial class or service coverage by peers)?

Q4.2 If you experienced infant loss, did the institution/department provide leave or other forms of support? Did you utilize leave or other forms of support?

Q4.3 Did you experience infertility, and if so, how did it affect your work?

Q4.4 Did you experience miscarriage/chemical pregnancy, and if so, how did it affect your work?

Q4.5 Did you experience a late-term pregnancy loss, and if so, how did it affect your work?

Q4.6 Did you experience infant loss, and if so, how did it affect your work?

Q4.7 Open ended: Please add anything else you want to tell us.

Q5.1 If you are or have been pregnant: Describe your experience being pregnant. From your perspective, was it a good pregnancy? Was it easy? Was it medically difficult? Did it require bedrest or work modification? Do you feel like it affected your work productivity?

Q5.2 If you are or have been pregnant: Describe your institution's/department's support for flexible scheduling to accommodate medical appointments.

Q5.3 If you have given birth: Describe your physical experience during maternity leave. How was your recovery?

Q5.4 How much time did you take or do you plan to take for maternity leave? Was this time paid?

Q5.5 If you have given birth: Describe your physical/mental/emotional health during the 18–24 months after your child was born. How did this affect your work?

Q5.6 If you have given birth: Did you experience postpartum issues that affected your sleep, eating, physical activity, relationships, productivity, etc.? How did you deal with these?

Q5.7 If you have given birth: Would you describe your postpartum issues as nonexistent, mild, moderate, or severe?

Q5.8 Describe your institution's/department's support for you and your family during the 18–24 months after your child was born (including flexible scheduling/missed work time for caregiving, etc.).

Q5.9 If your partner is currently or has been pregnant: Describe your institution's/department's support for flexible scheduling to accommodate medical appointments.

Q5.10 How much time did you take or do you plan to take for parental leave? Was this time paid?

Q5.11 Describe your institution's/department's support for you and your family during the 18–24 months after your child was born (including flexible scheduling/missed work time for caregiving, etc.).

Q5.12 How did the family formation process affect your work productivity?

Q5.13 Regarding child/family health: On average, how many times each month was your work affected by child/family illnesses?

Q5.14 If you have a child or children with special needs, how has this affected your work? Do you feel your institution/department provides adequate support?

Q5.15 Open ended: Please add anything else you want to tell us.

Q6.1 If you are currently or have been pregnant during graduate school: Describe your institution's/department's support for flexible scheduling to accommodate medical appointments.

Q6.2 How much time did you take or do you plan to take for maternity leave?

Q6.3 If you took, are taking, or plan to take maternity leave in graduate school, was/is/will this time be paid? (Feel free to elaborate.)
- Yes _____
- Not sure _____
- No _____

Q6.4 Describe your institution's/department's support for you and your family during the 18–24 months after your child was born (including flexible scheduling/missed work time for caregiving, etc.).

Q6.5 How did the family formation process affect your work?

Q6.6 Do you feel you had adequate support from your committee and/or other advisors?
- Extremely adequate
- Moderately adequate
- Slightly adequate
- Neither adequate nor inadequate
- Slightly inadequate
- Moderately inadequate
- Extremely inadequate
- Other _____

Q6.7 If your partner is currently or has been pregnant during your time in graduate school: How much time did you take or do you plan to take for maternity leave? Was this time paid?

Q6.8 Describe your institution's/department's support for you and your family during the 18–24 months after your child was born (including flexible scheduling/missed work time for caregiving, etc.).

Q6.9 If your partner is currently or has been pregnant during your time in graduate school: How did the family formation process affect your work?

Q6.10 Open ended: Please add anything else you want to tell us.

Q7.1 What strategies do you use to balance work and home responsibilities?

Q7.2 On average how much sleep do you get per night?
- Less than 3 hours
- 3–4 hours
- 4–5 hours
- 5–6 hours
- 6–7 hours

- 7–8 hours
- 8–9 hours
- More than 9 hours

Q7.3 Do you have uninterrupted or continuous (fulfilling) sleep?
- Yes
- No
- Sometimes
- Other _____

Q7.4 If you coparent: How do you and your partner divide home responsibilities?

Q7.5 What is the best advice you have been given (or have given) about the work-life balance?

Q7.6 Of the following, which do you prioritize (choose three): work, family, self-care/exercise, friends, sleep.

Q7.7 For parents of older children, when did things get easier?

Q7.8 What strategies do you use to maximize your work productivity?

Q7.9 What strategies do you use to maximize your connection to home?

Q7.10 What strategies do you use for self-care?

Q7.11 Open ended: Please add anything else you want to tell us.

Q8.1 If you are or were on the tenure track, how did childbearing or family formation affect your progression toward tenure?

Q8.2 To the best of your knowledge, does parenthood affect progression toward tenure for others in your institution/department?

Q8.3 If you are not or were not in a tenure-track position, how did childbearing or family formation affect your or your department's expectations of work productivity, career progress, or potential?

Q8.4 How did childbearing or family formation affect the job search process (e.g., timing of entering the job market, search location, or disclosure of family status) and/or the outcome of your job search?

Q8.5 Open ended: Please add anything else you want to tell us.

Q9.1 If you are the parent of an older child who has left home: How does your work-life balance now compare to when your child was younger?

Q9.2 From your perspective, is the workload in your institution/department balanced across parents of young children and parents of older children? If not, what do you feel should change?

Q9.3 How have official policies and unofficial norms regarding family formation changed in your department/in the discipline/in academia over time?

Q9.4 Open ended: Please add anything else you want to tell us.

Q10.1 If you are the partner of someone who gave birth: If you took parental leave for the birth or adoption of a child, describe negotiating this process.

Q10.2 Have others in your institution/department taken parental leave when their partners have given birth or when they have adopted a child?

Q10.3 How did taking parental leave affect your progression toward tenure?

Q10.4 In what ways do you support your partner's work productivity (e.g., attending conferences, overnight feedings)?

Q10.5 Open ended: Please add anything else you want to tell us.

Q10.6 Concerning grandparents: If you are a grandparent, what role have you played in support of your child (the academic) vis-à-vis grandchild care?

Q10.7 If you are an academic who is a grandparent, what role have you played in support of your child (academic or non-academic) vis-à-vis grandchild care?

Q10.8 If you are a parent, what role do grandparents play as caregivers for your child(ren)?

Q10.9 Open ended: Please add anything else you want to tell us.

Q11.1 If you have breastfed or are currently breastfeeding: What lactation facilities does your department/university provide?

Q11.2 What factors influenced your decision to breastfeed (or not)?

Q11.3 How long did you or do you plan to breastfeed?

Q11.4 What is your experience breastfeeding at conferences?

Q11.5 Describe any difficulties you experienced in breastfeeding (i.e., mastitis, low supply, difficulty pumping).

Q11.6 Did you exclusively breastfeed?

Q11.7 Open ended: Please add anything else you want to tell us.

References

Ainley, Kirsten, Ida Danewid, and Joanne Yao. 2017. "Challenging the Gender Citation Gap: What Journals Can Do." *International Affairs Blog*. https://medium.com/international-affairs-blog/challenging-the-gender-citation-gap-what-journals-can-do-f79e0b831055.

American College of Obstetricians and Gynecologists. 2018. "Early Pregnancy Loss." ACOG Clinical. November 2018. https://www.acog.org/en/Clinical/Clinical Guidance/Practice Bulletin/Articles/2018/11/Early Pregnancy Loss.

American Political Science Association. n.d. "Project on Women and Minorities (P-WAM)." https://www.apsanet.org/RESOURCES/Data-on-the-Profession/Dashboards/P-WAM.

Amir, L. H. 2006. "Breastfeeding: Managing 'Supply' Difficulties." *Australian Family Physician* 35 (9): 686.

Anderson, Jenny. 2016. "The Ultimate Efficiency Hack: Have Kids (We're Serious) Women with Children Outperform Those Who Don't Have Children over a 30-Year Career Research Shows." *Quartz*. October 11, 2016. https://qz.com/802254/the-ultimate-efficiency-hack-have-kids/.

Antecol, Heather, Kelly Bedard, and Jenna Stearns. 2016. "Equal but Inequitable: Who Benefits from Gender-Neutral Tenure Clock Stopping Policies?" IZA Discussion Papers.

———. 2018. "Equal but Inequitable: Who Benefits from Gender-Neutral Tenure Clock Stopping Policies?" *American Economic Review* 108 (9): 2420–41.

"Anuario de las mujeres 2017: Mes por mes, los hitos claves de un año 'feminista.'" n.d. Clarín.com. Accessed November 13, 2019. https://www.clarin.com/entremujeres/genero/anuario-mujeres-2017-mes-mes-hitos-claves-ano-feminista_0_SJvyBXOGf.html.

Applebaum, B. 2019. "Remediating Campus Climate: Implicit Bias Training Is Not Enough." *Studies in Philosophy and Education* 38 (2): 129–41. https://doi.org/10.1007/s11217-018-9644-1.

Armenti, Carmen. 2004. "Women Faculty Seeking Tenure and Parenthood: Lessons from Previous Generations." *Cambridge Journal of Education* 34 (1): 65–83.

Artz, Benjamin, Amanda H. Goodall, and Andrew J. Oswald. 2018. "Do Women Ask?" *Industrial Relations: A Journal of Economy and Society* 57 (4): 611–36. https://doi.org/10.1111/irel.12214.

Baker, Sara Farrell. 2017. "Postpartum Traditions around the World: How Does the U.S. Measure Up?" *Scary Mommy*. November 5, 2017. https://www.scarymommy.com/postpartum-care-is-better-other-countries/.

Bartlett, John. 2018. "Chile's #MeToo Moment: Students Protest against Sexual Harassment." *The Guardian*. July 9, 2018. https://www.theguardian.com/world /2018/jul/09/chile-metoo-sexual-harassment-universities.

Bellas, Marcia L., and Robert Kevin Toutkoushian. 1999. "Faculty Time Allocations and Research Productivity: Gender, Race and Family Effects." *Review of Higher Education* 22 (4): 367–85.

Bertrand, Marianne, and Sendhil Mullainathan. 2003. "Are Emily and Greg More Employable than Lakisha and Jamal? A Field Experiment on Labor Market Discrimination." Working Paper 9873. National Bureau of Economic Research. https://doi.org/10.3386/w9873.

Bessette, Lee. 2013. "Bad Female Academic: Just Say No." *Inside Higher Ed*. January 23, 2013. https://www.insidehighered.com/blogs/college-ready-writing/bad -female-academic-just-say-no.

Blofield, Merike, and Juliana Martínez Franzoni. 2015. "Maternalism, Co-responsibility, and Social Equity: A Typology of Work-Family Policies." *Social Politics: International Studies in Gender, State and Society* 22 (1): 38–59. https://doi.org/10.1093/sp /jxu015.

Bowles, Hannah Riley, Linda Babcock, and Lei Lai. 2007. "Social Incentives for Gender Differences in the Propensity to Initiate Negotiations: Sometimes It Does Hurt to Ask." *Organizational Behavior and Human Decision Processes* 103 (1): 84–103.

Brenhouse, Hillary. 2013. "Why Are America's Postpartum Practices So Rough on New Mothers?" *The Daily Beast*. August 15, 2013. http://www.thedailybeast.com /witw/articles/2013/08/15/america-s-postpartum-practices.html.

Breuning, Marijke, and Kathryn Sanders. 2007. "Gender and Journal Authorship in Eight Prestigious Political Science Journals." *PS: Political Science and Politics* 40 (2): 347–51.

Breuning, Marijke, Benjamin Isaak Gross, Ayal Feinberg, Melissa Martinez, Ramesh Sharma, and John Ishiyama. 2018. "Clearing the Pipeline? Gender and the Review Process at the American Political Science Review." *PS: Political Science and Politics* 51 (3): 629–34. https://doi.org/10.1017/S1049096518000069.

Broderick, Nichole A., and Arturo Casadevall. 2017. "Disequilibrium in Gender Ratios among Authors Who Contributed Equally." *BioRxiv*, 241554.

Bunnefeld, Lynsey. 2019. "Shared Parental Leave: Making It Work for the Whole Family." *Nature*. October 9, 2019. https://www.nature.com/articles/d41586-019 -03019-z.

Calderone, Karen L. 1990. "The Influence of Gender on the Frequency of Pain and Sedative Medication Administered to Postoperative Patients." *Sex Roles* 23 (11–12): 713–25.

Cardozo, Karen M. 2017. "Academic Labor: Who Cares?" *Critical Sociology* 43 (3): 405–28. https://doi.org/10.1177/0896920516641733.

Carlsen, Audrey, and Maya Salam y Claire Cain Miller. 2018. "Cómo #MeToo ha cambiado los centros del poder." *New York Times*, October 25, 2018. https://www .nytimes.com/es/2018/10/25/metoo-mujeres-hombres-remplazos/.

Casadevall, Arturo, Gregg L. Semenza, Sarah Jackson, Gordon Tomaselli, and Rexford S. Ahima. 2019. "Reducing Bias: Accounting for the Order of Co–First Authors." *Journal of Clinical Investigation* 129 (6).

Chen, Esther H., Frances S. Shofer, Anthony J. Dean, Judd E. Hollander, William G. Baxt, Jennifer L. Robey, Keara L. Sease, and Angela M. Mills. 2008. "Gender Disparity in Analgesic Treatment of Emergency Department Patients with Acute Abdominal Pain." *Academic Emergency Medicine: Official Journal of the Society for Academic Emergency Medicine* 15 (5): 414–18. https://doi.org/10.1111/j.1553-2712 .2008.00100.x.

Chenoweth, Erica, Page Fortna, Sara Mitchell, Burcu Savun, Jessica Weeks, and Kathleen Cunningham. 2016. "How to Get Tenure (If You're a Woman)." *Foreign Policy.* April 19, 2016. http://foreignpolicy.com/2016/04/19/how-to-get-tenure-if -youre-a-woman-academia-stephen-walt/.

Chronister, Jay L., Bruce M. Gansneder, Elizabeth Harper, and Roger G. Baldwin. 1997. "Full-Time Non-Tenure-Track Faculty: Gender Differences." *NEA Higher Education Research Center Update* 3 (5): n5.

Ciciolla, Lucia, and Suniya S. Luthar. 2019. "Invisible Household Labor and Ramifications for Adjustment: Mothers as Captains of Households." *Sex Roles* 81 (7–8): 1–20.

Clark Blickenstaff, Jacob. 2005. "Women and Science Careers: Leaky Pipeline or Gender Filter?" *Gender and Education* 17 (4): 369–86.

Claypool, Vicki Hesli, Brian David Janssen, Dongkyu Kim, and Sara McLaughlin Mitchell. 2017. "Determinants of Salary Dispersion among Political Science Faculty: The Differential Effects of Where You Work (Institutional Characteristics) and What You Do (Negotiate and Publish)." *PS: Political Science and Politics* 50 (1): 146–56.

Colgan, Jeff. 2015. "New Evidence on Gender Bias in IR Syllabi." *Duck of Minerva* (blog). August 27, 2015. http://duckofminerva.com/2015/08/new-evidence-on -gender-bias-in-ir-syllabi.html.

Colligan, Thomas W., and Eileen M. Higgins. 2006. "Workplace Stress: Etiology and Consequences." *Journal of Workplace Behavioral Health* 21 (2): 89–97.

Collins, Emily I. M., Anna L. Cox, Jon Bird, and Daniel Harrison. 2014. "Social Networking Use and RescueTime: The Issue of Engagement." *Proceedings of the 2014 ACM International Joint Conference on Pervasive and Ubiquitous Computing: Adjunct Publication,* 687–90. Association for Computing Machinery.

Collins, Patricia Hill. 2016. "Shifting the Center: Race, Class, and Feminist Theorizing about Motherhood." In *Mothering: Ideology, Experience, and Agency,* edited by Evelyn Nakano Glenn, Grace Chang, Linda Rennie Forcey, 45–65. New York: Routledge. https://www.taylorfrancis.com/books/e/9781315538891/chapters/10 .4324/9781315538891-3.

Connelly, Rachel, and Kristen Ghodsee. 2011. *Professor Mommy: Finding Work-Family Balance in Academia.* New York: Rowman & Littlefield.

Crawford, Kerry, and Leah Windsor. 2019. "Best Practices for Normalizing Parents in the Academy: Higher- and Lower-Order Processes and Women and Parents' Success." *PS: Political Science and Politics,* October 2019.

Crow, Sheryl. 2002. "Soak Up the Sun." *C'mon, C'mon.*

Davidson, Deborah, and Debra Langan. 2006. "The Breastfeeding Incident: Teaching and Learning through Transgression." *Studies in Higher Education* 31 (4): 439–52.

Dayal, Anjali K., Madison V. Schramm, and Alexandra M. Stark. 2017. "Writing Women Back In." *Duck of Minerva* (blog). May 31, 2017. http://duckofminerva .com/2017/05/writing-women-back-in.html.

Dion, Michelle. 2008. "All-Knowing or All-Nurturing? Student Expectations, Gender Roles, and Practical Suggestions for Women in the Classroom." *PS: Political Science and Politics* 41 (4): 853–56.

Duffy, Meghan. 2013. "Implicit Biases and Evaluating Job Candidates (Updated)." *Dynamic Ecology* (blog). November 6, 2013. https://dynamicecology.wordpress .com/2013/11/06/implicit-biases-evaluating-job-candidates/.

Duhigg, Charles. 2017. "If GoDaddy Can Turn the Corner on Sexism, Who Can't?" *New York Times.* July 23, 2017. https://www.nytimes.com/2017/07/23/business /godaddy-tv-ads-sexism.html.

Duke, Katy. 2006. "Faking Happiness at Work Can Make You Ill." *BMJ : British Medical Journal* 332 (7544): 747.

Epifanio, Mariaelisa, and Vera E. Troeger. 2013. "How Much Do Children Really Cost? Maternity Benefits and Career Opportunities of Women in Academia." 171. Competitive Advantage in the Global Economy (CAGE) Online Working Paper Series. https://ideas.repec.org/p/cge/wacage/171.html.

"Estudiantes ponen fin a toma feminista en Facultad de Derecho en la U. de Chile." 2018. *El Mostrador* (blog). July 9, 2018. https://www.elmostrador.cl/dia/2018/07 /09/estudiantes-ponen-fin-a-toma-feminista-en-facultad-de-derecho-en-la-u-de -chile/.

Evans, Elrena, and Caroline Grant. 2008. *Mama, PhD: Women Write about Motherhood and Academic Life.* New Brunswick, NJ: Rutgers University Press.

Fichtenbaum, Rudy. 2014. "From the President: Inequality, Corporatization, and the Casualization of Academic Labor." American Association of University Professors. October 2014. https://www.aaup.org/article/president-inequality-corporatization -and-casualization-academic-labor#.XouJFhNKg_N.

Flaherty, Colleen. 2020. "Early Journal Submission Data Suggest COVID-19 Is Tanking Women's Research Productivity." *Inside Higher Ed.* April 21, 2020. https://www .insidehighered.com/news/2020/04/21/early-journal-submission-data-suggest -covid-19-tanking-womens-research-productivity.

Folbre, Nancy. 1994. "Children as Public Goods." *American Economic Review* 84 (2): 86–90.

Foschi, Martha. 1996. "Double Standards in the Evaluation of Men and Women." *Social Psychology Quarterly* 59 (3): 237–54. https://doi.org/10.2307/2787021.

Foye, Meghann. 2016. *Meternity.* Original edition. Don Mills, Ontario: MIRA.

Gardner, Abby. 2020. "The Oscars Rejected This Frida Mom Postpartum Ad for Being 'Too Graphic'—and People Are Angry." *Glamour.* February 9, 2020. https://www .glamour.com/story/oscars-rejected-frida-mom-postpartum-ad-backlash.

Gardner, Susan K. 2012. "'I Couldn't Wait to Leave the Toxic Environment': A Mixed Methods Study of Women Faculty Satisfaction and Departure from One Research Institution." *NASPA Journal about Women in Higher Education* 5 (1): 71–95.

Geronimus, A. 1992. "The Weathering Hypothesis and the Health of African-American Women and Infants: Evidence and Speculations." *Ethnicity and Disease* 2 (3): 207–21. https://www.ncbi.nlm.nih.gov/pubmed/1467758.

Ginther, Donna K., and Kathy J. Hayes. 2003. "Gender Differences in Salary and Promotion for Faculty in the Humanities 1977–95." *Journal of Human Resources* 38 (1): 34–73.

Goddard, Stacie, Deborah Avant, Michael C. Desch, William C. Wohlforth, and Sean M. Lynn-Jones. 2017. "Policy Forum on the Gender Gap in Political Science." ISSF. September 22, 2017. https://issforum.org/forums/gender-gap.

Goldsmith Weil, Jael. 2017. "Milk Makes State: The Extension and Implementation of Chile's State Milk Programs, 1901–1971." *Historia (Santiago)* 50 (1): 79–104. https://doi.org/10.4067/S0717-71942017000100003.

———. 2020. "Constructing Maternalism from Paternalism: The Case of State Milk Programs." In *Motherhood, Social Policies and Women's Activism in Latin America*, edited by Alejandra Ramm and Jasmine Gideon, 69–95. Studies of the Americas. Cham: Springer International Publishing. https://doi.org/10.1007/978-3-030 -21402-9_4.

Goldstein, Katherine. 2018. "I Was a Sheryl Sandberg Superfan. Then Her 'Lean In' Advice Failed Me." *Vox*. December 6, 2018. https://www.vox.com/first-person /2018/12/6/18128838/michelle-obama-lean-in-sheryl-sandberg.

Greenwald, Anthony G., and Linda Hamilton Krieger. 2006. "Implicit Bias: Scientific Foundations." *California Law Review* 94 (4): 945–67.

Gregory, Vanessa. 2015. "Surviving a Failed Pregnancy." *Harper's Magazine*. June 2015. https://harpers.org/archive/2015/06/surviving-a-failed-pregnancy/.

Griffin, Deborah H. n.d. "Measuring Survey Nonresponse by Race and Ethnicity." United States Bureau of the Census. Accessed July 23, 2020. https://www.census.gov /content/dam/Census/library/working-papers/2002/acs/2002_Griffin_01.pdf.

Griffiths, Sarah. 2019. "The Effect of Childbirth No-One Talks About." *BBC*. April 24, 2019. http://www.bbc.com/future/story/20190424-the-hidden-trauma -of-childbirth.

Guarino, Cassandra M., and Victor M. H. Borden. 2017. "Faculty Service Loads and Gender: Are Women Taking Care of the Academic Family?" *Research in Higher Education* 58 (6): 672–94. https://doi.org/10.1007/s11162-017-9454-2.

Hancock, Kathleen J., Matthew A. Baum, and Marijke Breuning. 2013. "Women and Pre-tenure Scholarly Productivity in International Studies: An Investigation into the Leaky Career Pipeline." *International Studies Perspectives* 14 (4): 507–27. https://doi.org/10.1111/insp.12002.

———. 2015. "What Explains High Research Productivity? Evidence from a Survey of International Studies Scholars." Unpublished.

Hesli, Vicki L., Jae Mook Lee, and Sara McLaughlin Mitchell. 2012. "Predicting Rank Attainment in Political Science: What Else Besides Publications Affects Promotion?" *PS: Political Science and Politics* 45 (3): 475–92.

Hochschild, Arlie, and Anne Machung. 2012. *The Second Shift: Working Families and the Revolution at Home*. New York: Penguin.

Hoekzema, Elseline, Erika Barba-Müller, Cristina Pozzobon, Marisol Picado, Florencio Lucco, David García-García, Juan Carlos Soliva, Adolf Tobeña, Manuel Desco, and Eveline A. Crone. 2017. "Pregnancy Leads to Long-Lasting Changes in Human Brain Structure." *Nature Neuroscience* 20 (2): 287.

Hoffmann, Diane E., and Anita J. Tarzian. 2001. "The Girl Who Cried Pain: A Bias against Women in the Treatment of Pain." *The Journal of Law, Medicine and Ethics* 28: 13–27.

hooks, bell. 2013. "Dig Deep: Beyond Lean In." *The Feminist Wire*. October 28, 2013. https://thefeministwire.com/2013/10/17973/.

James, Al. 2017. *Work-Life Advantage: Sustaining Regional Learning and Innovation*. 2017. Hoboken: John Wiley and Sons.

June, Audrey Williams. 2012. "Ph.D.'s from Top Political-Science Programs Dominate Hiring, Research Finds." *Chronicle of Higher Education*, December 5, 2012. https://www.chronicle.com/article/PhDs-From-Top/136113.

Kadera, Kelly M. 1998. "Transmission, Barriers, and Constraints: A Dynamic Model of the Spread of War." *Journal of Conflict Resolution* 42 (3): 367–87.

Kadera, Kelly M., Mark J. C. Crescenzi, and Megan L. Shannon. 2003. "Democratic Survival, Peace, and War in the International System." *American Journal of Political Science* 47 (2): 234–47.

Kim, Jae Yun, Gráinne M. Fitzsimons, and Aaron C. Kay. 2018. "Lean In Messages Increase Attributions of Women's Responsibility for Gender Inequality." *Journal of Personality and Social Psychology* 115 (6): 974–1001. https://doi.org/10.1037/pspa0000129.

Kitchener, Caroline. 2020. "Women Academics Seem to Be Submitting Fewer Papers during Coronavirus. 'Never Seen Anything like It,' Says One Editor." *The Lily*. April 24, 2020. https://www.thelily.com/women-academics-seem-to-be-submitting-fewer-papers-during-coronavirus-never-seen-anything-like-it-says-one-editor/.

Kittilson, Miki Caul. 2008. "Representing Women: The Adoption of Family Leave in Comparative Perspective." *Journal of Politics* 70 (2): 323–34.

Krapf, Matthias, Heinrich W. Ursprung, and Christian Zimmermann. 2014. "Parenthood and Productivity of Highly Skilled Labor: Evidence from the Groves of Academe." IZA Discussion Paper No. 7904.

Kulis, S., and D. Sicotte. 2002. "Women Scientists in Academia: Geographically Constrained to Big Cities, College Clusters, or the Coasts?" *Research in Higher Education* 43 (1): 1–30.

Kulp, Amanda M. 2019. "Parenting on the Path to the Professoriate: A Focus on Graduate Student Mothers." *Research in Higher Education* 61 (May): 408–29.

Lee, Jennifer, Rebecca C. Miller, Lily J. Moloney, and Amy L. Prieto. 2018. "The Development of Strategies for Nanoparticle Synthesis: Considerations for Deepening Understanding of Inherently Complex Systems." *Journal of Solid State Chemistry* 273: 243–86.

Leeds, Brett Ashley, Leslie Schwindt-Bayer, Michael Alvarez, and Tiffany D. Barnes. 2014. "The Importance of Mentoring." *OUP Blog*. November 23, 2014. https://blog.oup.com/2014/11/mentorship-academic-career-political-science/.

Lennard, Anna C., Brent A. Scott, and Russell E. Johnson. 2019. "Turning Frowns (and Smiles) Upside Down: A Multilevel Examination of Surface Acting Positive and Negative Emotions on Well-Being." *Journal of Applied Psychology* 104 (9): 1164–80.

London School of Economics and Political Science. 2014. "The Leaky Pipeline: Women in Academia." *Equity, Diversity and Inclusion* (blog). March 14, 2014. http://blogs.lse.ac.uk/equityDiversityInclusion/2014/03/the-leaky-pipeline-women-in-academia/.

Long, J. Scott. 1990. "The Origins of Sex Differences in Science." *Social Forces* 84 (4): 1297–315.

Lor, Maichou, Barbara J. Bowers, Anna Krupp, and Nora Jacobson. 2017. "Tailored Explanation: A Strategy to Minimize Nonresponse in Demographic Items among

Low-Income Racial and Ethnic Minorities." *Survey Practice* 10 (3). https://www
.ncbi.nlm.nih.gov/pmc/articles/PMC5844486/.

Lundquist, Jennifer, and Joya Misra. 2017. "How to Find Mentors and Be a Good One Yourself (Essay)." *Inside Higher Ed.* July 13, 2017. https://www.insidehighered .com/advice/2017/07/13/how-find-mentors-and-be-good-one-yourself-essay.

Madera, Juan M., Michelle R. Hebl, and Randi C. Martin. 2009. "Gender and Letters of Recommendation for Academia: Agentic and Communal Differences." *Journal of Applied Psychology* 94 (6): 1591–99. https://doi.org/10.1037/a0016539.

Maliniak, Daniel, Ryan Powers, and Barbara F. Walter. 2013. "The Gender Citation Gap in International Relations." *International Organization* 67 (4): 889–922.

"Más de 30 universidades ya están movilizadas por demandas feministas." n.d. Cooperativa.cl. Accessed November 13, 2019. https://www.cooperativa.cl/noticias /pais/educacion/movimiento-estudiantil/mas-de-30-universidades-ya-estan -movilizadas-por-demandas-feministas/2018-05-29/123325.html.

Mason, Mary Ann, and Marc Goulden. 2002. "Do Babies Matter?" *Academe* 88 (6): 21.

Mason, Mary Ann, Nicholas H. Wolfinger, and Marc Goulden. 2013. *Do Babies Matter? Gender and Family in the Ivory Tower.* New Brunswick, NJ: Rutgers University Press.

Masuoka, Natalie. 2017. "Review: *Getting Paid while Taking Time: The Women's Movement and the Development of Paid Family Leave Policies in the United States,* by Megan Sholar." *Perspectives on Politics* 15 (4): 1165–66.

McMurtrie, Beth. 2013. "Political Science Is Rife with Gender Bias, Scholars Find." *Chronicle of Higher Education.* August 30, 2013. https://www.chronicle.com /article/Political-Science-Is-Rife-With/141319.

Merritt, Deborah J. 2008. "Bias, the Brain, and Student Evaluations of Teaching." *St. John's Law Review* 82: 235.

Miller, David I., and Jonathan Wai. 2015. "The Bachelor's to Ph.D. STEM Pipeline No Longer Leaks More Women than Men: A 30-Year Analysis." *Frontiers in Psychology* 6. https://doi.org/10.3389/fpsyg.2015.00037.

Minello, Alessandra. 2020. "The Pandemic and the Female Academic." *Nature.* April 2020. https://doi.org/10.1038/d41586-020-01135-9.

Mitchell, Kristina M. W., and Jonathan Martin. 2018. "Gender Bias in Student Evaluations." *PS: Political Science and Politics* 51 (3): 648–52. https://doi.org/10.1017 /S104909651800001X.

Mitchell, Sara McLaughlin, and Vicki L. Hesli. 2013. "Women Don't Ask? Women Don't Say No? Bargaining and Service in the Political Science Profession." *PS: Political Science and Politics* 46 (2): 355–69.

Mitchell, Sara McLaughlin, Samantha Lange, and Holly Brus. 2013. "Gendered Citation Patterns in International Relations Journals." *International Studies Perspectives* 14 (4): 485–92. https://doi.org/10.1111/insp.12026.

Molyneux, Maxine. 2000. "Twentieth-Century State Formations in Latin America." In *Hidden Histories of Gender and the State in Latin America*, edited by Elizabeth Dore and Maxine Molyneux. Durham, NC: Duke University Press.

Morrison, Emory, Elizabeth Rudd, and Maresi Nerad. n.d. "Onto, Up, Off the Academic Faculty Ladder: The Gendered Effects of Family on Career Transitions for a Cohort of Social Science PhDs." *Review of Higher Education* 34 (4): 525–53.

Morrow Jones, Hazel, and Janet M. Box-Steffensmeier. 2014. "Implicit Bias and Why It Matters to the Field of Political Methodology." *Political Methodologist* (blog).

March 31, 2014. https://thepoliticalmethodologist.com/2014/03/31/implicit-bias
-and-why-it-matters-to-the-field-of-political-methodology/.

Moss-Racusin, Corinne A., John F. Dovidio, Victoria L. Brescoll, Mark J. Graham, and Jo Handelsman. 2012. "Science Faculty's Subtle Gender Biases Favor Male Students." *Proceedings of the National Academy of Sciences* 109 (41): 16474–79. https://doi.org/10.1073/pnas.1211286109.

Mui, Ylan Q. 2014. "Study: Women with More Children Are More Productive at Work." *Washington Post.* October 30, 2014. https://www.washingtonpost.com /news/wonk/wp/2014/10/30/study-women-with-more-children-are-more -productive-at-work/.

Murdie, Amanda. 2017. "An Academic Woman's Rant of the Week: Service Discrepancies." *Duck of Minerva* (blog). April 12, 2017. http://duckofminerva.com/2017 /04/an-academic-womans-rant-of-the-week-service-discrepancies.html.

"My Expressed Breastmilk Doesn't Smell Fresh. What Can I Do?" 2011. *KellyMom. com* (blog). July 28, 2011. https://kellymom.com/bf/pumpingmoms/milkstorage /lipase-expressedmilk/.

Newport, Cal. 2016. *Deep Work: Rules for Focused Success in a Distracted World.* London: Hachette UK.

Norman, Abby. 2017. *Ask Me about My Uterus: A Quest to Make Doctors Believe in Women's Pain.* New York: Perseus.

Oprisko, Robert. 2012. "Superpowers: The American Academic Elite." *Georgetown Public Policy Review.* http://gppreview.com/2012/12/03/superpowers-the-american -academic-elite/.

Oprisko, Robert L. 2012. *Honor: A Phenomenology.* New York: Routledge.

Patton, Stacey. 2014. "Should You Check the 'Race Box'?" *Chronicle of Higher Education| Community* (blog). January 29, 2014. https://community.chronicle.com /news/302-should-you-check-the-race-box.

Penny, Laurie. 2017. "Most Women You Know Are Angry—and That's All Right." *Teen Vogue,* August 2, 2017. https://www.teenvogue.com/story/women-angry-anger -laurie-penny.

Peters, Terri. 2016. "A Hotel Told This Mom to Pump in the Bathroom . . . Bad Move." *TODAY.* August 18, 2016. https://www.today.com/parents/see-how-mom -responded-when-hotel-told-her-pump-breast-t101995.

Piazza, Jo. 2017. "What's the Etiquette for Breastfeeding at a Work Conference?" *Forbes.* March 8, 2017. https://www.forbes.com/sites/jopiazza/2017/03/08 /whats-the-etiquette-for-breastfeeding-at-a-work-conference/.

Pirtle, Whitney N. Laster. 2017. "Birthing Both a Baby and a Ph.D. as a Woman of Color." *Inside Higher Ed.* February 24, 2017. https://www.insidehighered.com /advice/2017/02/24/juggling-both-baby-and-grad-school-minority-student-essay.

———. 2018. "Motherhood while Black: The Hard Truth about Race and Parenthood." *Chronicle of Higher Education.* April 1, 2018. https://www.chronicle.com /interactives/the-awakening.

Powell, Kendall. 2019. "Why Scientist-Mums in the United States Need Better Parental-Support Policies." *Nature.* April 30, 2019. https://www.nature.com /articles/d41586-019-01315-2.

Pozen, Robert C. 2012a. *Extreme Productivity: Boost Your Results, Reduce Your Hours.* New York: HarperBusiness.

———. 2012b. "Measure Results, Not Hours, to Improve Work Efficiency." *New York Times*. October 6, 2012. https://www.nytimes.com/2012/10/07/business/measure-results-not-hours-to-improve-work-efficiency.html.

Primack, Brian A., Ariel Shensa, César G. Escobar-Viera, Erica L. Barrett, Jaime E. Sidani, Jason B. Colditz, and A. Everette James. 2017. "Use of Multiple Social Media Platforms and Symptoms of Depression and Anxiety: A Nationally-Representative Study among US Young Adults." *Computers in Human Behavior* 69: 1–9.

Pritlove, C., C. Juando-Prats, K. Ala-leppilampi, and J. A. Parsons. 2019. "The Good, the Bad, and the Ugly of Implicit Bias." *The Lancet* 393 (10171): 502–4. https://doi.org/10.1016/S0140-6736(18)32267-0.

Project Implicit. n.d. "Take a Test." Accessed June 18, 2018. https://implicit.harvard.edu/implicit/takeatest.html.

"Promotion and Self-Promotion." 2013. *The Economist*, August 31, 2013. https://www.economist.com/science-and-technology/2013/08/31/promotion-and-self-promotion.

"Recalendarización del año académico: el panorama de las universidades tras movilizaciones feministas." 2018. *El Dinamo* (blog). July 4, 2018. https://www.eldinamo.cl/educacion/2018/07/04/recalendarizacion-del-ano-academico-el-panorama-de-las-universidades-tras-movilizaciones-feministas/.

Robinson, Michael E., and Emily A. Wise. 2003. "Gender Bias in the Observation of Experimental Pain." *Pain* 104 (1–2): 259–64.

Romero, Aldemaro, Jr. 2017. "Best Practices for Recruiting and Retaining Diverse Faculty for Institutions of Higher Education." Committee on Cultural Diversity, Council of Colleges of Arts and Sciences. March 10, 2017. https://www.ccas.net/files/2018%20All%20Meetings/Romero%202017.pdf.

Ruiz, Miguel. 1997. *The Four Agreements: A Toltec Wisdom Book*. San Rafael, CA: Amber-Allen.

Sabaratnam, Meera. 2017. "Decolonising the Curriculum: What's All the Fuss About?" *SOAS* (blog). January 18, 2017. https://www.soas.ac.uk/blogs/study/decolonising-curriculum-whats-the-fuss/.

Sallee, Margaret W. 2014. *Faculty Fathers: Toward a New Ideal in the Research University*. Albany: State University of New York Press.

Sandberg, Sheryl. 2013. *Lean in: Women, Work, and the Will to Lead*. New York: Alfred A. Knopf.

Sarsons, Heather. 2017. "Recognition for Group Work: Gender Differences in Academia." *American Economic Review* 107 (5): 141–45. https://doi.org/10.1257/aer.p20171126.

Scott, Beth. 2013. "7 Things You Need to Know about Pregnancy Discrimination." *AAUW* (blog). October 31, 2013. https://www.aauw.org/2013/10/31/know-about-pregnancy-discrimination/.

Seltzer, Rena. 2015. *The Coach's Guide for Women Professors: Who Want a Successful Career and a Well-Balanced Life*. Sterling, VA: Stylus.

"Sexo, mentiras y denuncias: la Facultad de Filosofía y Humanidades de la Universidad de Chile y los casos de acoso y abusos." 2016. *El Mostrador* (blog). December 28, 2016. https://m.elmostrador.cl/noticias/pais/2016/12/27/sexo-mentiras-y-denuncias-la-facultad-de-filosofia-y-humanidades-de-la-universidad-de-chile-y-los-casos-de-acoso-y-abusos/.

Silver-Greenberg, Jessica, and Natalie Kitroeff. 2018. "Miscarrying at Work: The Phys-ical Toll of Pregnancy Discrimination." *New York Times*, October 21, 2018. https://www.nytimes.com/interactive/2018/10/21/business/pregnancy-discrimination-miscarriages.html.

Slaughter, Anne-Marie. 2012. "Why Women Still Can't Have It All." *The Atlantic*. June 13, 2012. https://www.theatlantic.com/magazine/archive/2012/07/why-women-still-cant-have-it-all/309020/.

———. 2015. *Why Women Still Can't Have It All*. Richmond, VA: OneWorld.

Staats, Cheryl. 2013. "State of the Science: Implicit Bias Review." Kirwan Institute for the Study of Race and Ethnicity, Ohio State University. http://www.kirwaninstitute.osu.edu/reports/2013/03_2013_SOTS-Implicit_Bias.pdf.

Stewart, Abigail J., and Virginia Valian. 2018. *An Inclusive Academy: Achieving Diversity and Excellence*. Cambridge, MA: MIT Press.

Sumner, Jane Lawrence. 2018. "The Gender Balance Assessment Tool (GBAT): A Web-Based Tool for Estimating Gender Balance in Syllabi and Bibliographies." *PS: Political Science and Politics* 51 (2). https://doi.org/10.1017/S1049096517002074.

Teele, Dawn Langan, and Kathleen Thelen. 2017. "Gender in the Journals: Publication Patterns in Political Science." *Political Science* 50 (2): 433–47.

Tinsley, Catherine H., Sandra I. Cheldelin, Andrea Kupfer Schneider, and Emily T. Amanatullah. 2009. "Women at the Bargaining Table: Pitfalls and Prospects." *Negotiation Journal* 25 (2): 233–48.

Trimeloni, Lauren, and Jeanne Spencer. 2016. "Diagnosis and Management of Breast Milk Oversupply." *Journal of the American Board of Family Medicine* 29 (1): 139–42. https://doi.org/10.3122/jabfm.2016.01.150164.

Trix, Frances, and Carolyn Psenka. 2003. "Exploring the Color of Glass: Letters of Recommendation for Female and Male Medical Faculty." *Discourse and Society* 14 (2): 191–220.

van Kessel, P., A. Hughes, G. A. Smith, and B. A. Alper. 2018. "Where Americans Find Meaning in Life." Pew Research Center Religion and Public Life. November 20, 2018. https://www.pewforum.org/2018/11/20/where-americans-find-meaning-in-life/.

Viglione, Giuliana. 2020. "Are Women Publishing Less during the Pandemic? Here's What the Data Say." *Nature* 581 (7809): 365–66. https://doi.org/10.1038/d41586-020-01294-9.

Voeten, Erik. 2013. "Introducing the Monkey Cage Gender Gap Symposium." *Washington Post*. September 30, 2013. https://www.washingtonpost.com/news/monkey-cage/wp/2013/09/30/introducing-the-monkey-cage-gender-gap-symposium/.

von Stein, Jana. 2013. "When Bad Things Happen to Untenured People." *Chronicle of Higher Education*, January 12, 2013. https://www.chronicle.com/article/When-Bad-Things-Happen-to/136539.

Wamsley, Laurel. 2018. "Michelle Obama's Take on 'Lean In'? That &#%! Doesn't Work." NPR. December 3, 2018. https://www.npr.org/2018/12/03/672898216/michelle-obamas-take-on-lean-in-that-doesn-t-work.

Ward, Kelly, and Lisa Wolf-Wendel. 2012. *Academic Motherhood: How Faculty Manage Work and Family*. New Brunswick, NJ: Rutgers University Press.

Whippman, Ruth. 2019. "Enough Leaning In. Let's Tell Men to Lean Out." *New York Times.* October 10, 2019. https://www.nytimes.com/2019/10/10/opinion/sunday /feminism-lean-in.html.

Wiegand, Krista, Debbie Lisle, Amanda Murdie, and James Scott. 2020. "Journal Submissions in Times of COVID-19: Is There a Gender Gap?" *Duck of Minerva* (blog). May 15, 2020. https://duckofminerva.com/2020/05/journal-submissions-in-times -of-covid-19-is-there-a-gender-gap.html.

Willis, Charmaine, and Nakissa Jahanbani. 2019. "How Men Can Help Combat Misogyny in Graduate Education." Times Higher Education. May 7, 2019. https://www.timeshighereducation.com/blog/how-men-can-help-combat -misogyny-graduate-education.

Windsor, Leah, and Kerry F. Crawford. 2020. "Snow Days, Holidays and Pandemic Quarantines: Why We Need to Be Looking after Parents." Medium. March 23, 2020. https://medium.com/international-affairs-blog/snow-days-holidays-and -pandemic-quarantines-why-we-need-to-be-looking-after-parents-a3dc38413548.

Winegar, Jessica. 2016. "The Miscarriage Penalty." *Chronicle of Higher Education.* November 29, 2016. http://www.chronicle.com/article/The-Miscarriage-Penalty /238526.

Wisler, Joelle. 2016. "Why Maternity Leave in the United States Really Sucks." *Scary Mommy.* September 9, 2016. https://www.scarymommy.com/maternity-leave-in -united-states-sucks/.

Wolfers, Justin. 2017. "A Family-Friendly Policy That's Friendliest to Male Professors." *New York Times.* December 21, 2017. https://www.nytimes.com/2016/06/26 /business/tenure-extension-policies-that-put-women-at-a-disadvantage.html.

Wolfinger, Nicholas H. 2013. "For Female Scientists, There's No Good Time to Have Children." *The Atlantic.* July 29, 2013. https://www.theatlantic.com/sexes/archive /2013/07/for-female-scientists-theres-no-good-time-to-have-children/278165/.

Wolfinger, Nicholas H., Mary Ann Mason, and Marc Goulden. 2008. "Problems in the Pipeline: Gender, Marriage, and Fertility in the Ivory Tower." *Journal of Higher Education* 79 (4): 388–405.

———. 2009. "Stay in the Game: Gender, Family Formation and Alternative Trajectories in the Academic Life Course." *Social Forces* 87 (3): 1591–621. https://doi .org/10.1353/sof.0.0182.

Wolf-Wendel, Lisa, Susan B. Twombly, and Suzanne Rice. 2004. *The Two-Body Problem: Dual-Career-Couple Hiring Practices in Higher Education.* Baltimore: Johns Hopkins University Press.

Wong, Kristin. 2018. "There's a Stress Gap between Men and Women: Here's Why It's Important." *New York Times.* December 6, 2018. https://www.nytimes.com/2018 /11/14/smarter-living/stress-gap-women-men.html.

Yakowicz, Will. n.d. "How to Remove Gender Bias from the Hiring Process." UC Davis ADVANCE. Accessed June 6, 2018. http://ucd-advance.ucdavis.edu/post /how-remove-gender-bias-hiring-process.

Yao, Joanne, and Andrew Delatolla. 2017. "Gender and Diversity in the IR Curriculum: Why Should We Care?" The Disorder of Things. April 20, 2017. https:// thedisorderofthings.com/2017/04/20/gender-and-diversity-in-the-ir-curriculum -why-should-we-care/.

Vignette Contributors

Susan Hannah Allen
David Andersen-Rodgers
Kelly Baker
Courtney Burns
Christina Fattore
Jael Goldsmith Weil
Kathleen J. Hancock
Kelly Kadera
Carolyn Kaldon
Lily Moloney
Madeleine Moloney
Maxwell Moloney
Sara McLaughlin Mitchell
Amanda Murdie
Erin Olsen-Telles
Whitney Pirtle
Nancy Rower
Susan Sell
Sahar Shafqat
Sarah Shair-Rosenfield
Krista E. Wiegand
Reed Wood

And several anonymous colleagues

Index

About the Authors

Kerry F. Crawford is an associate professor in the Department of Political Science at James Madison University. She is the author of *Wartime Sexual Violence: From Silence to Condemnation of a Weapon of War* (Georgetown University Press, 2017) and coauthor with David Andersen-Rodgers of *Human Security: Theory and Action* (Rowman & Littlefield, 2018).

Leah C. Windsor is a research assistant professor at the Institute for Intelligent Systems at the University of Memphis. She is a principal investigator of the Languages Across Cultures lab, where she studies the language of world leaders. Her recent work has been published in *PLOS ONE*, *Political Communication*, and *PS: Political Science and Politics*.